BLACKWOOD™

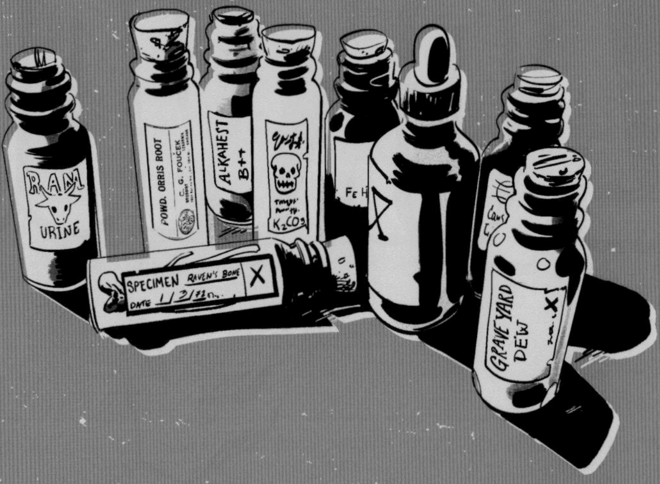
RAM
URINE
POWD. ORRIS ROOT
C. G. FOUČEK
ALKAHEST
B++
K_2CO_3
Fe H
SPECIMEN Raven's Bone
DATE 1/3/72
X
GRAVE YARD
DEW
X

BLACKWOOD

Written by **EVAN DORKIN**

Art by **VERONICA** and **ANDY FISH**

Letters by **GREG MCKENNA**

Color flats for issue #4 by **DANIEL HADDOCK**

Cover by **VERONICA FISH**

Chapter breaks by **VERONICA FISH**

DARK HORSE BOOKS

President & Publisher **MIKE RICHARDSON**

Editor **DANIEL CHABON**

Assistant Editor **CHUCK HOWITT**

Designer **SARAH TERRY**

Digital Art Technician **JOSIE CHRISTENSEN**

BLACKWOOD VOLUME 2: THE MOURNING AFTER

Collects issues #1–#4 of the Dark Horse Comics series *Blackwood: The Mourning After*.

Published by Dark Horse Books, a division of Dark Horse Comics LLC
10956 SE Main Street, Milwaukie, OR 97222

DarkHorse.com
To find a comics shop in your area, visit comicshoplocator.com

First edition: September 2020 ◆ Trade paperback ISBN 978-1-50671-692-3
Ebook ISBN 978-1-50671-693-0

1 3 5 7 9 10 8 6 4 2
Printed in China

Library of Congress Cataloging-in-Publication Data

Names: Dorkin, Evan, author. | Fish, Veronica, artist. | Fish, Andy,
    artist. | McKenna, Greg, letterer.
Title: The mourning after / written by Evan Dorkin ; art by Veronica and
    Andy Fish ; letters by Greg McKenna ; cover by Veronica Fish.
Description: First edition. | Milwaukie, OR : Dark Horse Books, 2020. |
    Series: Blackwood ; v. 2 | "Collects issues 1 through 6 of the Dark
    Horse Comics series Blackwood: The Mourning After."
Identifiers: LCCN 2020014412 (print) | LCCN 2020014413 (ebook) | ISBN
    9781506716923 (trade paperback) | ISBN 9781506716930 (ebook)
Subjects: LCSH: Comic books, strips, etc.
Classification: LCC PN6728.B524 D675 2020 (print) | LCC PN6728.B524
    (ebook) | DDC 741.5/973--dc23
LC record available at https://lccn.loc.gov/2020014412
LC ebook record available at https://lccn.loc.gov/2020014413

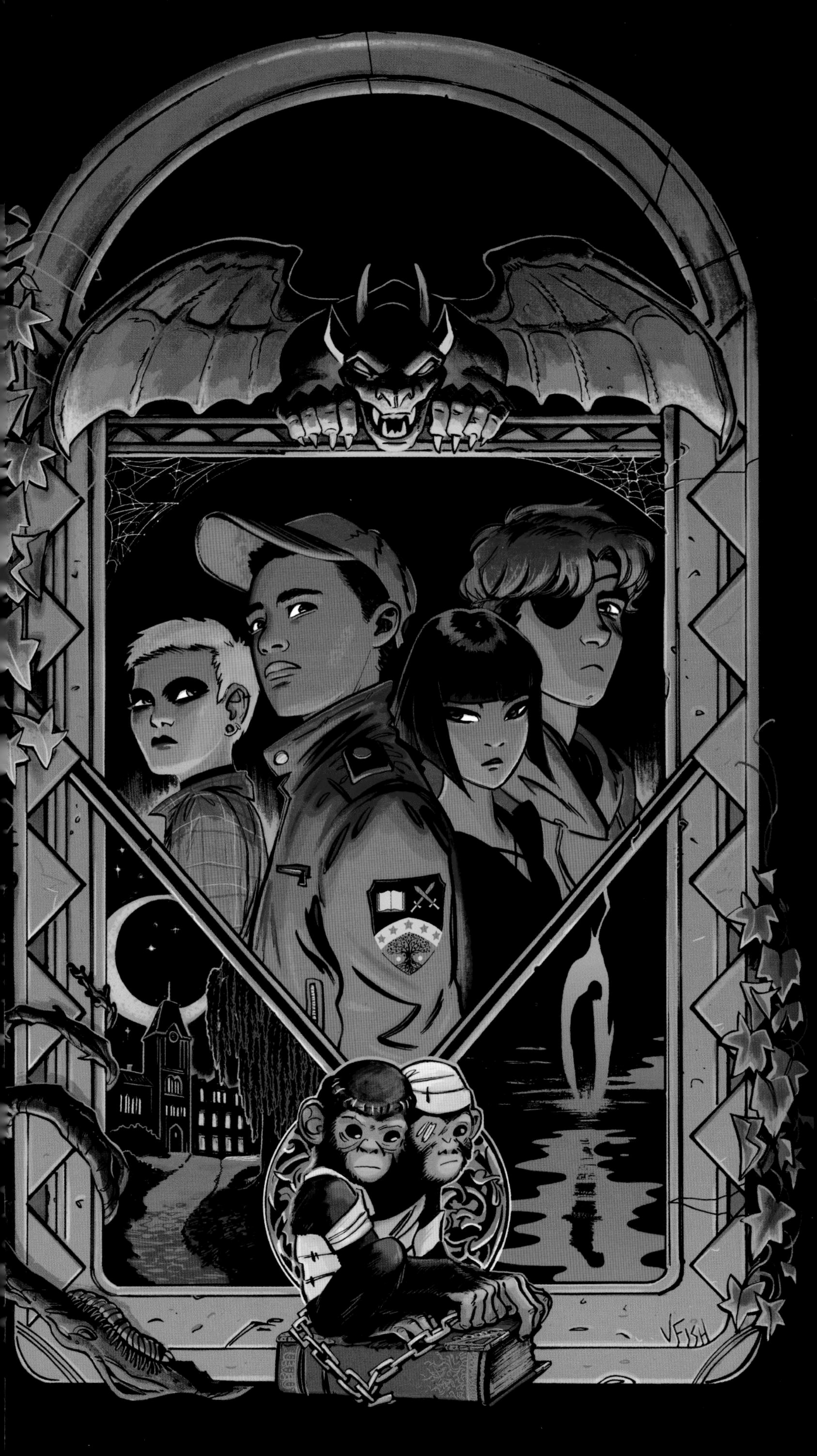
VFISH

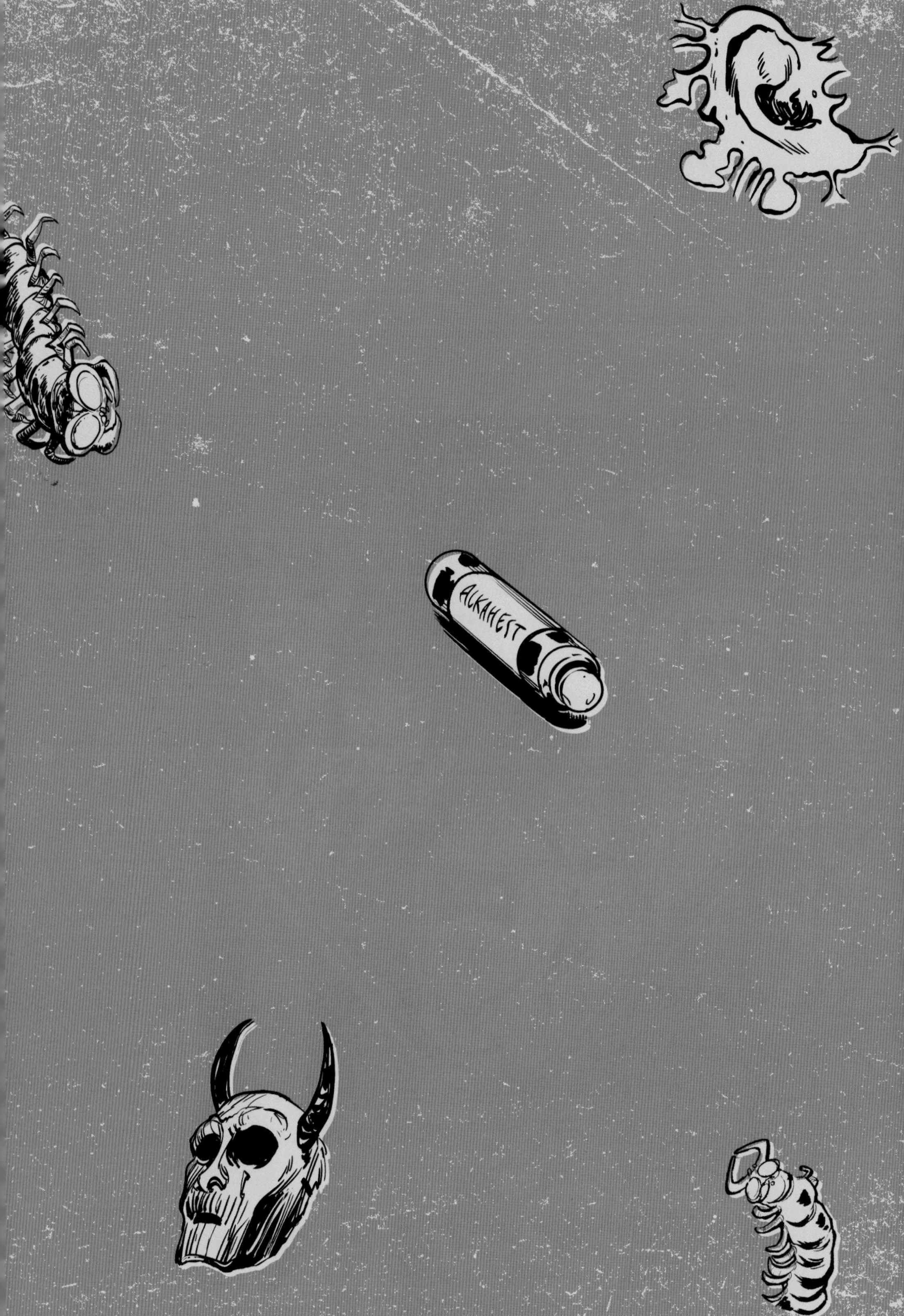
ALKAHEST

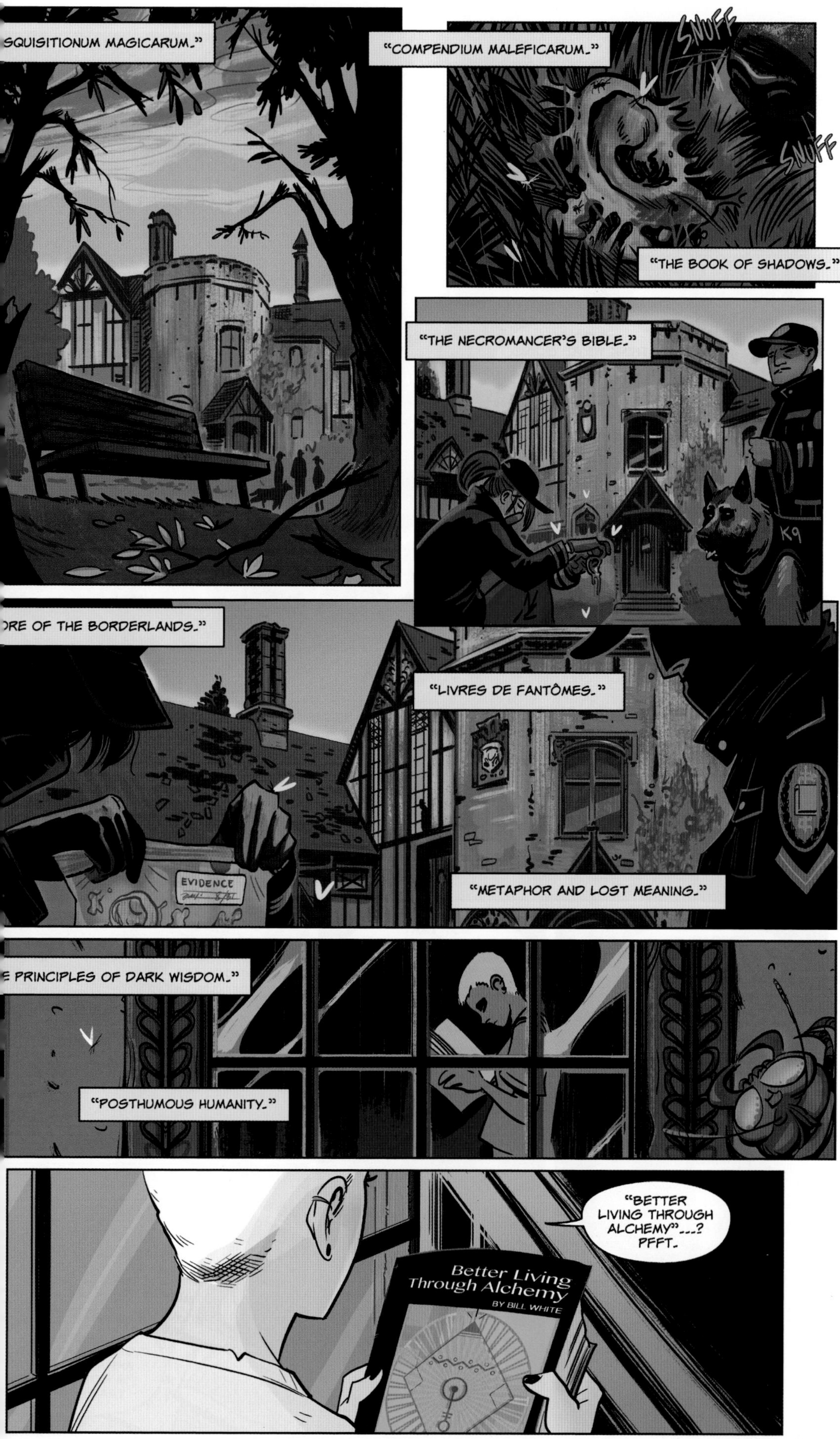
SQUISITIONUM MAGICARUM."
"COMPENDIUM MALEFICARUM."
SNUFF
SNUFF
"THE BOOK OF SHADOWS."
"THE NECROMANCER'S BIBLE."
K9
ORE OF THE BORDERLANDS."
"LIVRES DE FANTÔMES."
EVIDENCE
"METAPHOR AND LOST MEANING."
E PRINCIPLES OF DARK WISDOM."
"POSTHUMOUS HUMANITY."
"BETTER LIVING THROUGH ALCHEMY"...? PFFT.
Better Living Through Alchemy
BY BILL WHITE

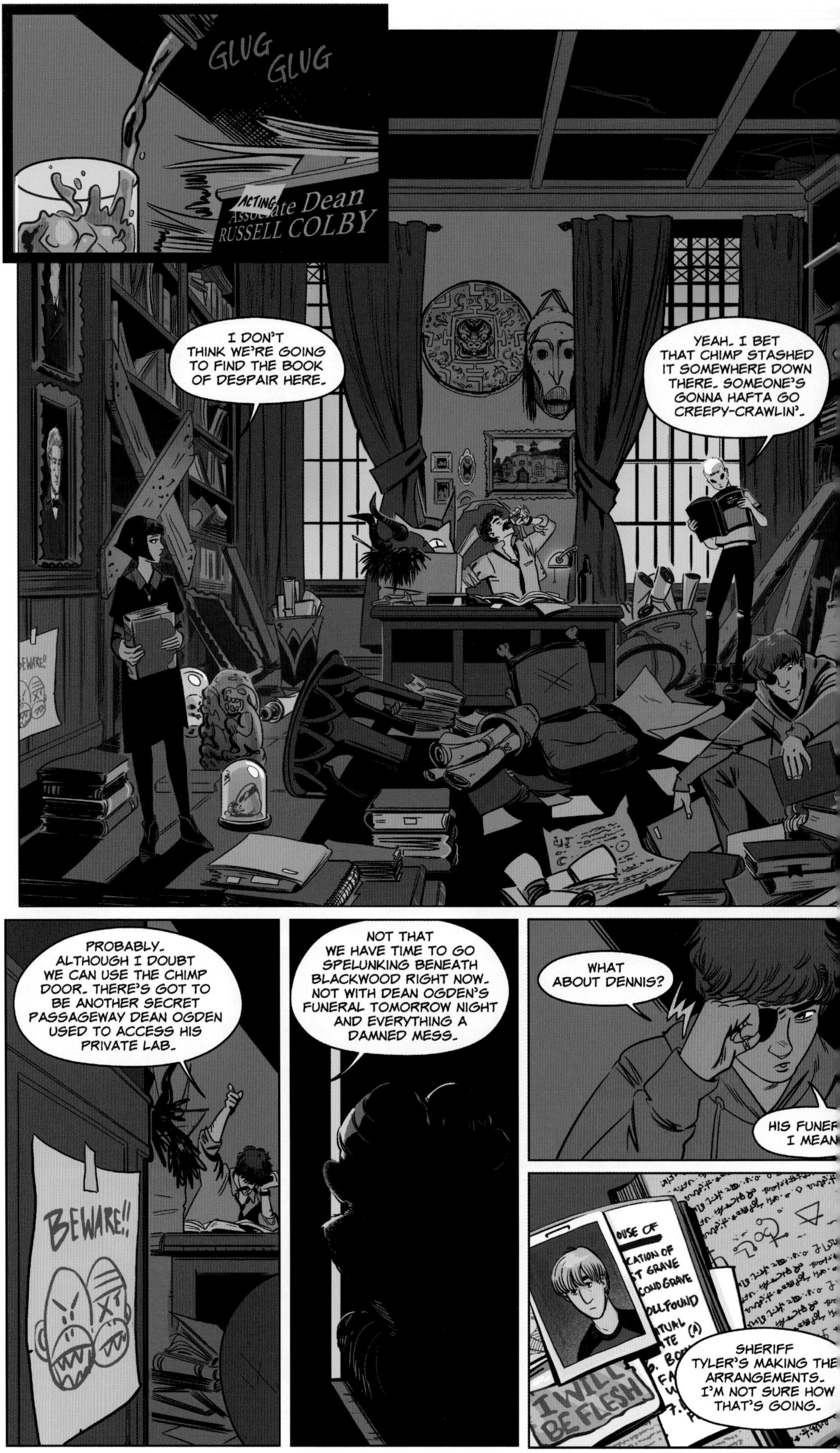
GLUG GLUG
ACTING Associate Dean RUSSELL COLBY
I DON'T THINK WE'RE GOING TO FIND THE BOOK OF DESPAIR HERE.
YEAH. I BET THAT CHIMP STASHED IT SOMEWHERE DOWN THERE. SOMEONE'S GONNA HAFTA GO CREEPY-CRAWLIN'.
BEWARE!!
PROBABLY. ALTHOUGH I DOUBT WE CAN USE THE CHIMP DOOR. THERE'S GOT TO BE ANOTHER SECRET PASSAGEWAY DEAN OGDEN USED TO ACCESS HIS PRIVATE LAB.
BEWARE!!
NOT THAT WE HAVE TIME TO GO SPELUNKING BENEATH BLACKWOOD RIGHT NOW. NOT WITH DEAN OGDEN'S FUNERAL TOMORROW NIGHT AND EVERYTHING A DAMNED MESS.
WHAT ABOUT DENNIS?
HIS FUNER
I MEAN
I WILL BE FLESH
SHERIFF TYLER'S MAKING THE ARRANGEMENTS. I'M NOT SURE HOW THAT'S GOING.

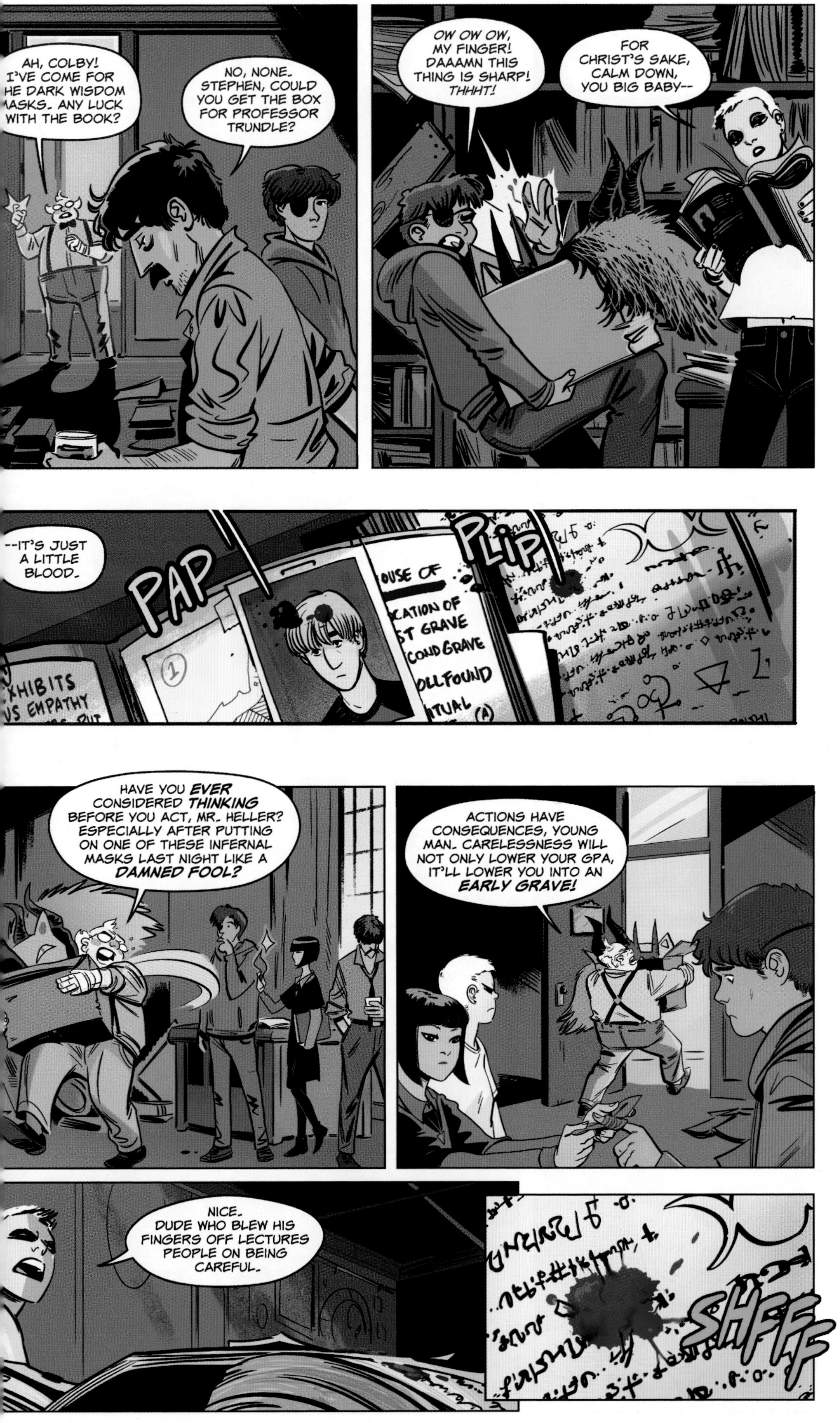
AH, COLBY! I'VE COME FOR THE DARK WISDOM MASKS. ANY LUCK WITH THE BOOK?
NO, NONE. STEPHEN, COULD YOU GET THE BOX FOR PROFESSOR TRUNDLE?
OW OW OW, MY FINGER! DAAAMN THIS THING IS SHARP! THHHT!
FOR CHRIST'S SAKE, CALM DOWN, YOU BIG BABY--
--IT'S JUST A LITTLE BLOOD.
PAP
PLIP
HAVE YOU EVER CONSIDERED THINKING BEFORE YOU ACT, MR. HELLER? ESPECIALLY AFTER PUTTING ON ONE OF THESE INFERNAL MASKS LAST NIGHT LIKE A DAMNED FOOL?
ACTIONS HAVE CONSEQUENCES, YOUNG MAN. CARELESSNESS WILL NOT ONLY LOWER YOUR GPA, IT'LL LOWER YOU INTO AN EARLY GRAVE!
NICE. DUDE WHO BLEW HIS FINGERS OFF LECTURES PEOPLE ON BEING CAREFUL.
SHFFF

SO, ARE WE GONNA HAVE TO ACTUALLY *READ* THIS KIND OF STUFF? I MEAN...IF WE WANT TO LEARN MAGIC?

OH, GOD... IT SOUNDS EVEN DUMBER WHEN *YOU* SAY IT...

HUH? WHAT DOES?

"MAGI

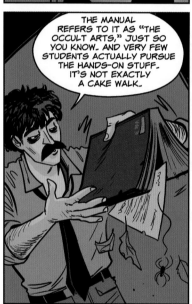

THE MANUAL REFERS TO IT AS "THE OCCULT ARTS," JUST SO YOU KNOW... AND VERY FEW STUDENTS ACTUALLY PURSUE THE HANDS-ON STUFF... IT'S NOT EXACTLY A CAKE WALK...

REALLY? WHAT'S THE POINT IF YOU CAN'T LEARN WITCH CRAP?

SHOVE

PSYCHIC RESEARCHERS, ALCHEMICAL ENGINEERS, OCCULT ARCHIVISTS-- WHERE DO YOU THINK THEY ALL COME FROM?

HELL IF I KNOW... IT'S LIKE THINKING ABOUT WHERE THE BOOGEYMAN COMES FROM...

SHRUG

YOU DON'T WANT TO KNOW THAT...

BELIEVE ME...

IT'S A NASTY STORY...

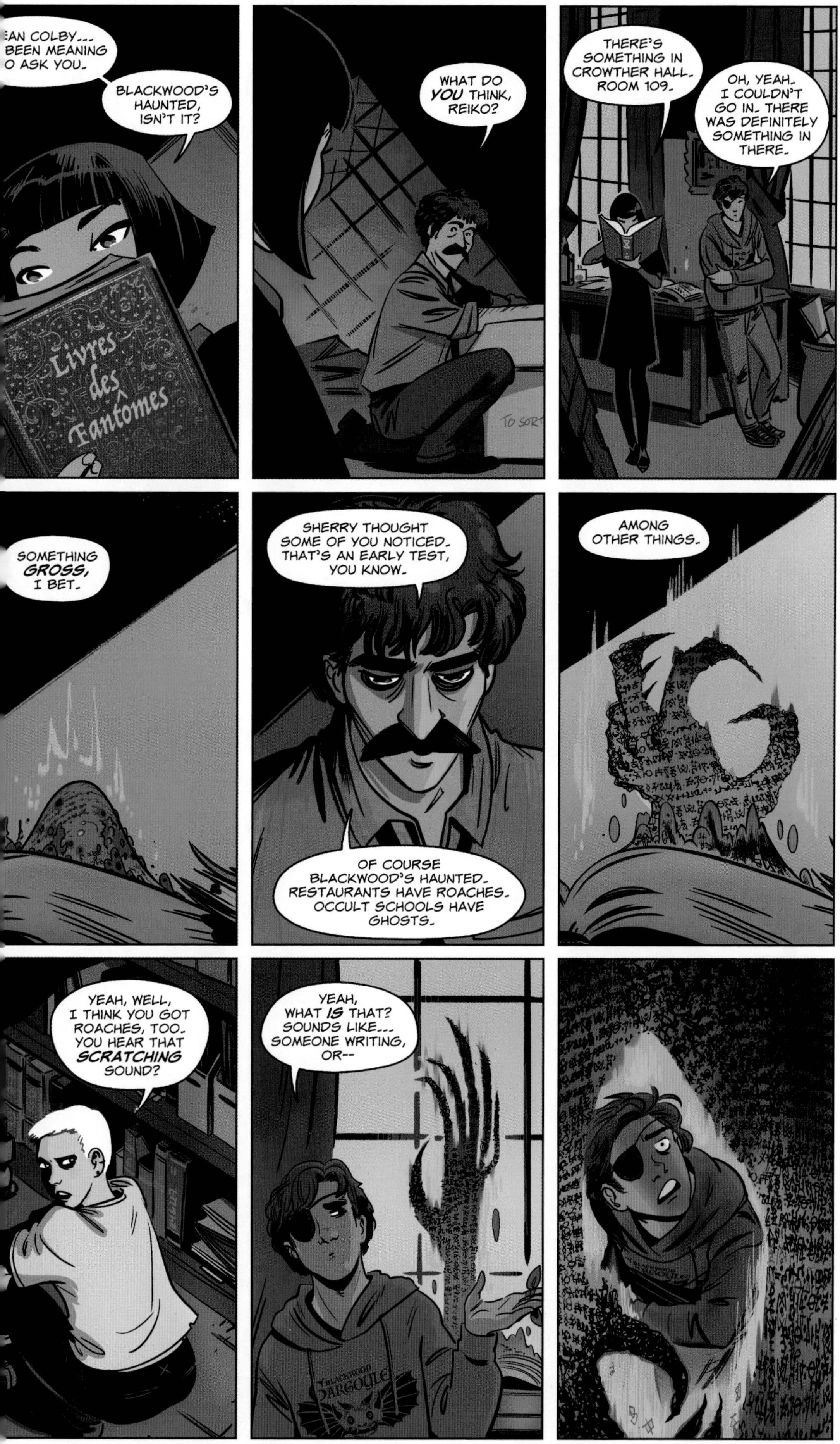
EAN COLBY... BEEN MEANING O ASK YOU.
BLACKWOOD'S HAUNTED, ISN'T IT?
Livres des Fantômes
WHAT DO YOU THINK, REIKO?
TO SORT
THERE'S SOMETHING IN CROWTHER HALL. ROOM 109.
OH, YEAH. I COULDN'T GO IN. THERE WAS DEFINITELY SOMETHING IN THERE.
SOMETHING GROSS, I BET.
SHERRY THOUGHT SOME OF YOU NOTICED. THAT'S AN EARLY TEST, YOU KNOW.
OF COURSE BLACKWOOD'S HAUNTED. RESTAURANTS HAVE ROACHES. OCCULT SCHOOLS HAVE GHOSTS.
AMONG OTHER THINGS.
YEAH, WELL, I THINK YOU GOT ROACHES, TOO. YOU HEAR THAT SCRATCHING SOUND?
YEAH, WHAT IS THAT? SOUNDS LIKE... SOMEONE WRITING, OR--
BLACKWOOD GARGOYLE

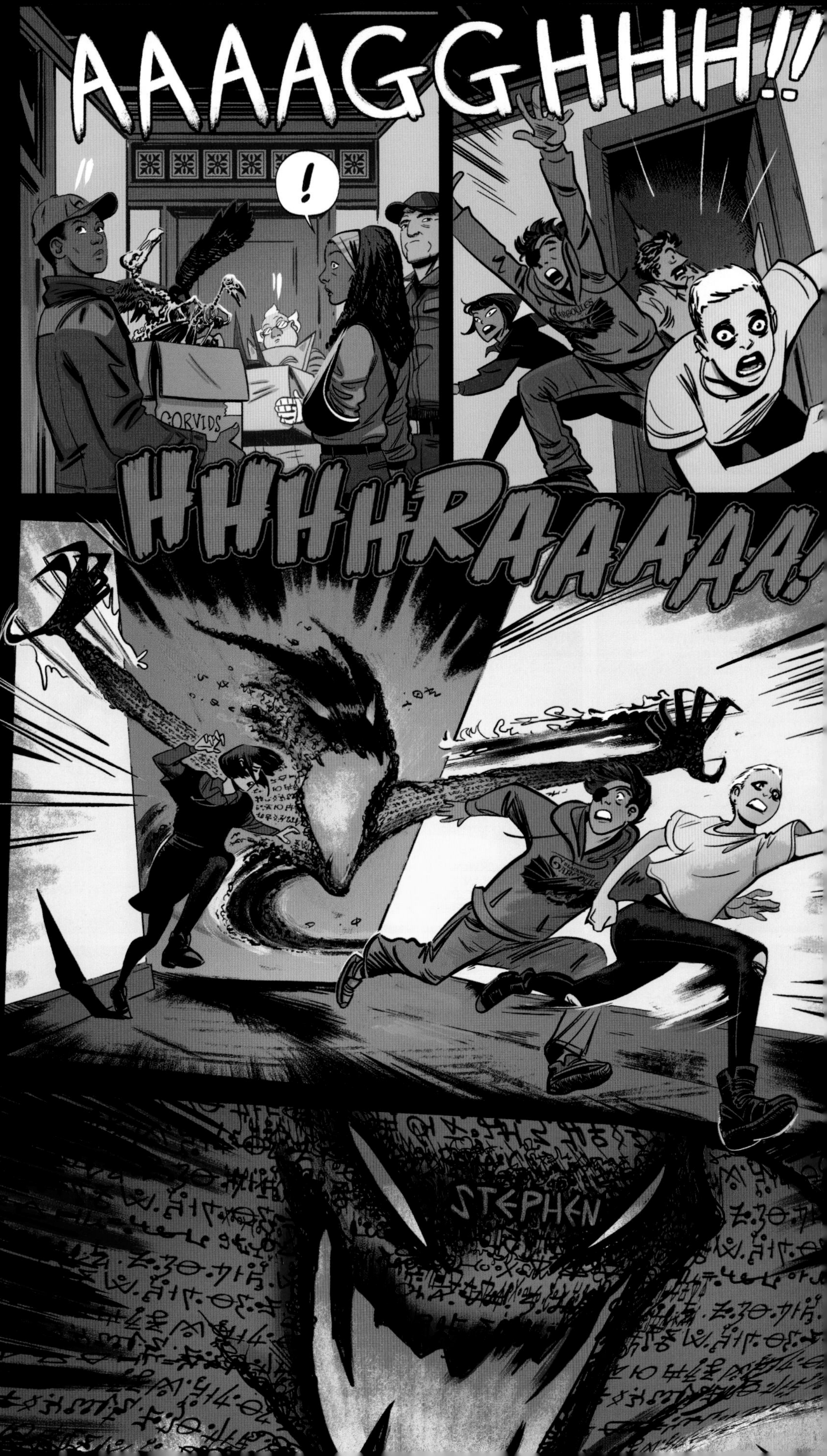
AAAAGGHHH!!
!
CORVIDS
GARGOYLES
HHHHRAAAAAA
STEPHEN

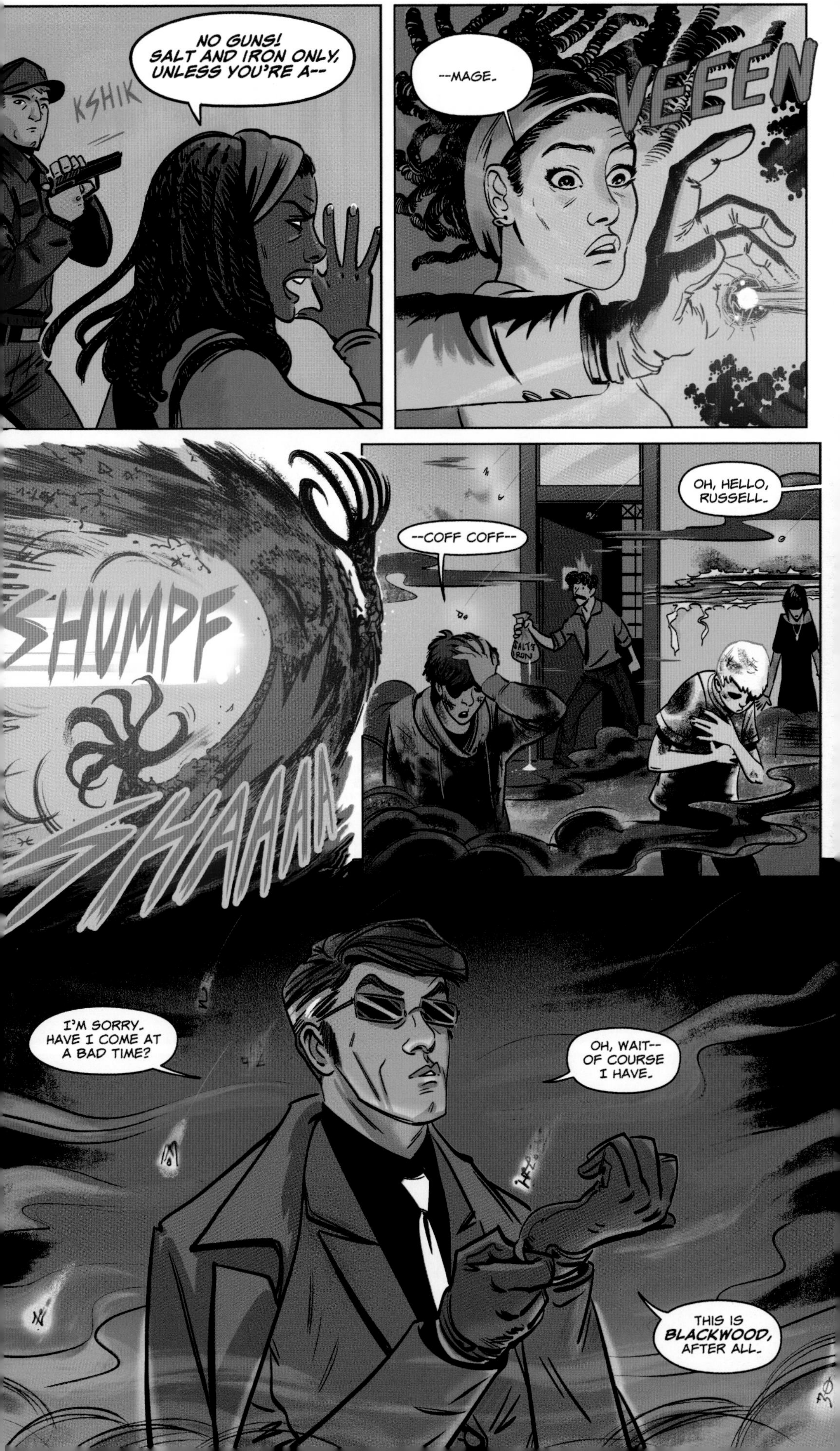

KSHIK
NO GUNS! SALT AND IRON ONLY, UNLESS YOU'RE A--
--MAGE.
VEEEN
SHUMPF
SHAAAAA
--COFF COFF--
OH, HELLO, RUSSELL.
SALT 'N IRON
I'M SORRY. HAVE I COME AT A BAD TIME?
OH, WAIT-- OF COURSE I HAVE.
THIS IS BLACKWOOD, AFTER ALL.

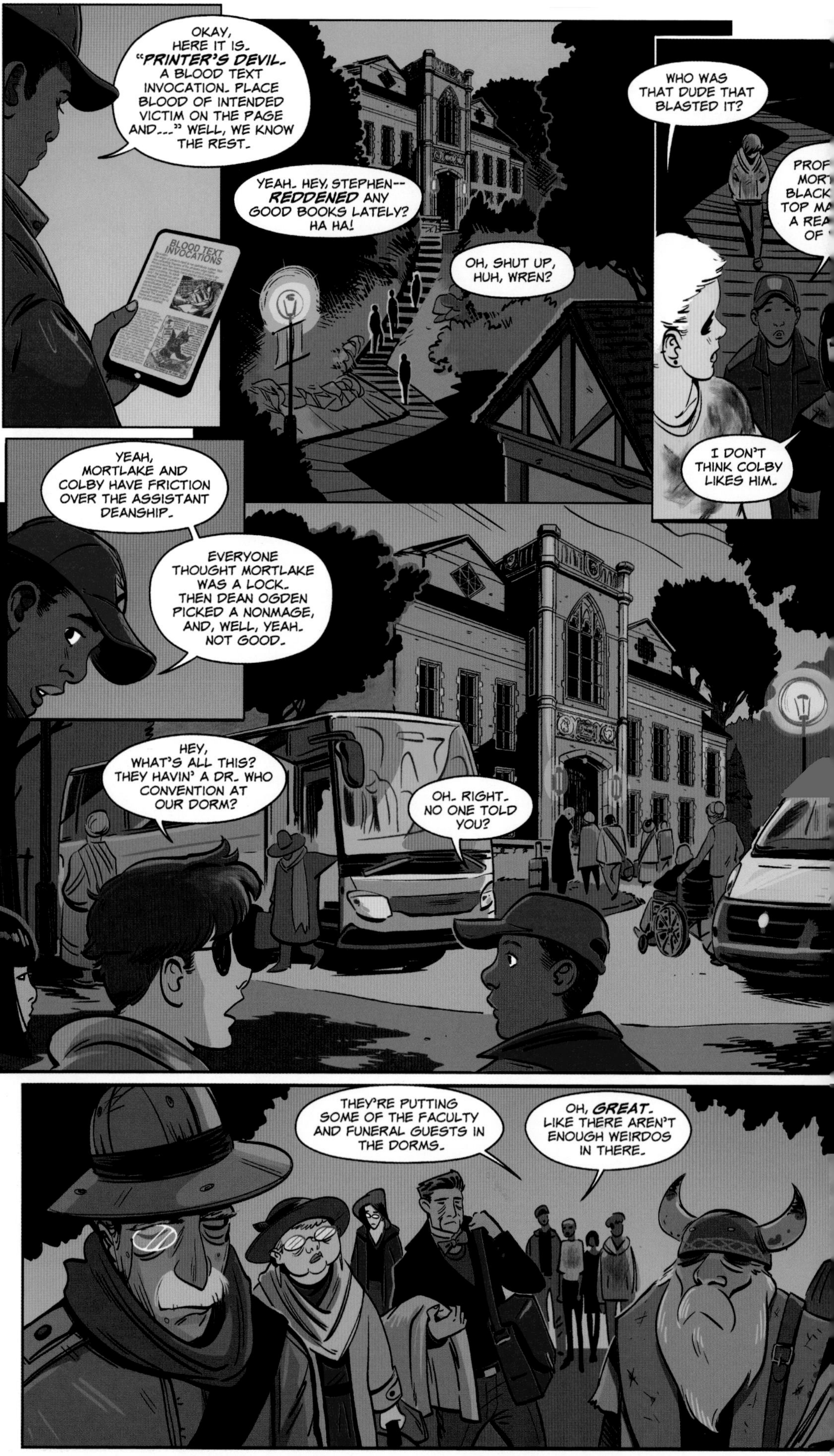

OKAY, HERE IT IS. "PRINTER'S DEVIL. A BLOOD TEXT INVOCATION. PLACE BLOOD OF INTENDED VICTIM ON THE PAGE AND..." WELL, WE KNOW THE REST.
BLOOD TEXT INVOCATIONS
YEAH. HEY, STEPHEN-- REDDENED ANY GOOD BOOKS LATELY? HA HA!
OH, SHUT UP, HUH, WREN?
WHO WAS THAT DUDE THAT BLASTED IT?
I DON'T THINK COLBY LIKES HIM.
YEAH, MORTLAKE AND COLBY HAVE FRICTION OVER THE ASSISTANT DEANSHIP.
EVERYONE THOUGHT MORTLAKE WAS A LOCK. THEN DEAN OGDEN PICKED A NONMAGE, AND, WELL, YEAH. NOT GOOD.
HEY, WHAT'S ALL THIS? THEY HAVIN' A DR. WHO CONVENTION AT OUR DORM?
OH. RIGHT. NO ONE TOLD YOU?
THEY'RE PUTTING SOME OF THE FACULTY AND FUNERAL GUESTS IN THE DORMS.
OH, GREAT. LIKE THERE AREN'T ENOUGH WEIRDOS IN THERE.

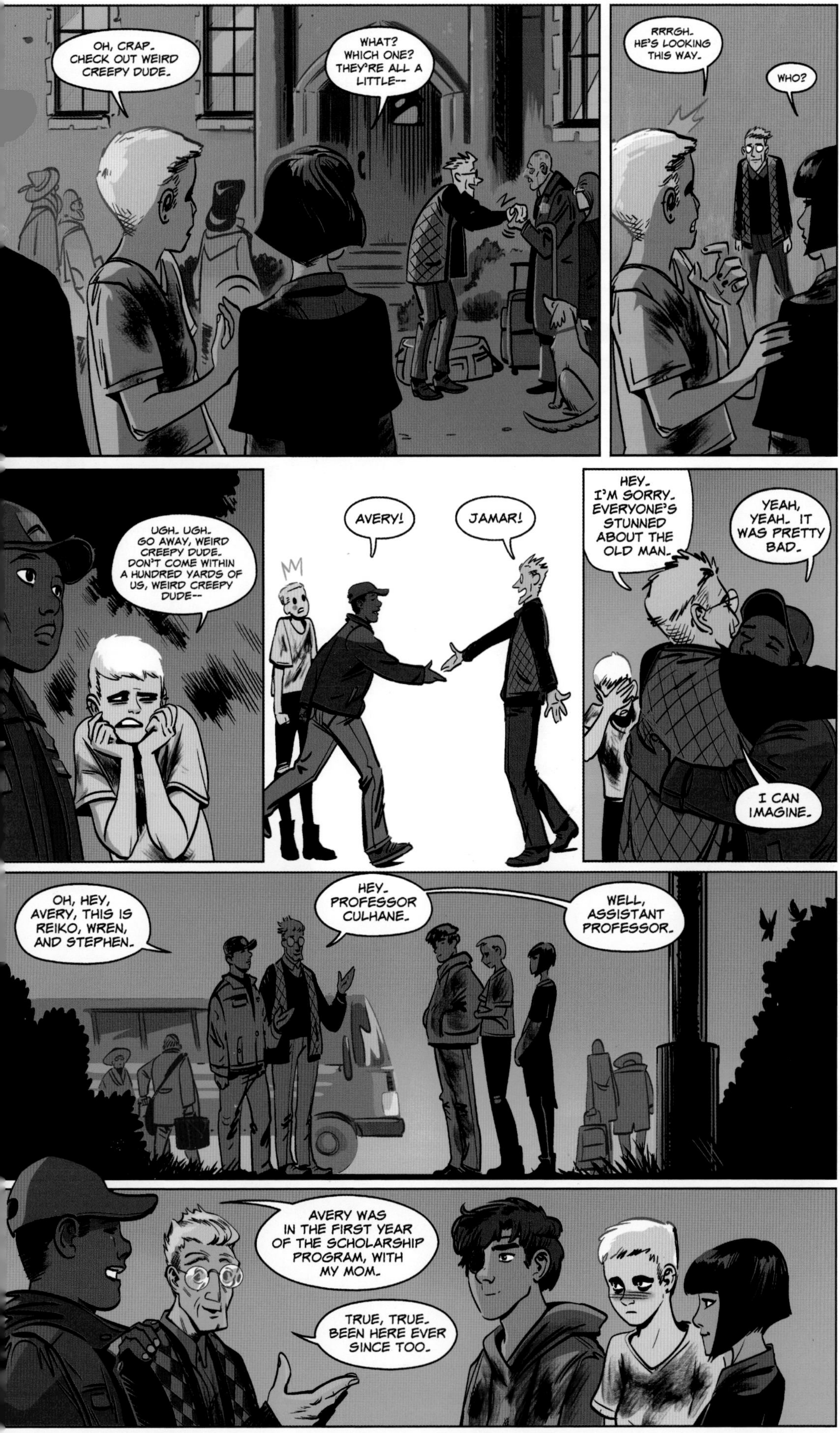
OH, CRAP. CHECK OUT WEIRD CREEPY DUDE.
WHAT? WHICH ONE? THEY'RE ALL A LITTLE--
RRRGH. HE'S LOOKING THIS WAY.
WHO?
UGH. UGH. GO AWAY, WEIRD CREEPY DUDE. DON'T COME WITHIN A HUNDRED YARDS OF US, WEIRD CREEPY DUDE--
AVERY!
JAMAR!
HEY. I'M SORRY. EVERYONE'S STUNNED ABOUT THE OLD MAN.
YEAH, YEAH. IT WAS PRETTY BAD.
I CAN IMAGINE.
OH, HEY, AVERY, THIS IS REIKO, WREN, AND STEPHEN.
HEY. PROFESSOR CULHANE.
WELL, ASSISTANT PROFESSOR.
AVERY WAS IN THE FIRST YEAR OF THE SCHOLARSHIP PROGRAM, WITH MY MOM.
TRUE, TRUE. BEEN HERE EVER SINCE TOO.

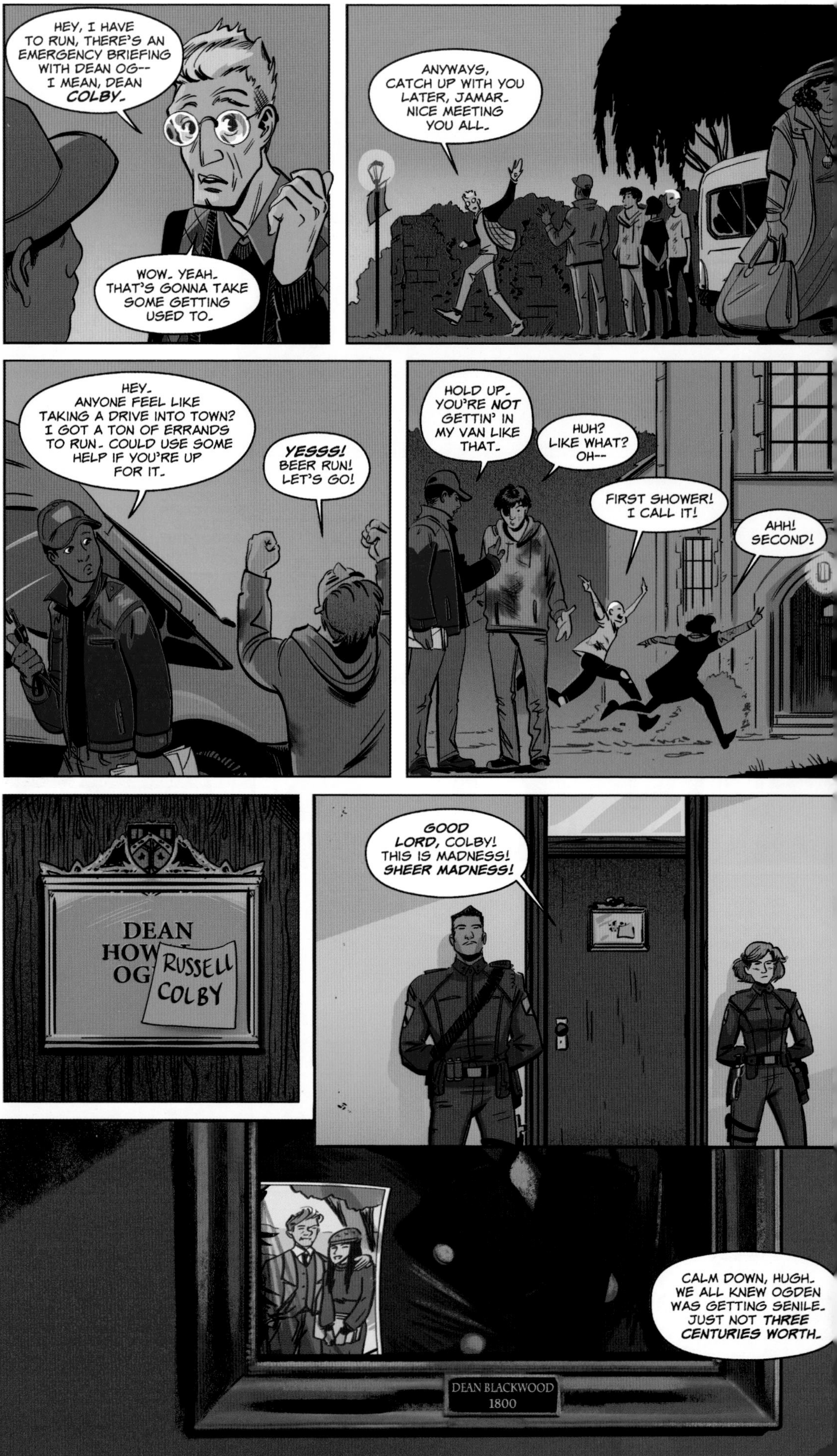
HEY, I HAVE TO RUN, THERE'S AN EMERGENCY BRIEFING WITH DEAN OG-- I MEAN, DEAN COLBY.
WOW. YEAH. THAT'S GONNA TAKE SOME GETTING USED TO.
ANYWAYS, CATCH UP WITH YOU LATER, JAMAR. NICE MEETING YOU ALL.
HEY. ANYONE FEEL LIKE TAKING A DRIVE INTO TOWN? I GOT A TON OF ERRANDS TO RUN. COULD USE SOME HELP IF YOU'RE UP FOR IT.
YESSS! BEER RUN! LET'S GO!
HOLD UP. YOU'RE NOT GETTIN' IN MY VAN LIKE THAT.
HUH? LIKE WHAT? OH--
FIRST SHOWER! I CALL IT!
AHH! SECOND!
DEAN HOW OG
RUSSELL COLBY
GOOD LORD, COLBY! THIS IS MADNESS! SHEER MADNESS!
CALM DOWN, HUGH. WE ALL KNEW OGDEN WAS GETTING SENILE. JUST NOT THREE CENTURIES WORTH.
DEAN BLACKWOOD 1800

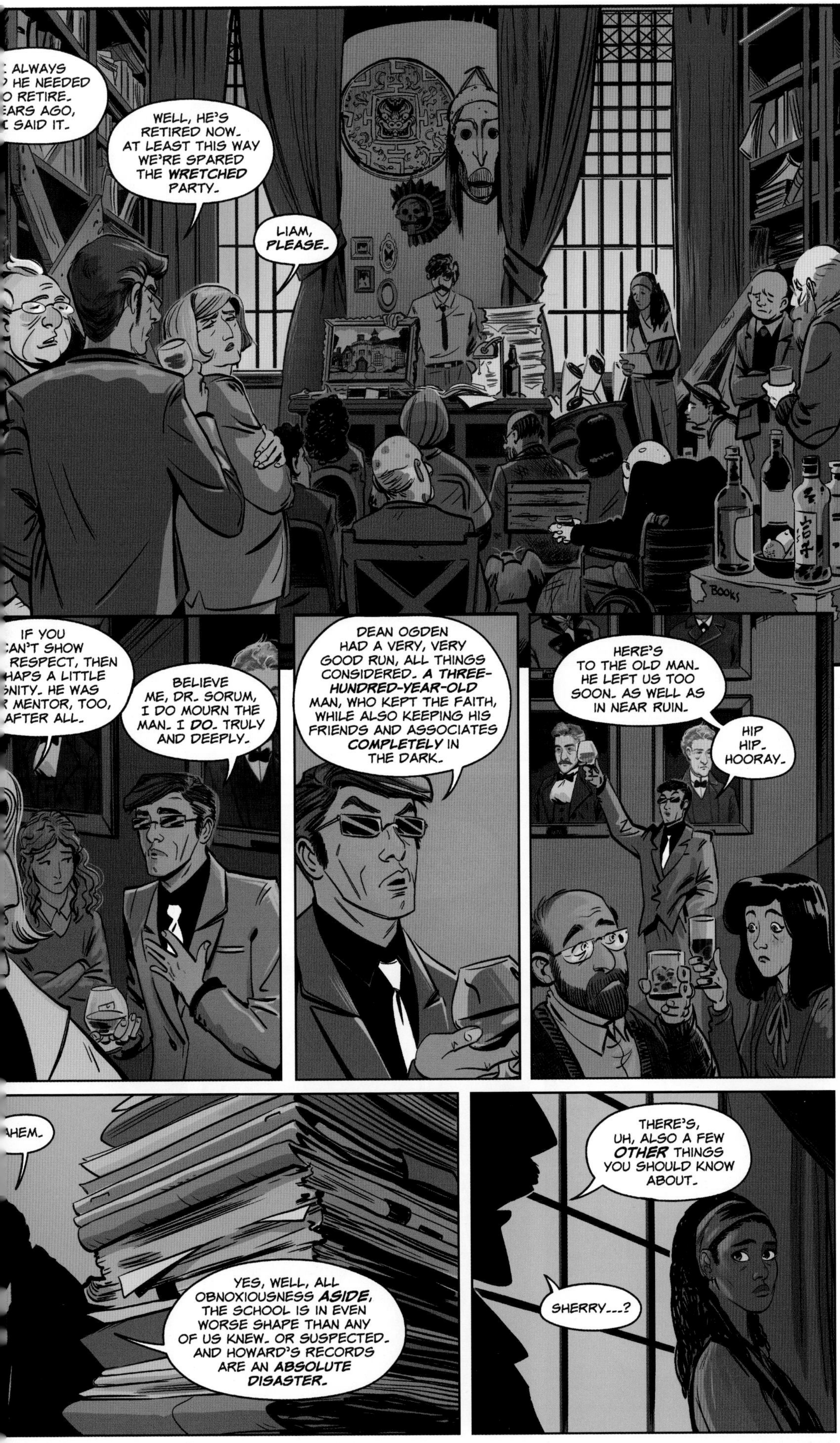
ALWAYS HE NEEDED RETIRE. EARS AGO, SAID IT.
WELL, HE'S RETIRED NOW. AT LEAST THIS WAY WE'RE SPARED THE WRETCHED PARTY.
LIAM, PLEASE.
BOOKS
IF YOU AN'T SHOW RESPECT, THEN HAPS A LITTLE NITY. HE WAS MENTOR, TOO, AFTER ALL.
BELIEVE ME, DR. SORUM, I DO MOURN THE MAN. I DO. TRULY AND DEEPLY.
DEAN OGDEN HAD A VERY, VERY GOOD RUN, ALL THINGS CONSIDERED. A THREE-HUNDRED-YEAR-OLD MAN, WHO KEPT THE FAITH, WHILE ALSO KEEPING HIS FRIENDS AND ASSOCIATES COMPLETELY IN THE DARK.
HERE'S TO THE OLD MAN. HE LEFT US TOO SOON. AS WELL AS IN NEAR RUIN.
HIP HIP. HOORAY.
AHEM.
YES, WELL, ALL OBNOXIOUSNESS ASIDE, THE SCHOOL IS IN EVEN WORSE SHAPE THAN ANY OF US KNEW. OR SUSPECTED. AND HOWARD'S RECORDS ARE AN ABSOLUTE DISASTER.
THERE'S, UH, ALSO A FEW OTHER THINGS YOU SHOULD KNOW ABOUT.
SHERRY...?

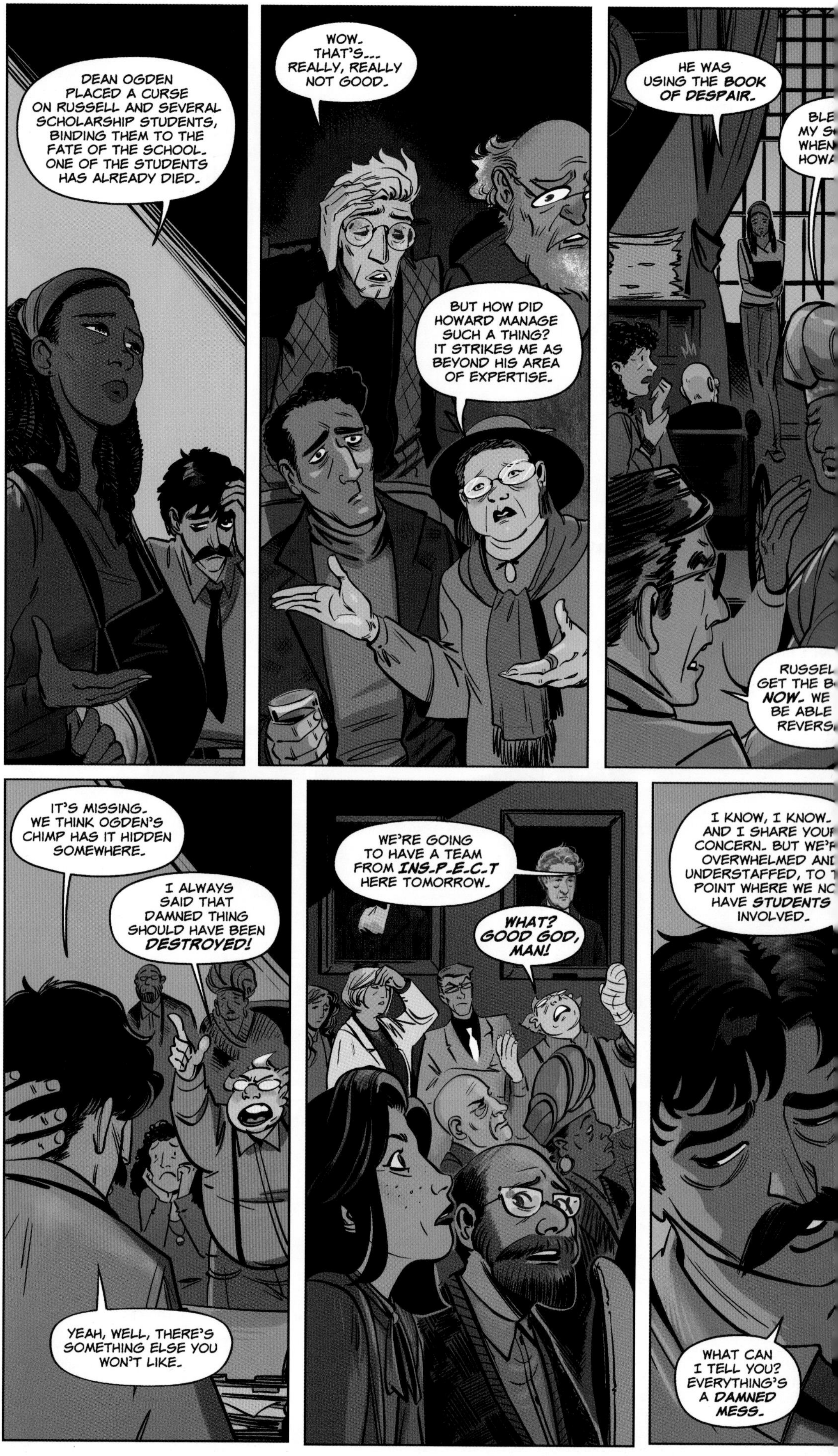

DEAN OGDEN PLACED A CURSE ON RUSSELL AND SEVERAL SCHOLARSHIP STUDENTS, BINDING THEM TO THE FATE OF THE SCHOOL. ONE OF THE STUDENTS HAS ALREADY DIED.
WOW. THAT'S... REALLY, REALLY NOT GOOD.
BUT HOW DID HOWARD MANAGE SUCH A THING? IT STRIKES ME AS BEYOND HIS AREA OF EXPERTISE.
HE WAS USING THE BOOK OF DESPAIR.
BLE MY S WHEN HOWA
RUSSEL GET THE B NOW. WE BE ABLE REVERS
IT'S MISSING. WE THINK OGDEN'S CHIMP HAS IT HIDDEN SOMEWHERE.
I ALWAYS SAID THAT DAMNED THING SHOULD HAVE BEEN DESTROYED!
YEAH, WELL, THERE'S SOMETHING ELSE YOU WON'T LIKE.
WE'RE GOING TO HAVE A TEAM FROM INS.P.E.C.T HERE TOMORROW.
WHAT? GOOD GOD, MAN!
I KNOW, I KNOW. AND I SHARE YOU CONCERN. BUT WE'R OVERWHELMED AND UNDERSTAFFED, TO T POINT WHERE WE NO HAVE STUDENTS INVOLVED.
WHAT CAN I TELL YOU? EVERYTHING'S A DAMNED MESS.

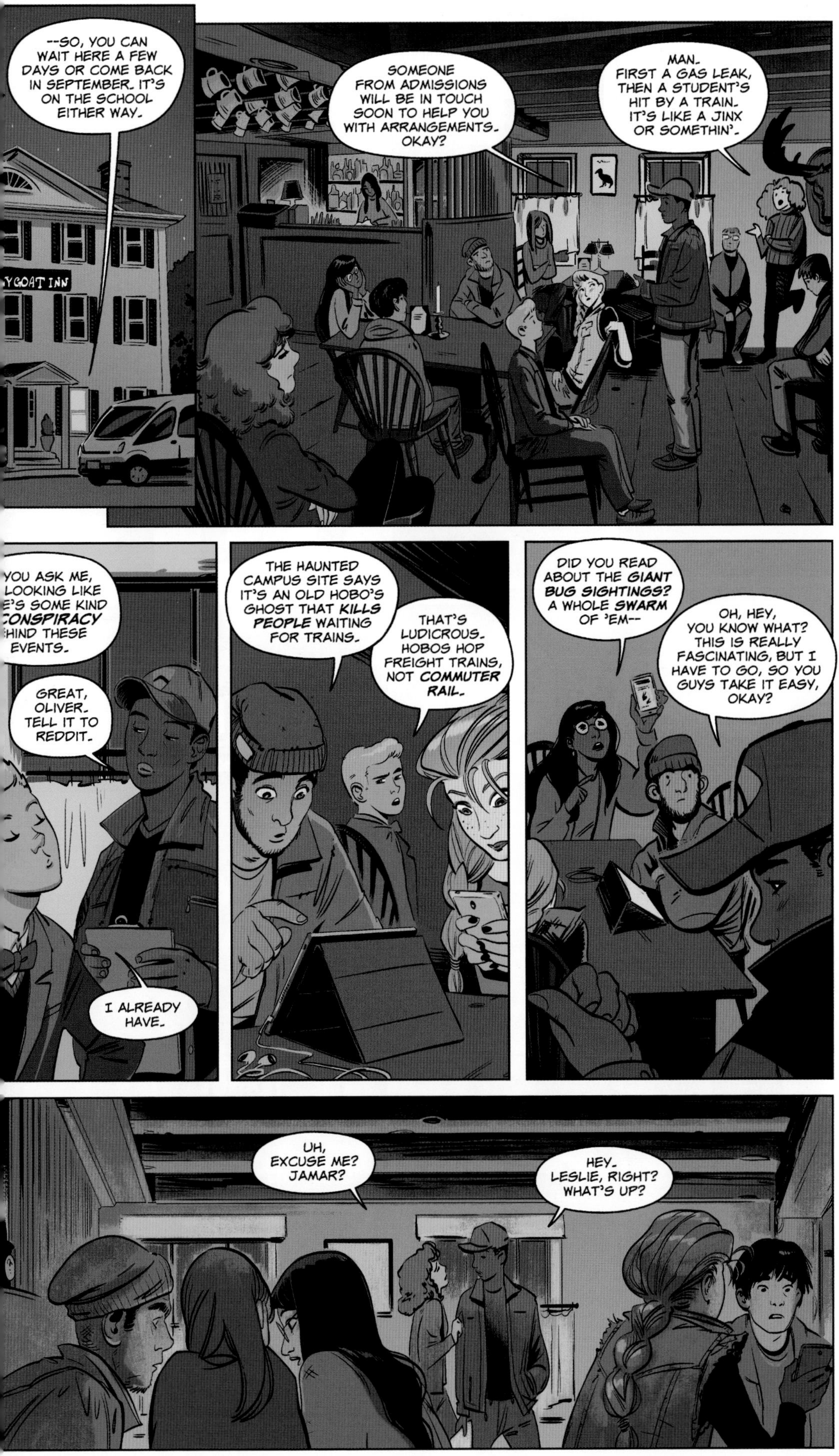
--SO, YOU CAN WAIT HERE A FEW DAYS OR COME BACK IN SEPTEMBER. IT'S ON THE SCHOOL EITHER WAY.
YGOAT INN
SOMEONE FROM ADMISSIONS WILL BE IN TOUCH SOON TO HELP YOU WITH ARRANGEMENTS. OKAY?
MAN. FIRST A GAS LEAK, THEN A STUDENT'S HIT BY A TRAIN. IT'S LIKE A JINX OR SOMETHIN'.
YOU ASK ME, LOOKING LIKE E'S SOME KIND CONSPIRACY HIND THESE EVENTS.
GREAT, OLIVER. TELL IT TO REDDIT.
I ALREADY HAVE.
THE HAUNTED CAMPUS SITE SAYS IT'S AN OLD HOBO'S GHOST THAT KILLS PEOPLE WAITING FOR TRAINS.
THAT'S LUDICROUS. HOBOS HOP FREIGHT TRAINS, NOT COMMUTER RAIL.
DID YOU READ ABOUT THE GIANT BUG SIGHTINGS? A WHOLE SWARM OF 'EM--
OH, HEY, YOU KNOW WHAT? THIS IS REALLY FASCINATING, BUT I HAVE TO GO, SO YOU GUYS TAKE IT EASY, OKAY?
UH, EXCUSE ME? JAMAR?
HEY. LESLIE, RIGHT? WHAT'S UP?

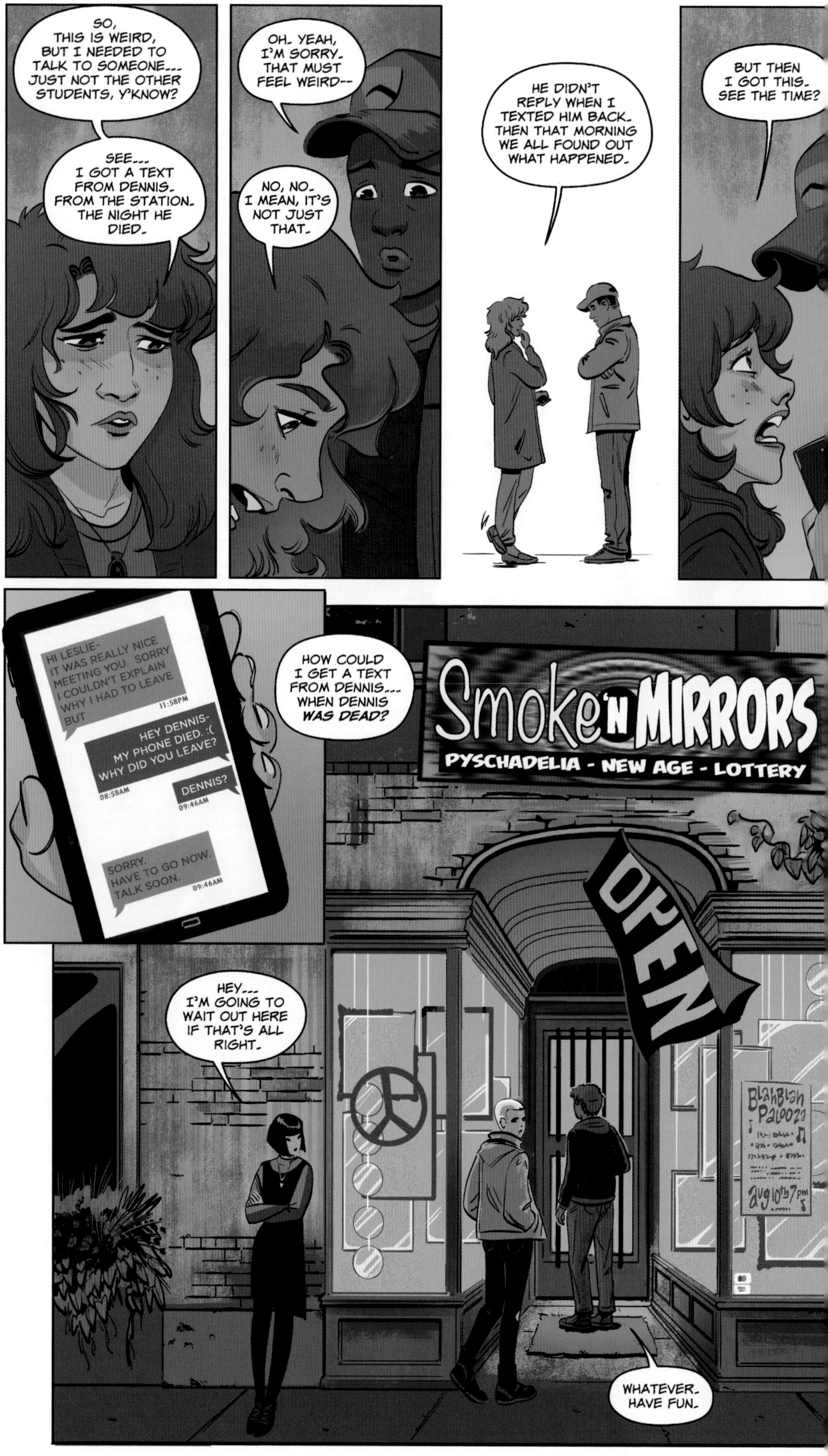
SO, THIS IS WEIRD, BUT I NEEDED TO TALK TO SOMEONE... JUST NOT THE OTHER STUDENTS, Y'KNOW?
SEE... I GOT A TEXT FROM DENNIS. FROM THE STATION. THE NIGHT HE DIED.
OH. YEAH, I'M SORRY. THAT MUST FEEL WEIRD--
NO, NO. I MEAN, IT'S NOT JUST THAT.
HE DIDN'T REPLY WHEN I TEXTED HIM BACK. THEN THAT MORNING WE ALL FOUND OUT WHAT HAPPENED.
BUT THEN I GOT THIS. SEE THE TIME?
HI LESLIE- IT WAS REALLY NICE MEETING YOU. SORRY I COULDN'T EXPLAIN WHY I HAD TO LEAVE BUT
11:58PM
HEY DENNIS- MY PHONE DIED. :(WHY DID YOU LEAVE?
08:58AM
DENNIS?
09:46AM
SORRY. HAVE TO GO NOW. TALK SOON.
09:46AM
HOW COULD I GET A TEXT FROM DENNIS... WHEN DENNIS WAS DEAD?
Smoke'N MIRRORS
PYSCHADELIA - NEW AGE - LOTTERY
OPEN
HEY... I'M GOING TO WAIT OUT HERE IF THAT'S ALL RIGHT.
BlahBlah Palooza
Aug 10th 7pm
WHATEVER. HAVE FUN.

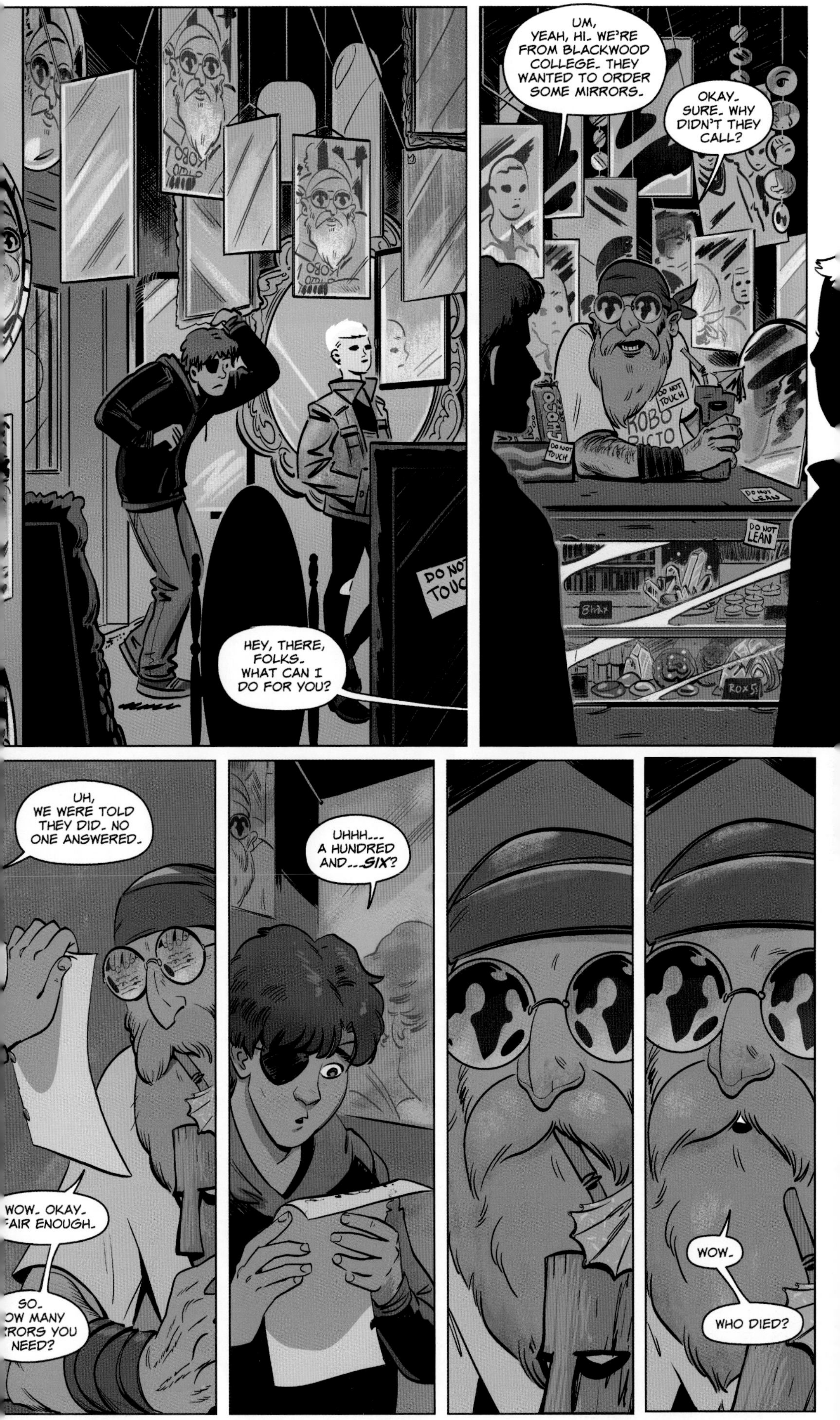
DO NOT TOUCH
HEY, THERE, FOLKS. WHAT CAN I DO FOR YOU?
UM, YEAH, HI. WE'RE FROM BLACKWOOD COLLEGE. THEY WANTED TO ORDER SOME MIRRORS.
OKAY. SURE. WHY DIDN'T THEY CALL?
DO NOT TOUCH
DO NOT TOUCH
DO NOT LEAN
DO NOT LEAN
UH, WE WERE TOLD THEY DID. NO ONE ANSWERED.
WOW. OKAY. FAIR ENOUGH.
SO. OW MANY RRORS YOU NEED?
UHHH... A HUNDRED AND...SIX?
WOW.
WHO DIED?

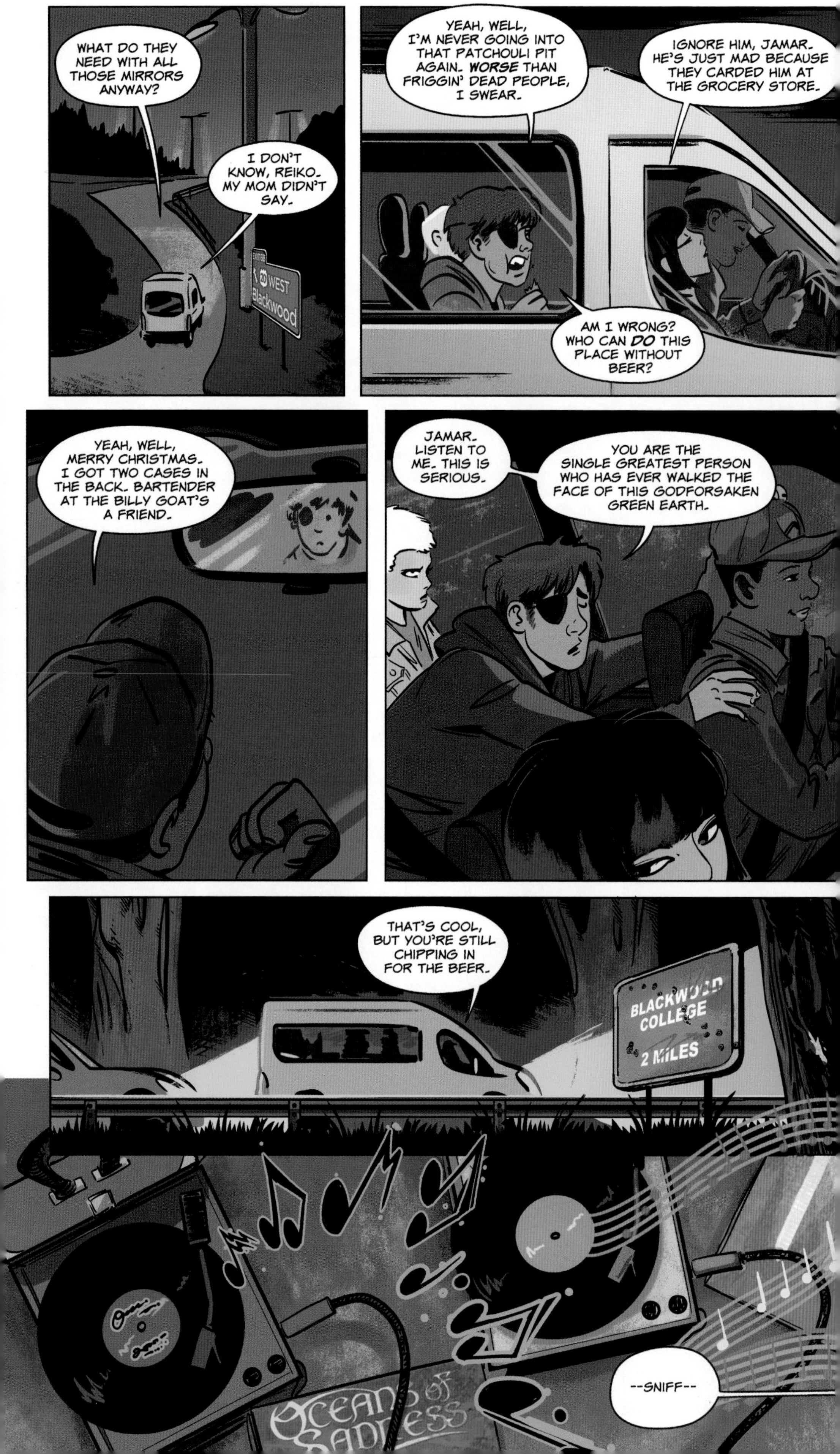
WHAT DO THEY NEED WITH ALL THOSE MIRRORS ANYWAY?
I DON'T KNOW, REIKO. MY MOM DIDN'T SAY.
EXIT 5B
20 WEST
Blackwood
YEAH, WELL, I'M NEVER GOING INTO THAT PATCHOULI PIT AGAIN. WORSE THAN FRIGGIN' DEAD PEOPLE, I SWEAR.
IGNORE HIM, JAMAR. HE'S JUST MAD BECAUSE THEY CARDED HIM AT THE GROCERY STORE.
AM I WRONG? WHO CAN DO THIS PLACE WITHOUT BEER?
YEAH, WELL, MERRY CHRISTMAS. I GOT TWO CASES IN THE BACK. BARTENDER AT THE BILLY GOAT'S A FRIEND.
JAMAR. LISTEN TO ME. THIS IS SERIOUS.
YOU ARE THE SINGLE GREATEST PERSON WHO HAS EVER WALKED THE FACE OF THIS GODFORSAKEN GREEN EARTH.
THAT'S COOL, BUT YOU'RE STILL CHIPPING IN FOR THE BEER.
BLACKWOOD COLLEGE
2 MILES
OCEANS OF SADNESS
--SNIFF--

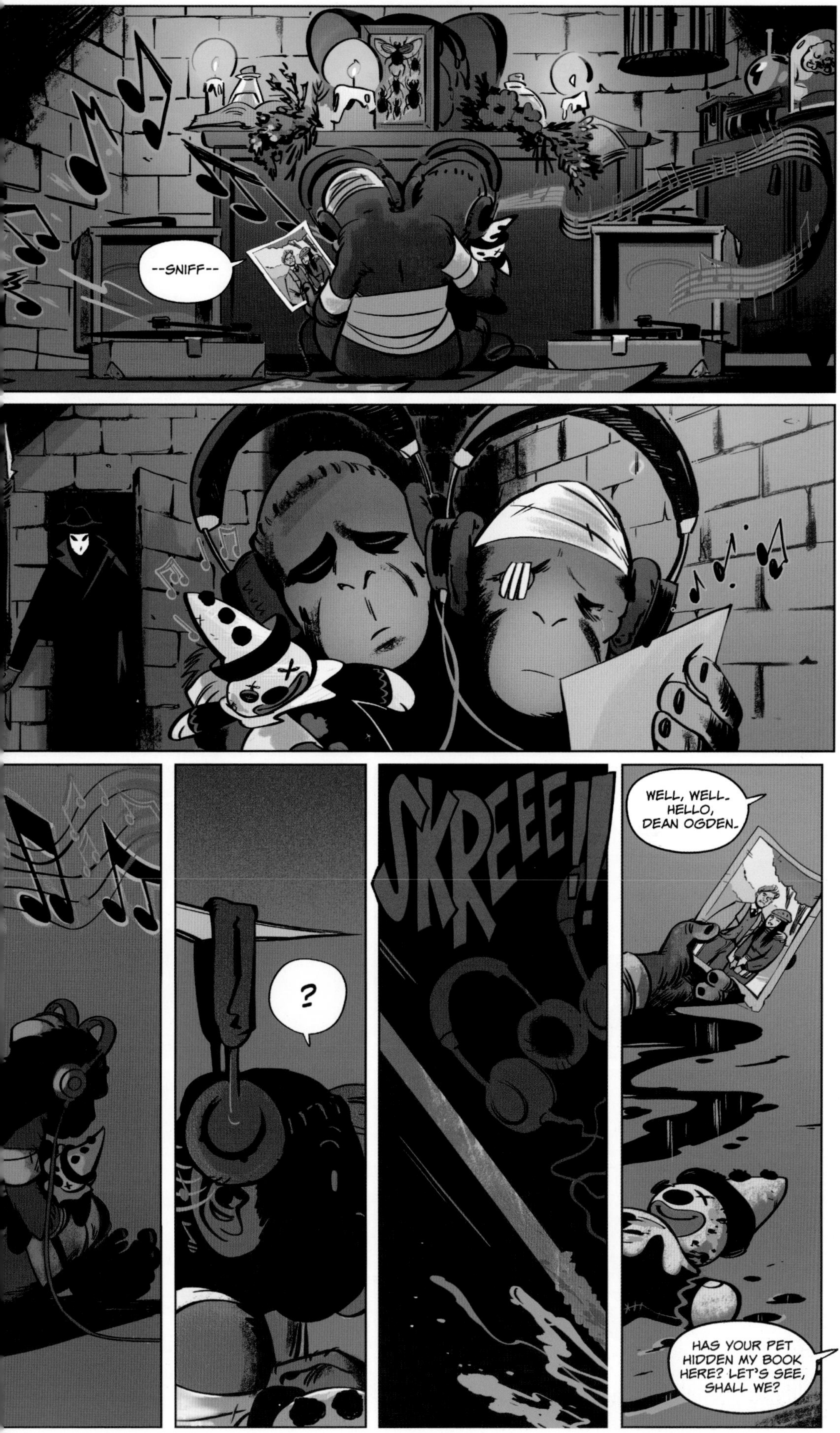
--SNIFF--
?
SKREEE!!
WELL, WELL. HELLO, DEAN OGDEN.
HAS YOUR PET HIDDEN MY BOOK HERE? LET'S SEE, SHALL WE?

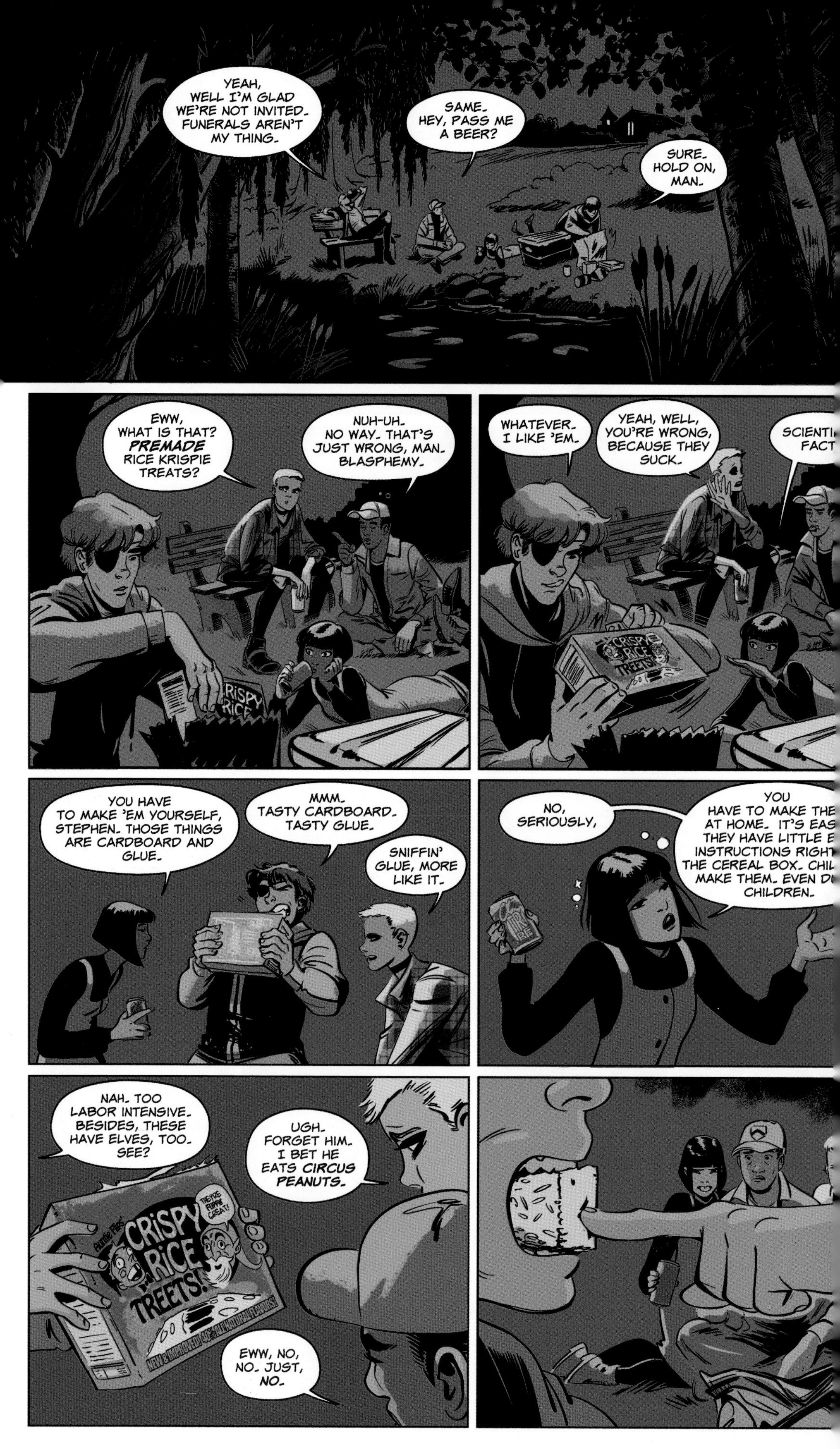
YEAH, WELL I'M GLAD WE'RE NOT INVITED. FUNERALS AREN'T MY THING.
SAME. HEY, PASS ME A BEER?
SURE. HOLD ON, MAN.
EWW, WHAT IS THAT? *PREMADE* RICE KRISPIE TREATS?
NUH-UH. NO WAY. THAT'S JUST WRONG, MAN. BLASPHEMY.
CRISPY RICE
WHATEVER. I LIKE 'EM.
YEAH, WELL, YOU'RE WRONG, BECAUSE THEY SUCK.
SCIENTI FACT
CRISPY RICE TREETS!
YOU HAVE TO MAKE 'EM YOURSELF, STEPHEN. THOSE THINGS ARE CARDBOARD AND GLUE.
MMM. TASTY CARDBOARD. TASTY GLUE.
SNIFFIN' GLUE, MORE LIKE IT.
NO, SERIOUSLY,
YOU HAVE TO MAKE THE AT HOME. IT'S EAS THEY HAVE LITTLE E INSTRUCTIONS RIGHT THE CEREAL BOX. CHIL MAKE THEM. EVEN D CHILDREN.
NAH. TOO LABOR INTENSIVE. BESIDES, THESE HAVE ELVES, TOO. SEE?
UGH. FORGET HIM. I BET HE EATS *CIRCUS PEANUTS*.
CRISPY RICE TREETS!
THEY'RE FLIPPIN' GREAT!
EWW, NO, NO. JUST, *NO*.

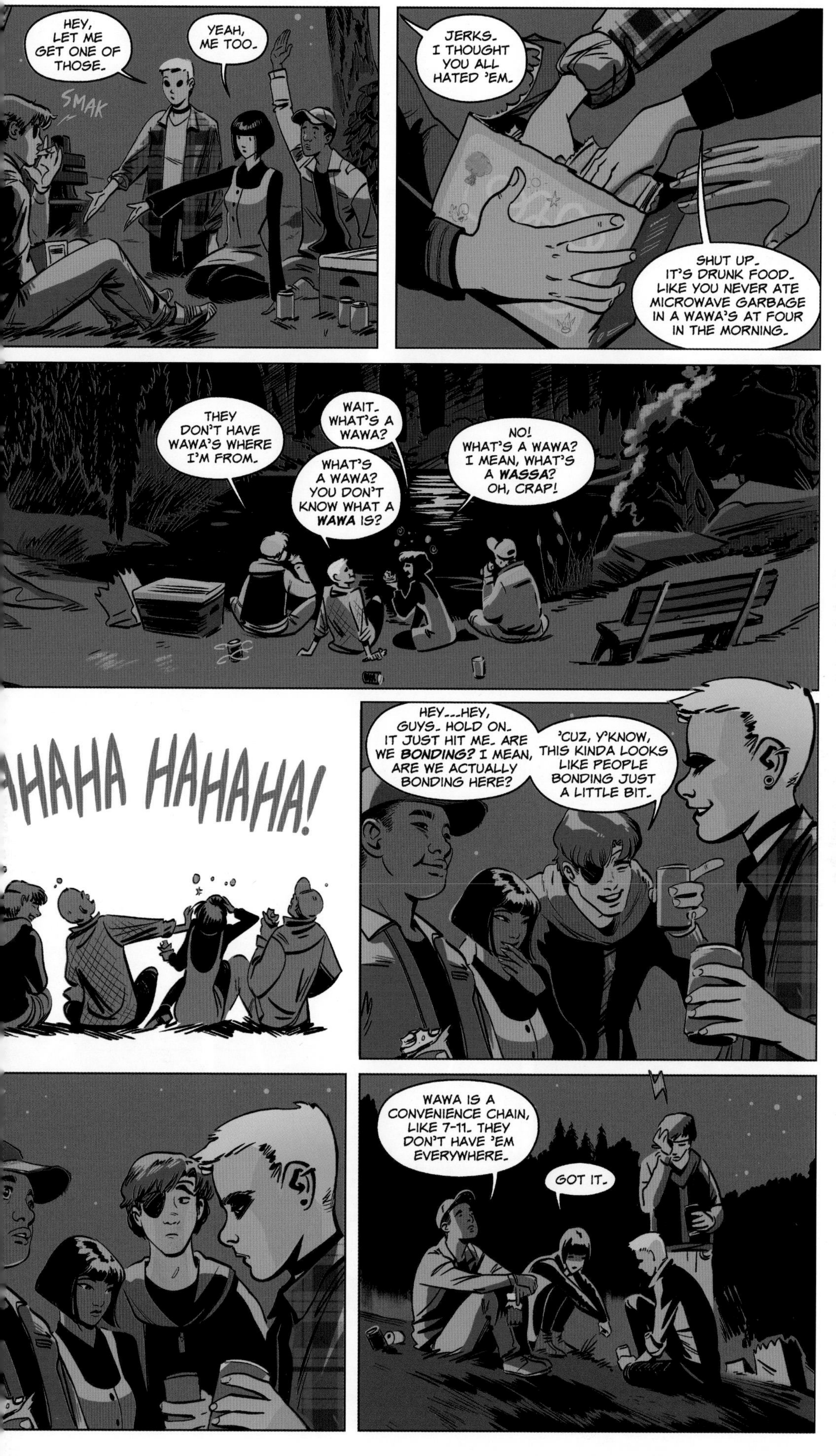
HEY, LET ME GET ONE OF THOSE.
YEAH, ME TOO.
SMAK
JERKS. I THOUGHT YOU ALL HATED 'EM.
SHUT UP. IT'S DRUNK FOOD. LIKE YOU NEVER ATE MICROWAVE GARBAGE IN A WAWA'S AT FOUR IN THE MORNING.
THEY DON'T HAVE WAWA'S WHERE I'M FROM.
WAIT. WHAT'S A WAWA?
WHAT'S A WAWA? YOU DON'T KNOW WHAT A WAWA IS?
NO! WHAT'S A WAWA? I MEAN, WHAT'S A WASSA? OH, CRAP!
AHAHA HAHAHA!
HEY...HEY, GUYS. HOLD ON. IT JUST HIT ME. ARE WE BONDING? I MEAN, ARE WE ACTUALLY BONDING HERE?
'CUZ, Y'KNOW, THIS KINDA LOOKS LIKE PEOPLE BONDING JUST A LITTLE BIT.
WAWA IS A CONVENIENCE CHAIN, LIKE 7-11. THEY DON'T HAVE 'EM EVERYWHERE.
GOT IT.

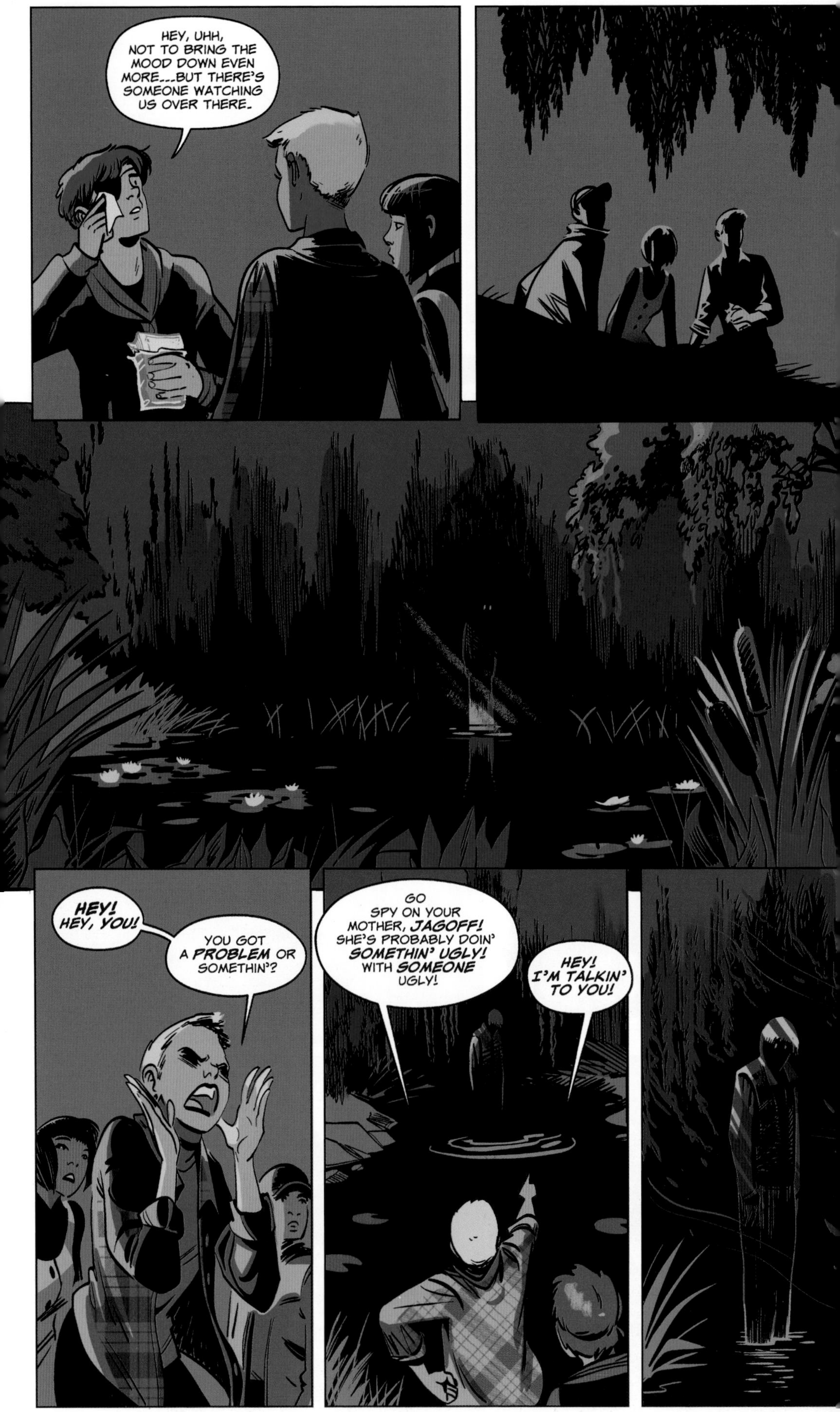
HEY, UHH, NOT TO BRING THE MOOD DOWN EVEN MORE...BUT THERE'S SOMEONE WATCHING US OVER THERE.
HEY! HEY, YOU!
YOU GOT A PROBLEM OR SOMETHIN'?
GO SPY ON YOUR MOTHER, JAGOFF! SHE'S PROBABLY DOIN' SOMETHIN' UGLY! WITH SOMEONE UGLY!
HEY! I'M TALKIN' TO YOU!

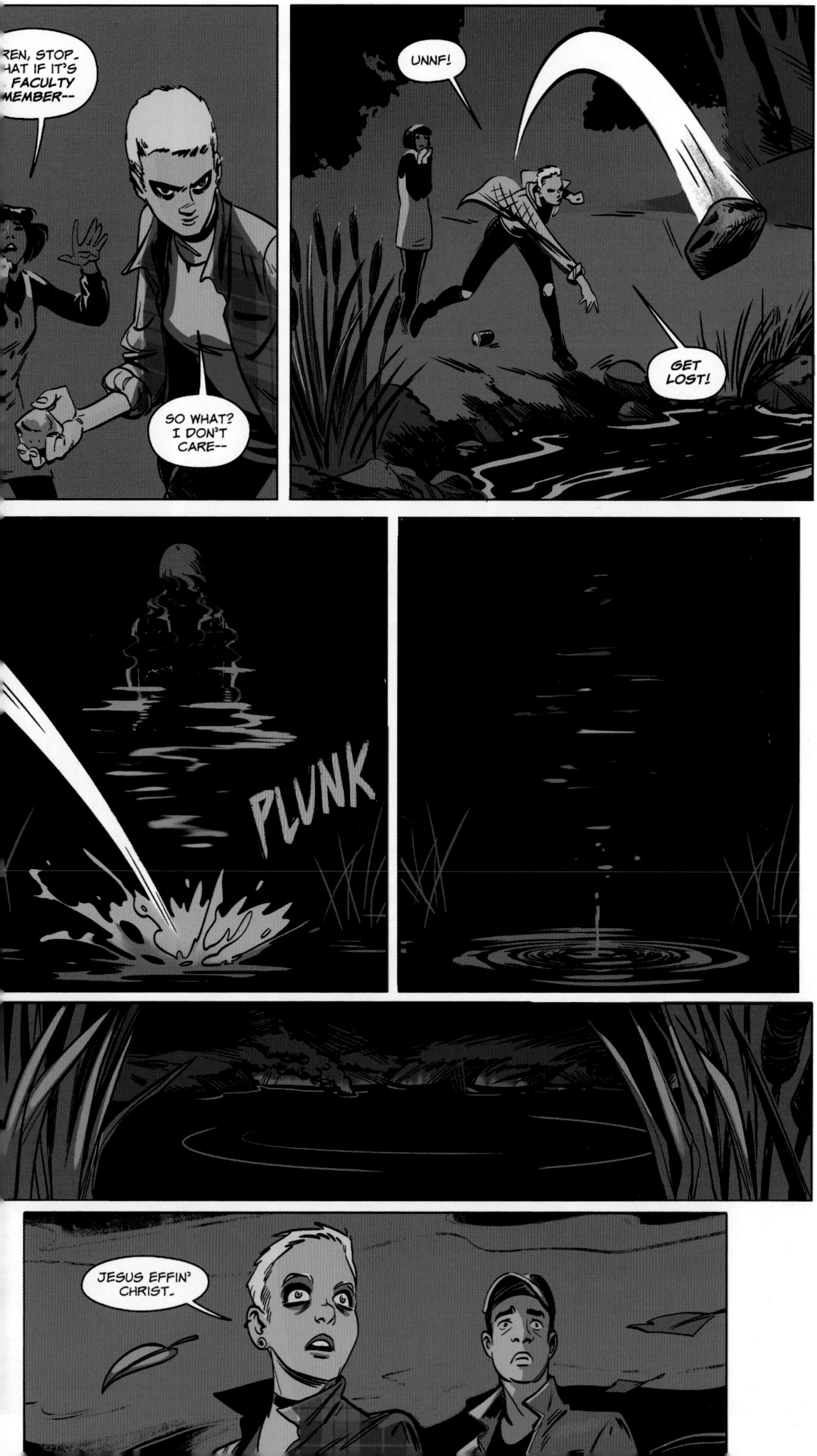

REN, STOP. HAT IF IT'S FACULTY MEMBER--
SO WHAT? I DON'T CARE--
UNNF!
GET LOST!
PLUNK
JESUS EFFIN' CHRIST.

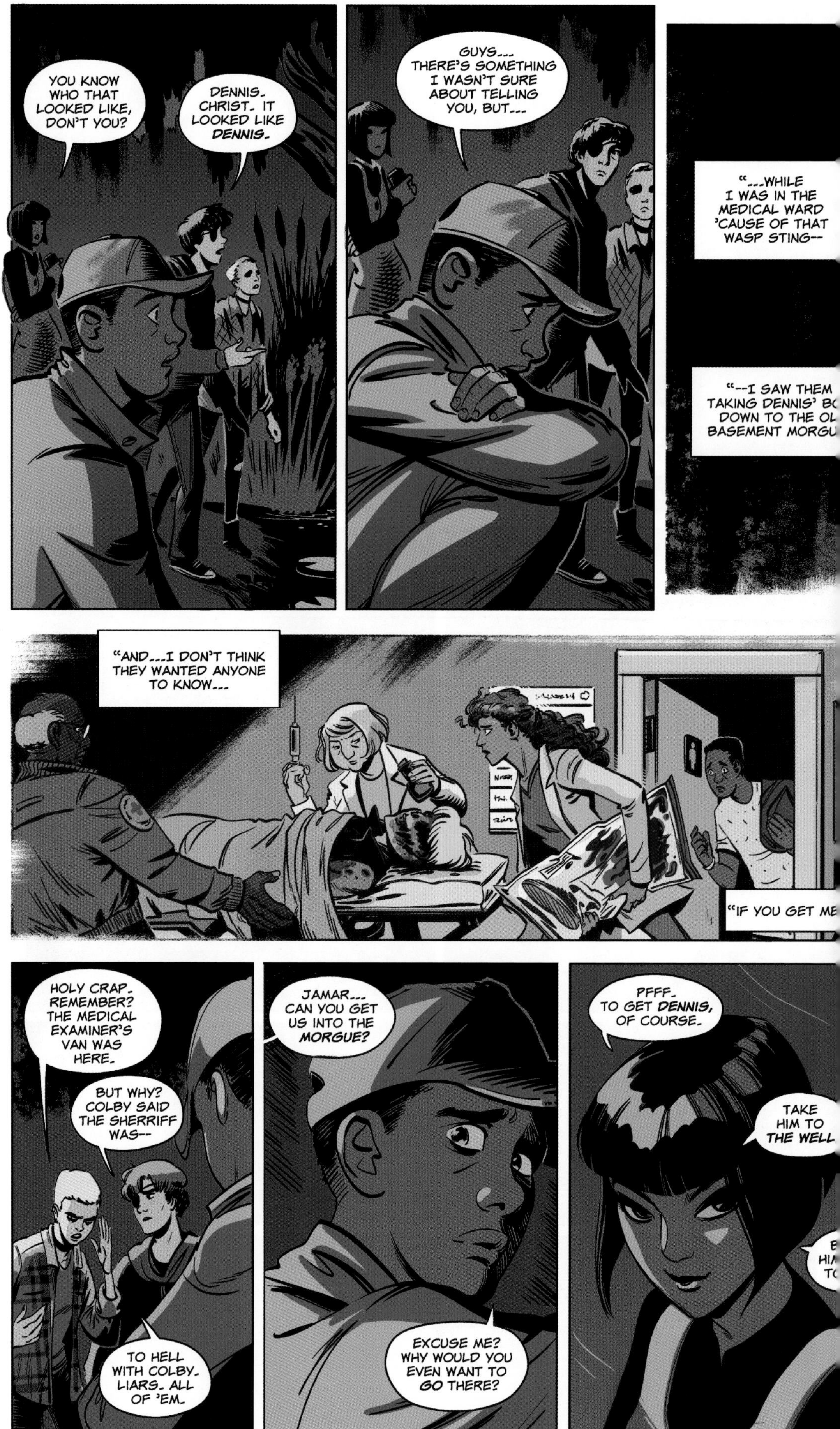

YOU KNOW WHO THAT LOOKED LIKE, DON'T YOU?
DENNIS. CHRIST. IT LOOKED LIKE DENNIS.
GUYS... THERE'S SOMETHING I WASN'T SURE ABOUT TELLING YOU, BUT...
"...WHILE I WAS IN THE MEDICAL WARD 'CAUSE OF THAT WASP STING--
"--I SAW THEM TAKING DENNIS' BO DOWN TO THE OL BASEMENT MORGU
"AND...I DON'T THINK THEY WANTED ANYONE TO KNOW...
"IF YOU GET ME
HOLY CRAP. REMEMBER? THE MEDICAL EXAMINER'S VAN WAS HERE.
BUT WHY? COLBY SAID THE SHERRIFF WAS--
TO HELL WITH COLBY. LIARS. ALL OF 'EM.
JAMAR... CAN YOU GET US INTO THE MORGUE?
EXCUSE ME? WHY WOULD YOU EVEN WANT TO GO THERE?
PFFF. TO GET DENNIS, OF COURSE.
TAKE HIM TO THE WELL

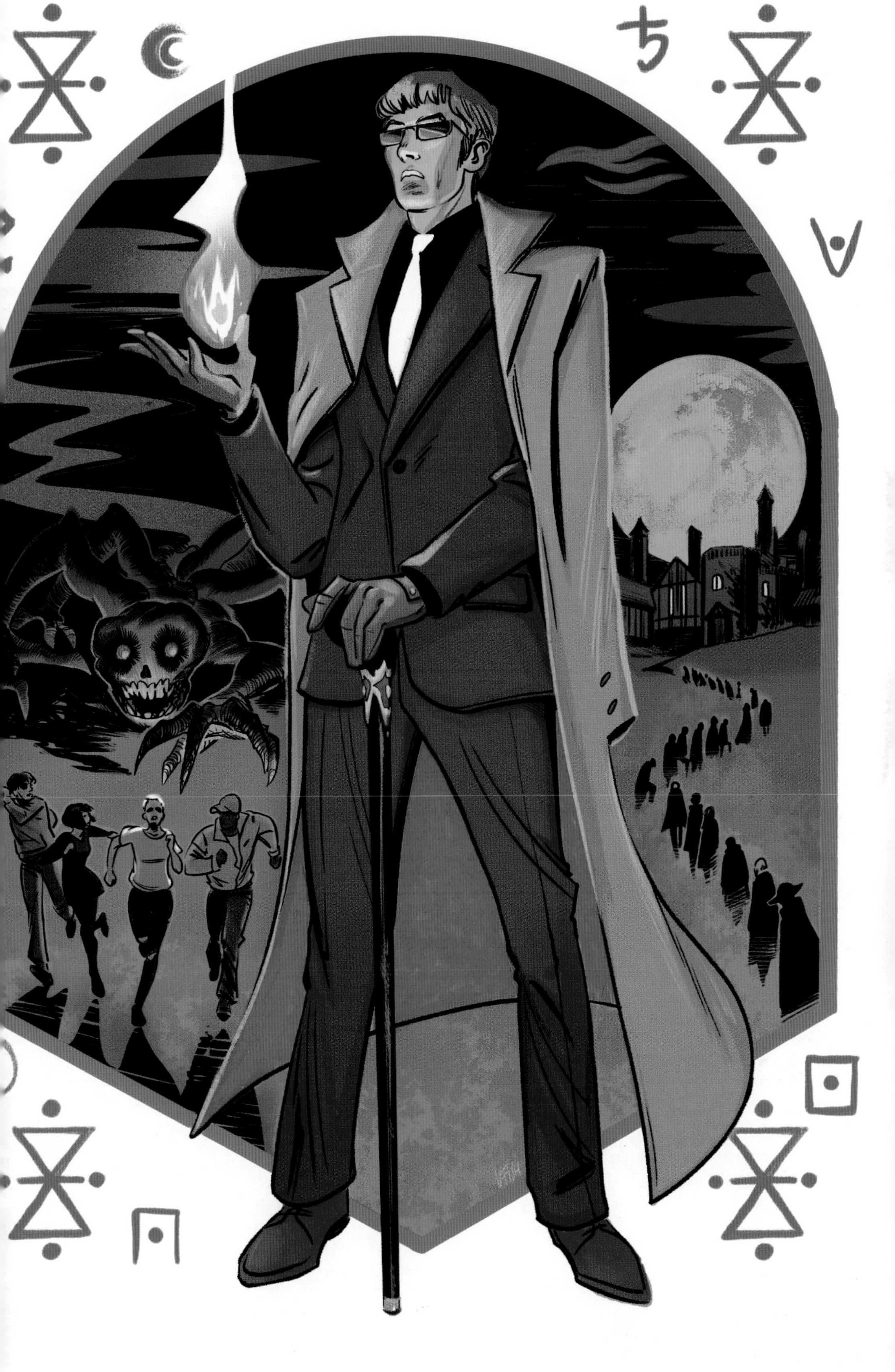

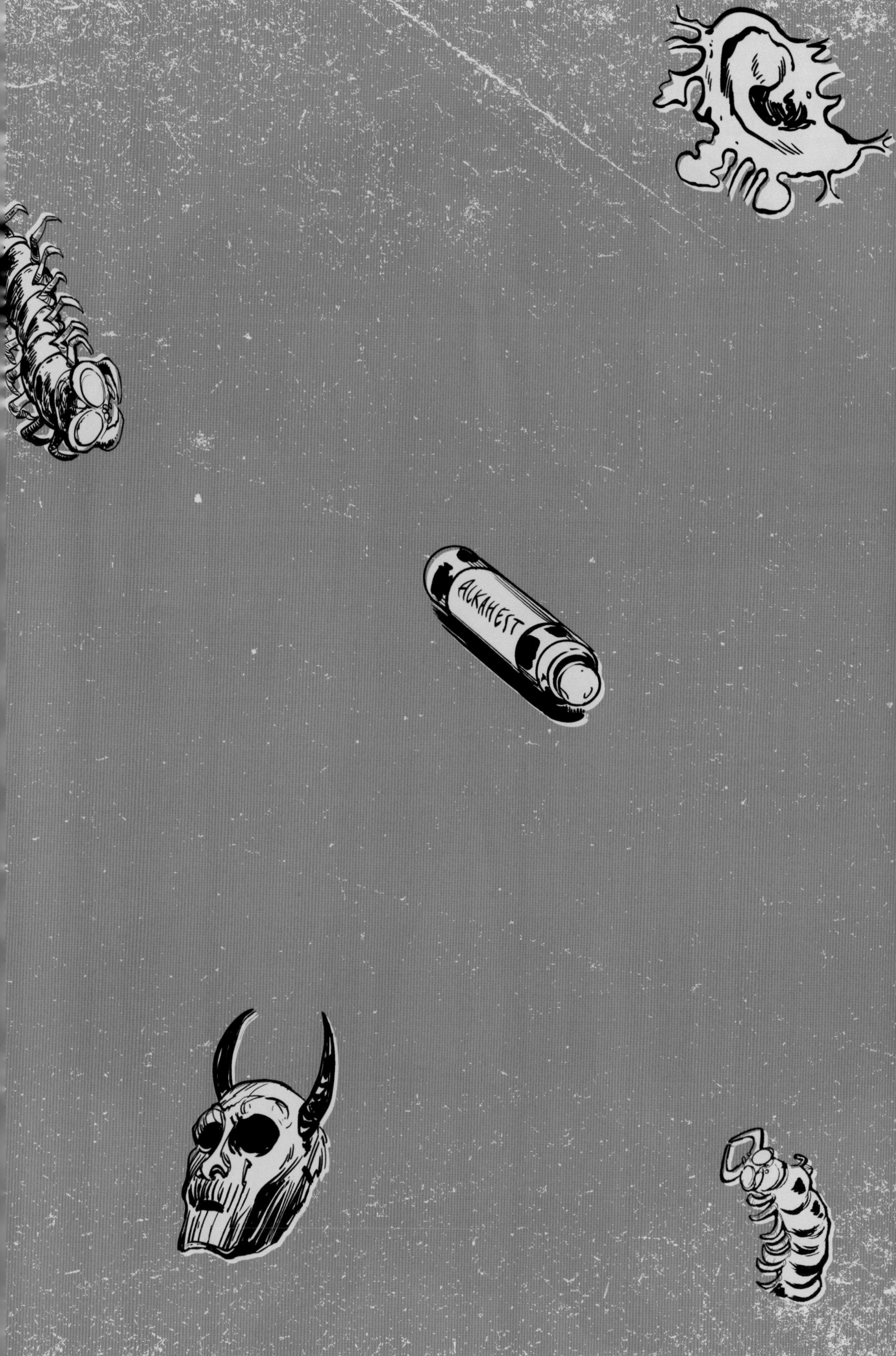
ALKAHEST

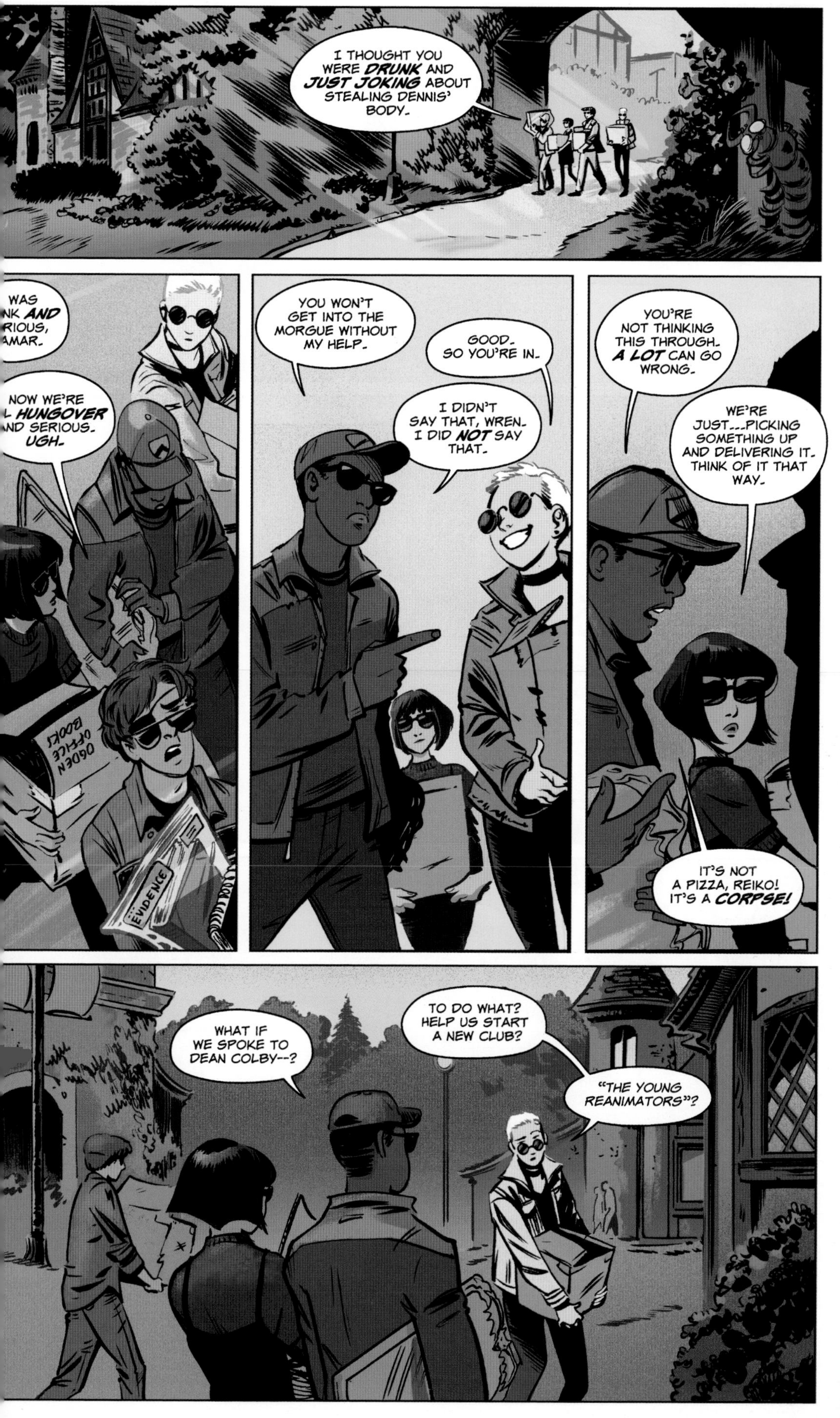

I THOUGHT YOU WERE DRUNK AND JUST JOKING ABOUT STEALING DENNIS' BODY.
WAS
NK AND
RIOUS,
AMAR.
NOW WE'RE
L HUNGOVER
AND SERIOUS.
UGH.
EVIDENCE
YOU WON'T GET INTO THE MORGUE WITHOUT MY HELP.
GOOD. SO YOU'RE IN.
I DIDN'T SAY THAT, WREN. I DID NOT SAY THAT.
YOU'RE NOT THINKING THIS THROUGH. A LOT CAN GO WRONG.
WE'RE JUST...PICKING SOMETHING UP AND DELIVERING IT. THINK OF IT THAT WAY.
IT'S NOT A PIZZA, REIKO! IT'S A CORPSE!
WHAT IF WE SPOKE TO DEAN COLBY--?
TO DO WHAT? HELP US START A NEW CLUB?
"THE YOUNG REANIMATORS"?

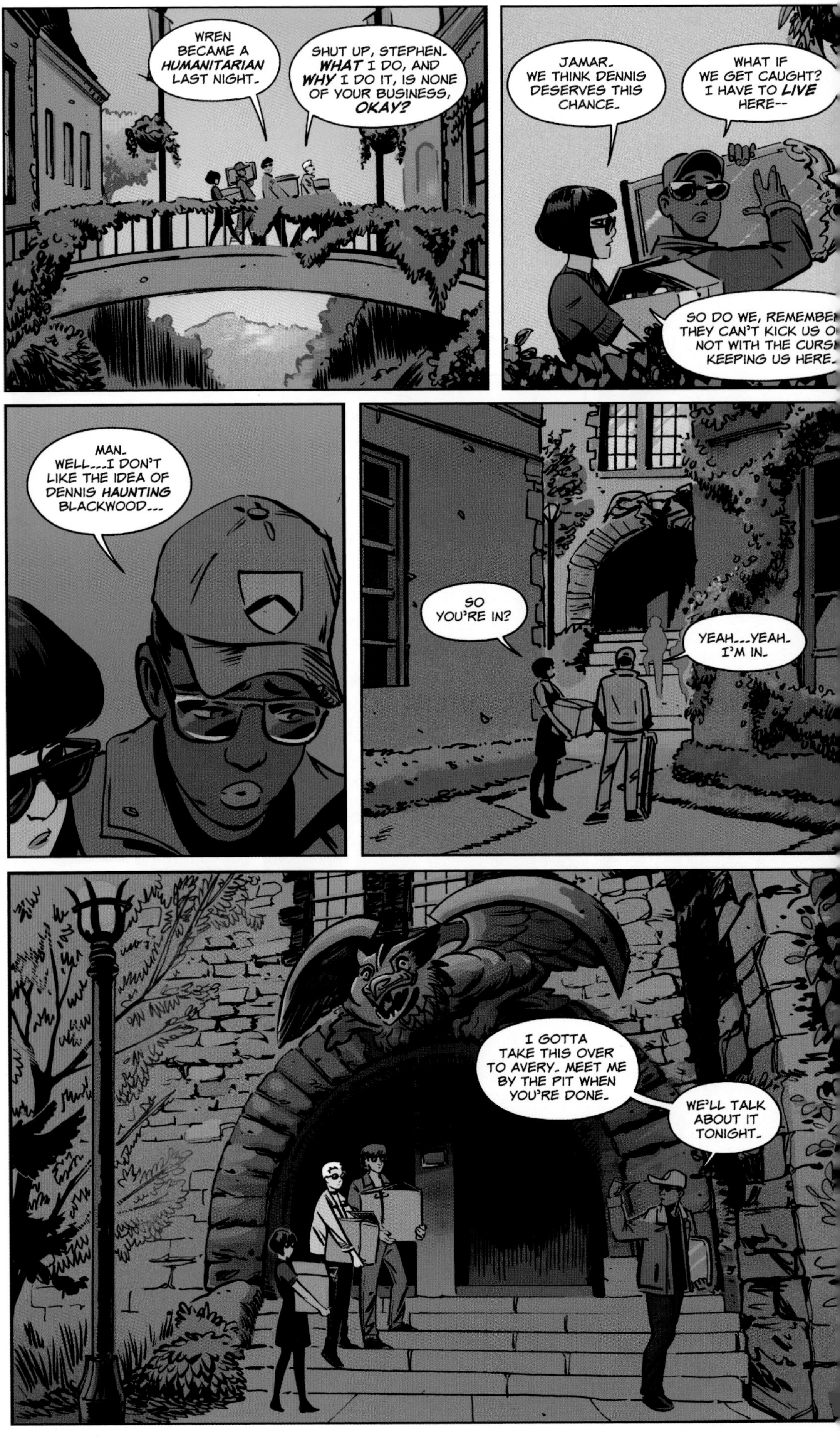
WREN BECAME A *HUMANITARIAN* LAST NIGHT.
SHUT UP, STEPHEN. ***WHAT*** I DO, AND ***WHY*** I DO IT, IS NONE OF YOUR BUSINESS, ***OKAY?***
JAMAR. WE THINK DENNIS DESERVES THIS CHANCE.
WHAT IF WE GET CAUGHT? I HAVE TO ***LIVE*** HERE--
SO DO WE, REMEMBE
THEY CAN'T KICK US O
NOT WITH THE CURS
KEEPING US HERE.
MAN. WELL...I DON'T LIKE THE IDEA OF DENNIS ***HAUNTING*** BLACKWOOD...
SO YOU'RE IN?
YEAH...YEAH. I'M IN.
I GOTTA TAKE THIS OVER TO AVERY. MEET ME BY THE PIT WHEN YOU'RE DONE.
WE'LL TALK ABOUT IT TONIGHT.

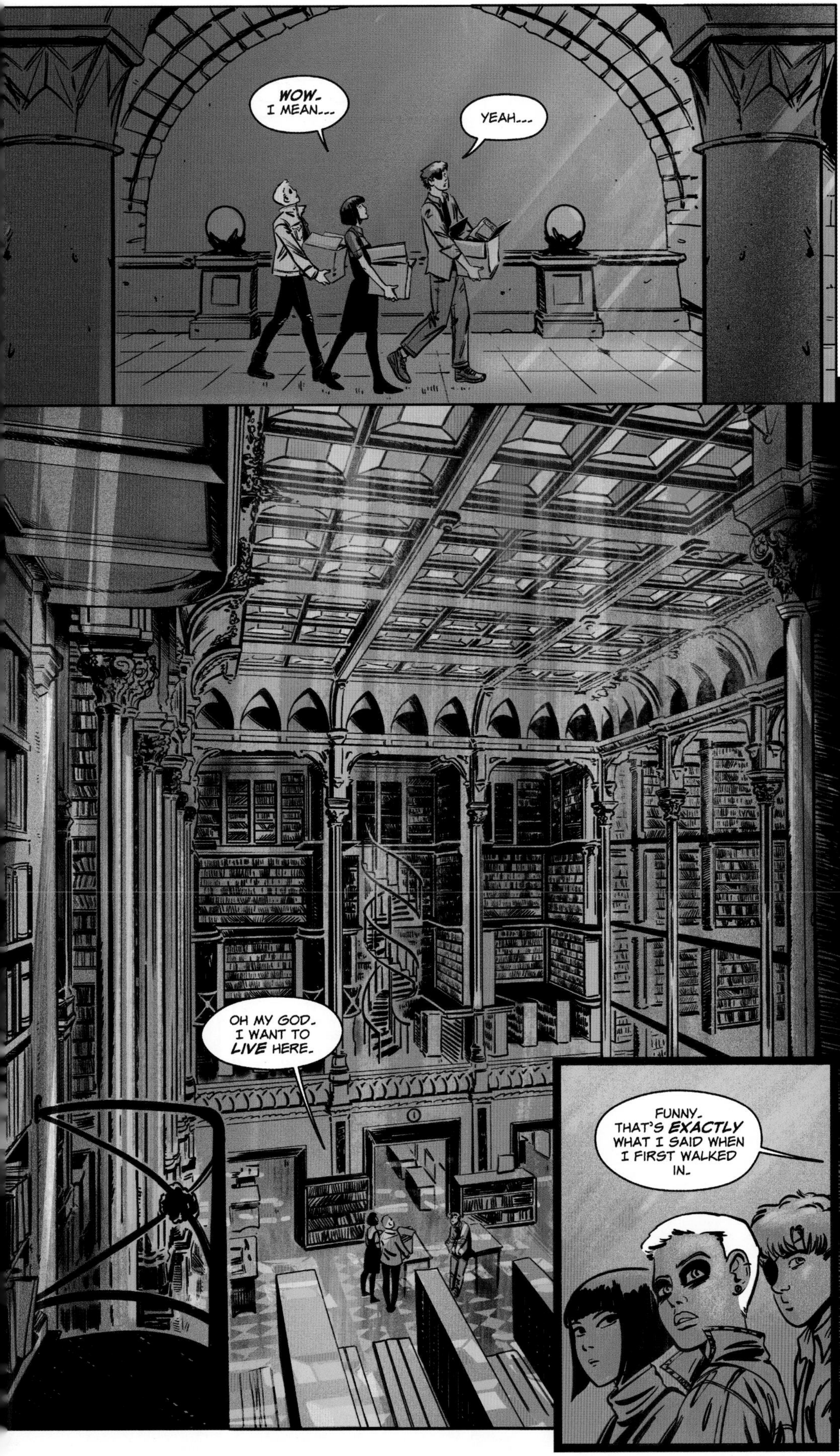
WOW. I MEAN...
YEAH...
OH MY GOD. I WANT TO LIVE HERE.
FUNNY. THAT'S EXACTLY WHAT I SAID WHEN I FIRST WALKED IN.

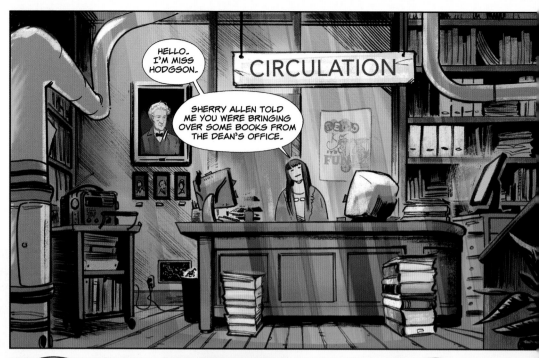

CIRCULATION

HELLO. I'M MISS HODGSON.

SHERRY ALLEN TOLD ME YOU WERE BRINGING OVER SOME BOOKS FROM THE DEAN'S OFFICE.

YOU CAN JUST PUT THEM ON THE COUNTER.

OH, *GOOD*. THEY BAGGED *THE BLOOD TEXT*. HEARD YOU HAD SOME TROUBLE WITH THAT ONE.

POOR DEAN OGDEN. WONDERFUL MAN, BUT HE NEVER RETURNED ANYTHING. CLASSIC BOOK HOARDER.

I'M SURPRISED THE LIBRARY'S OPEN DURING BREAK. DOESN'T IT GET LONELY HERE?

OH, NO. YOU'RE N— ALONE WITH — AND OF CO— WE HAVE CATS

OH, YOU WON'T SEE THEM. NOT UNTIL THEY WANT YOU TO. THEY ARE *CATS*, AFTER ALL.

YEAH. WELL, WE SHOULD GET GOING. C'MON REIKO. YOU CAN MOVE IN LATER.

IT.... WAS NICE MEETING YOU. I'LL BE BACK. *SOON*.

COME BACK ANYTIME. SOMEONE WILL ALWAYS BE HERE.

THE LIBRARY NEVER CLOSES.

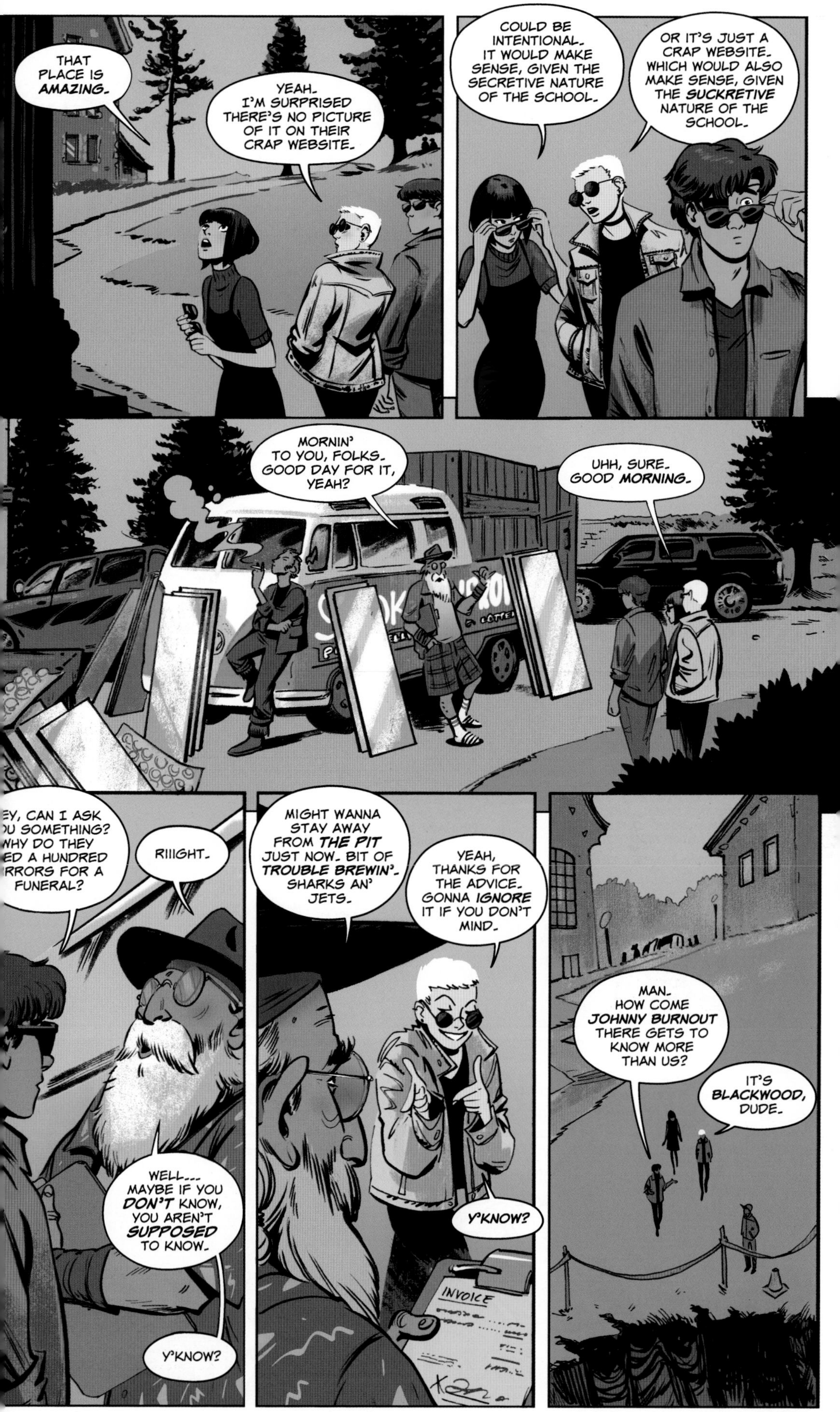
THAT PLACE IS **AMAZING**.
YEAH. I'M SURPRISED THERE'S NO PICTURE OF IT ON THEIR CRAP WEBSITE.
COULD BE INTENTIONAL. IT WOULD MAKE SENSE, GIVEN THE SECRETIVE NATURE OF THE SCHOOL.
OR IT'S JUST A CRAP WEBSITE. WHICH WOULD ALSO MAKE SENSE, GIVEN THE ***SUCKRETIVE*** NATURE OF THE SCHOOL.
MORNIN' TO YOU, FOLKS. GOOD DAY FOR IT, YEAH?
UHH, SURE. GOOD **MORNING**.
EY, CAN I ASK OU SOMETHING? WHY DO THEY ED A HUNDRED RRORS FOR A FUNERAL?
RIIIGHT.
WELL... MAYBE IF YOU ***DON'T*** KNOW, YOU AREN'T ***SUPPOSED*** TO KNOW.
Y'KNOW?
MIGHT WANNA STAY AWAY FROM ***THE PIT*** JUST NOW. BIT OF ***TROUBLE BREWIN'***. SHARKS AN' JETS.
YEAH, THANKS FOR THE ADVICE. GONNA ***IGNORE*** IT IF YOU DON'T MIND.
Y'KNOW?
INVOICE
MAN. HOW COME ***JOHNNY BURNOUT*** THERE GETS TO KNOW MORE THAN US?
IT'S ***BLACKWOOD,*** DUDE.

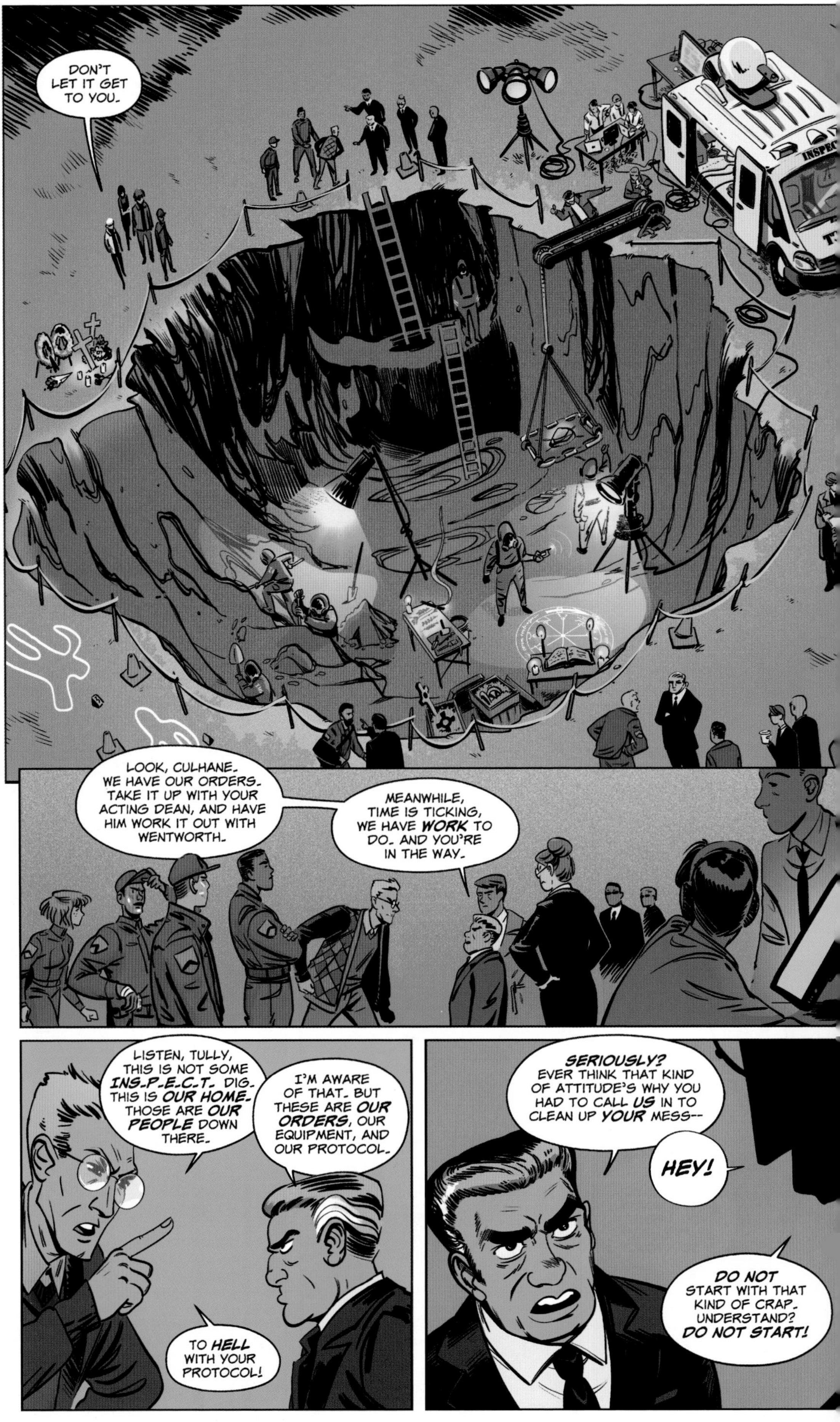
DON'T LET IT GET TO YOU.
INSPEC
LOOK, CULHANE. WE HAVE OUR ORDERS. TAKE IT UP WITH YOUR ACTING DEAN, AND HAVE HIM WORK IT OUT WITH WENTWORTH.
MEANWHILE, TIME IS TICKING, WE HAVE WORK TO DO. AND YOU'RE IN THE WAY.
LISTEN, TULLY, THIS IS NOT SOME INS.P.E.C.T. DIG. THIS IS OUR HOME. THOSE ARE OUR PEOPLE DOWN THERE.
I'M AWARE OF THAT. BUT THESE ARE OUR ORDERS, OUR EQUIPMENT, AND OUR PROTOCOL.
TO HELL WITH YOUR PROTOCOL!
SERIOUSLY? EVER THINK THAT KIND OF ATTITUDE'S WHY YOU HAD TO CALL US IN TO CLEAN UP YOUR MESS--
HEY!
DO NOT START WITH THAT KIND OF CRAP. UNDERSTAND? DO NOT START!

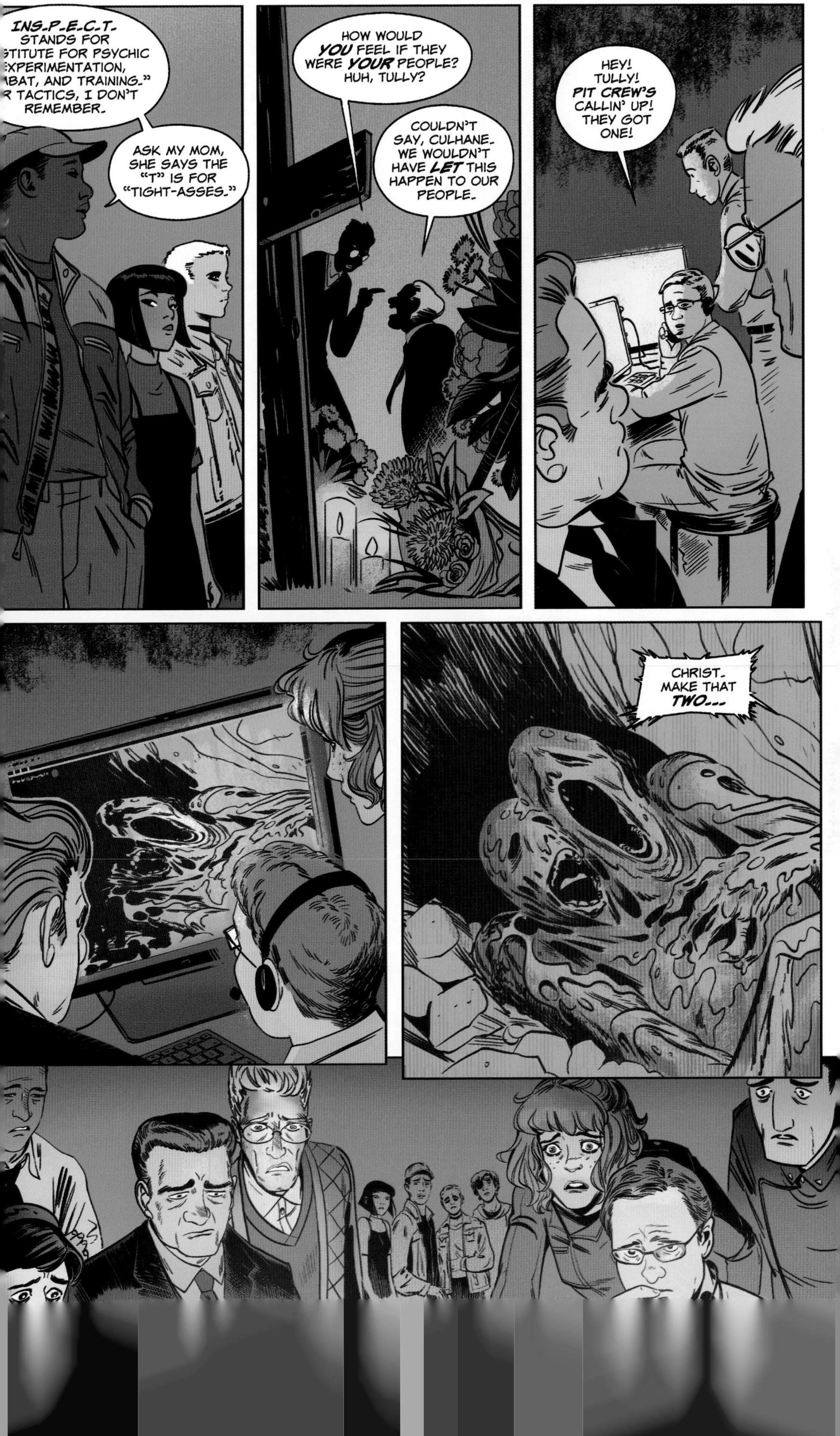
INS.P.E.C.T. STANDS FOR
STITUTE FOR PSYCHIC
EXPERIMENTATION,
BAT, AND TRAINING."
R TACTICS, I DON'T REMEMBER.
ASK MY MOM, SHE SAYS THE "T" IS FOR "TIGHT-ASSES."
HOW WOULD YOU FEEL IF THEY WERE YOUR PEOPLE? HUH, TULLY?
COULDN'T SAY, CULHANE. WE WOULDN'T HAVE LET THIS HAPPEN TO OUR PEOPLE.
HEY! TULLY! PIT CREW'S CALLIN' UP! THEY GOT ONE!
CHRIST. MAKE THAT TWO...

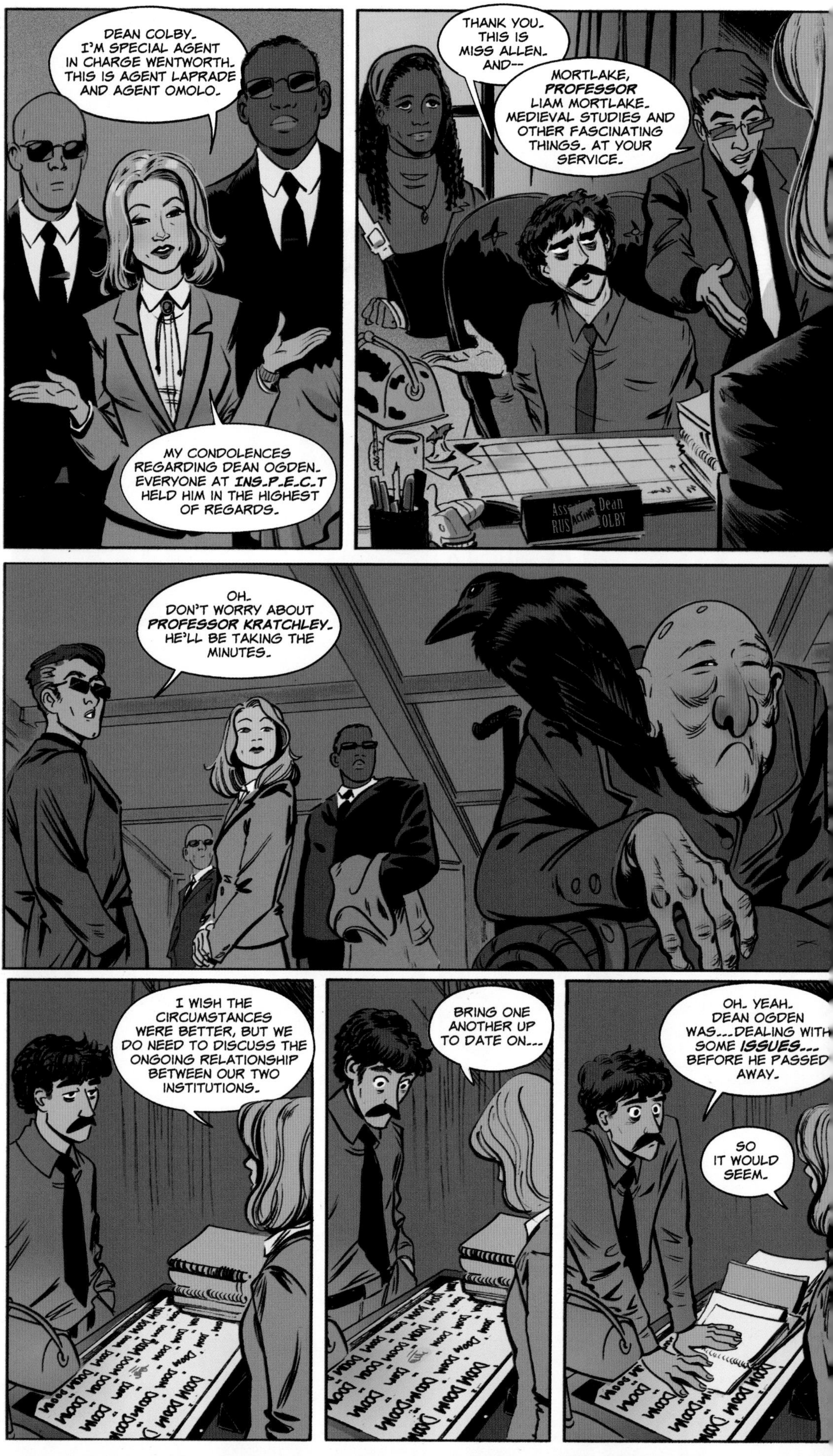
DEAN COLBY. I'M SPECIAL AGENT IN CHARGE WENTWORTH. THIS IS AGENT LAPRADE AND AGENT OMOLO.
MY CONDOLENCES REGARDING DEAN OGDEN. EVERYONE AT INS.P.E.C.T HELD HIM IN THE HIGHEST OF REGARDS.
THANK YOU. THIS IS MISS ALLEN. AND--
MORTLAKE, **PROFESSOR** LIAM MORTLAKE. MEDIEVAL STUDIES AND OTHER FASCINATING THINGS. AT YOUR SERVICE.
OH. DON'T WORRY ABOUT **PROFESSOR KRATCHLEY.** HE'LL BE TAKING THE MINUTES.
I WISH THE CIRCUMSTANCES WERE BETTER, BUT WE DO NEED TO DISCUSS THE ONGOING RELATIONSHIP BETWEEN OUR TWO INSTITUTIONS.
BRING ONE ANOTHER UP TO DATE ON...
OH. YEAH. DEAN OGDEN WAS...DEALING WITH SOME ***ISSUES...*** BEFORE HE PASSED AWAY.
SO IT WOULD SEEM.

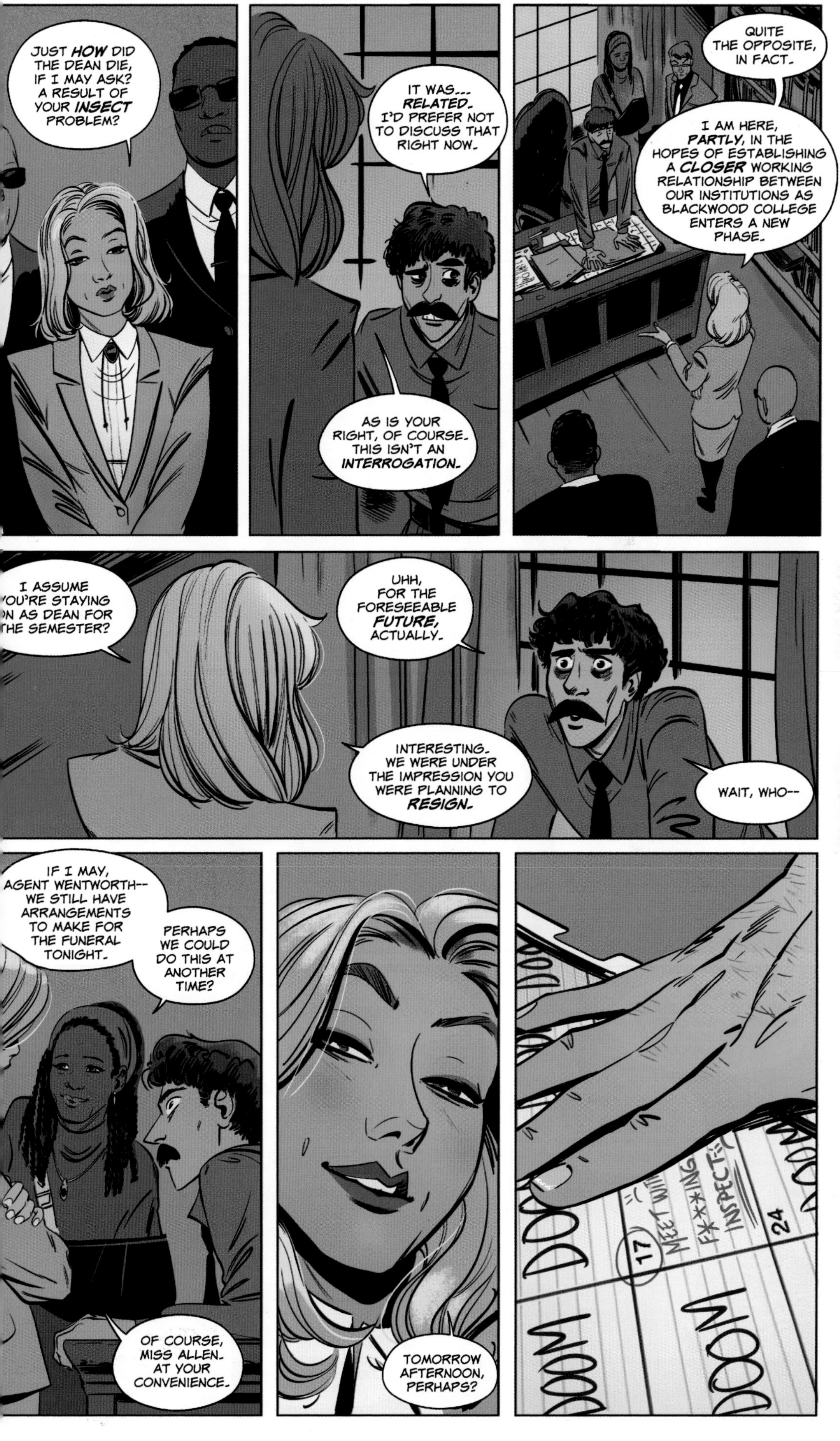
JUST HOW DID THE DEAN DIE, IF I MAY ASK? A RESULT OF YOUR INSECT PROBLEM?
IT WAS... RELATED. I'D PREFER NOT TO DISCUSS THAT RIGHT NOW.
AS IS YOUR RIGHT, OF COURSE. THIS ISN'T AN INTERROGATION.
QUITE THE OPPOSITE, IN FACT.
I AM HERE, PARTLY, IN THE HOPES OF ESTABLISHING A CLOSER WORKING RELATIONSHIP BETWEEN OUR INSTITUTIONS AS BLACKWOOD COLLEGE ENTERS A NEW PHASE.
I ASSUME YOU'RE STAYING ON AS DEAN FOR THE SEMESTER?
UHH, FOR THE FORESEEABLE FUTURE, ACTUALLY.
INTERESTING. WE WERE UNDER THE IMPRESSION YOU WERE PLANNING TO RESIGN.
WAIT, WHO--
IF I MAY, AGENT WENTWORTH-- WE STILL HAVE ARRANGEMENTS TO MAKE FOR THE FUNERAL TONIGHT.
PERHAPS WE COULD DO THIS AT ANOTHER TIME?
OF COURSE, MISS ALLEN. AT YOUR CONVENIENCE.
TOMORROW AFTERNOON, PERHAPS?
17
MEET WITH
F***ING
INSPECT
24
DOOM
DOOM
DOOM

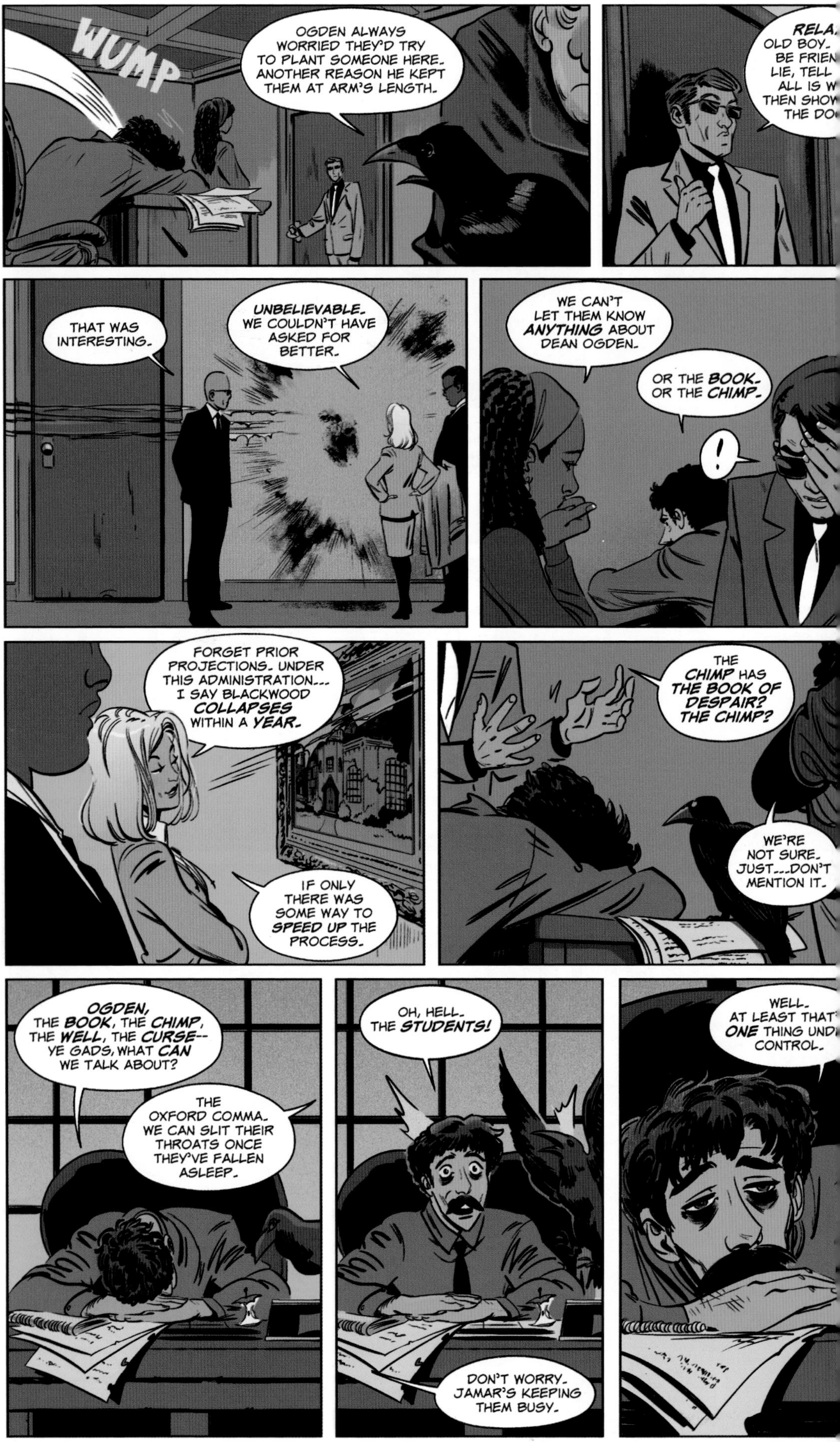
WUMP
OGDEN ALWAYS WORRIED THEY'D TRY TO PLANT SOMEONE HERE. ANOTHER REASON HE KEPT THEM AT ARM'S LENGTH.
RELA
OLD BOY.
BE FRIEN
LIE, TELL
ALL IS W
THEN SHOW
THE DO
THAT WAS INTERESTING.
UNBELIEVABLE. WE COULDN'T HAVE ASKED FOR BETTER.
WE CAN'T LET THEM KNOW ANYTHING ABOUT DEAN OGDEN.
OR THE BOOK. OR THE CHIMP.
!
FORGET PRIOR PROJECTIONS. UNDER THIS ADMINISTRATION... I SAY BLACKWOOD COLLAPSES WITHIN A YEAR.
IF ONLY THERE WAS SOME WAY TO SPEED UP THE PROCESS.
THE CHIMP HAS THE BOOK OF DESPAIR? THE CHIMP?
WE'RE NOT SURE. JUST...DON'T MENTION IT.
OGDEN, THE BOOK, THE CHIMP, THE WELL, THE CURSE-- YE GADS, WHAT CAN WE TALK ABOUT?
THE OXFORD COMMA. WE CAN SLIT THEIR THROATS ONCE THEY'VE FALLEN ASLEEP.
OH, HELL. THE STUDENTS!
DON'T WORRY. JAMAR'S KEEPING THEM BUSY.
WELL. AT LEAST THAT'
ONE THING UND
CONTROL.

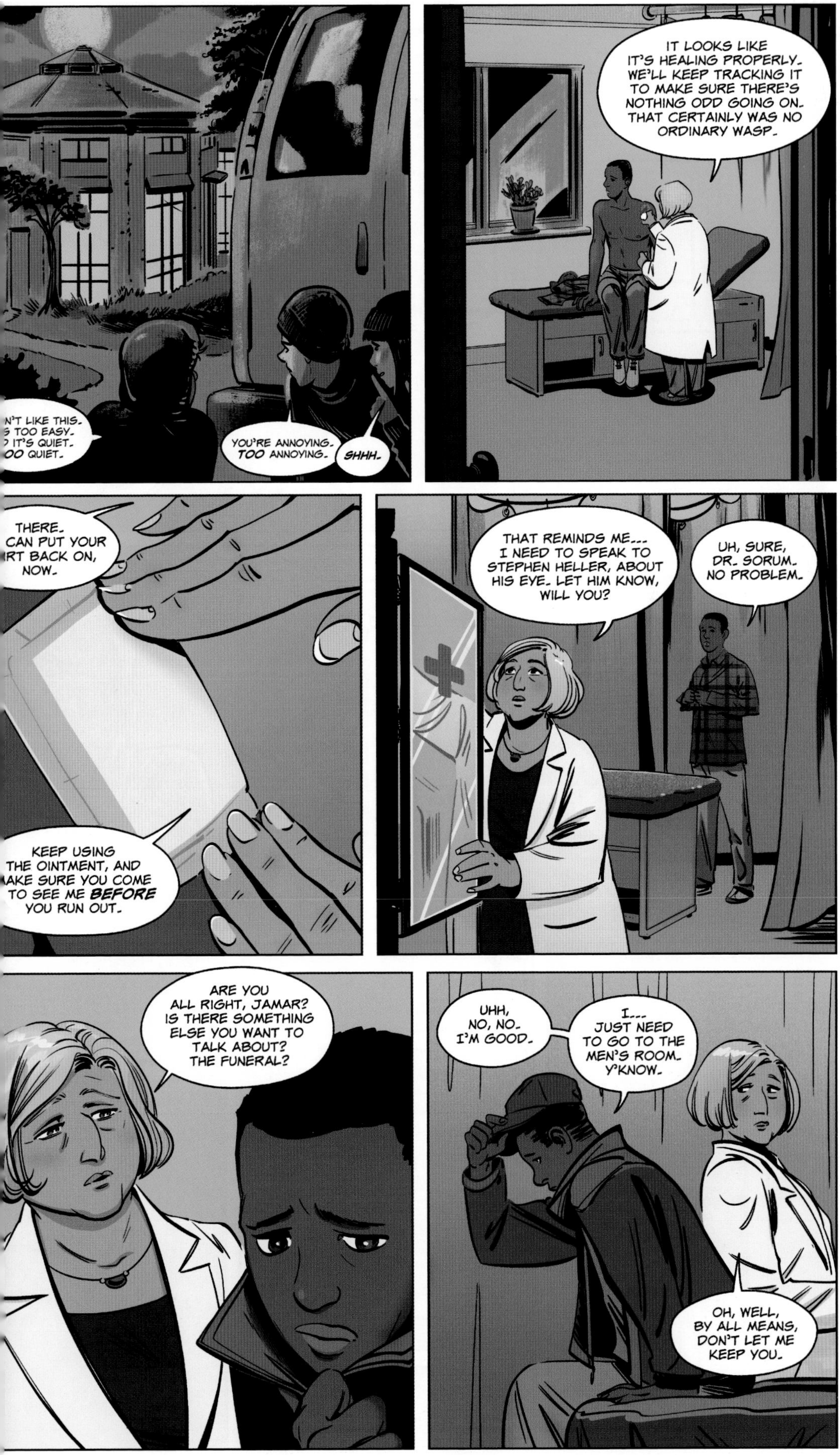
N'T LIKE THIS.
S TOO EASY.
D IT'S QUIET.
OO QUIET.
YOU'RE ANNOYING. TOO ANNOYING.
SHHH.
IT LOOKS LIKE IT'S HEALING PROPERLY. WE'LL KEEP TRACKING IT TO MAKE SURE THERE'S NOTHING ODD GOING ON. THAT CERTAINLY WAS NO ORDINARY WASP.
THERE. CAN PUT YOUR RT BACK ON, NOW.
KEEP USING THE OINTMENT, AND AKE SURE YOU COME TO SEE ME BEFORE YOU RUN OUT.
THAT REMINDS ME... I NEED TO SPEAK TO STEPHEN HELLER, ABOUT HIS EYE. LET HIM KNOW, WILL YOU?
UH, SURE, DR. SORUM. NO PROBLEM.
ARE YOU ALL RIGHT, JAMAR? IS THERE SOMETHING ELSE YOU WANT TO TALK ABOUT? THE FUNERAL?
UHH, NO, NO. I'M GOOD.
I... JUST NEED TO GO TO THE MEN'S ROOM. Y'KNOW.
OH, WELL, BY ALL MEANS, DON'T LET ME KEEP YOU.

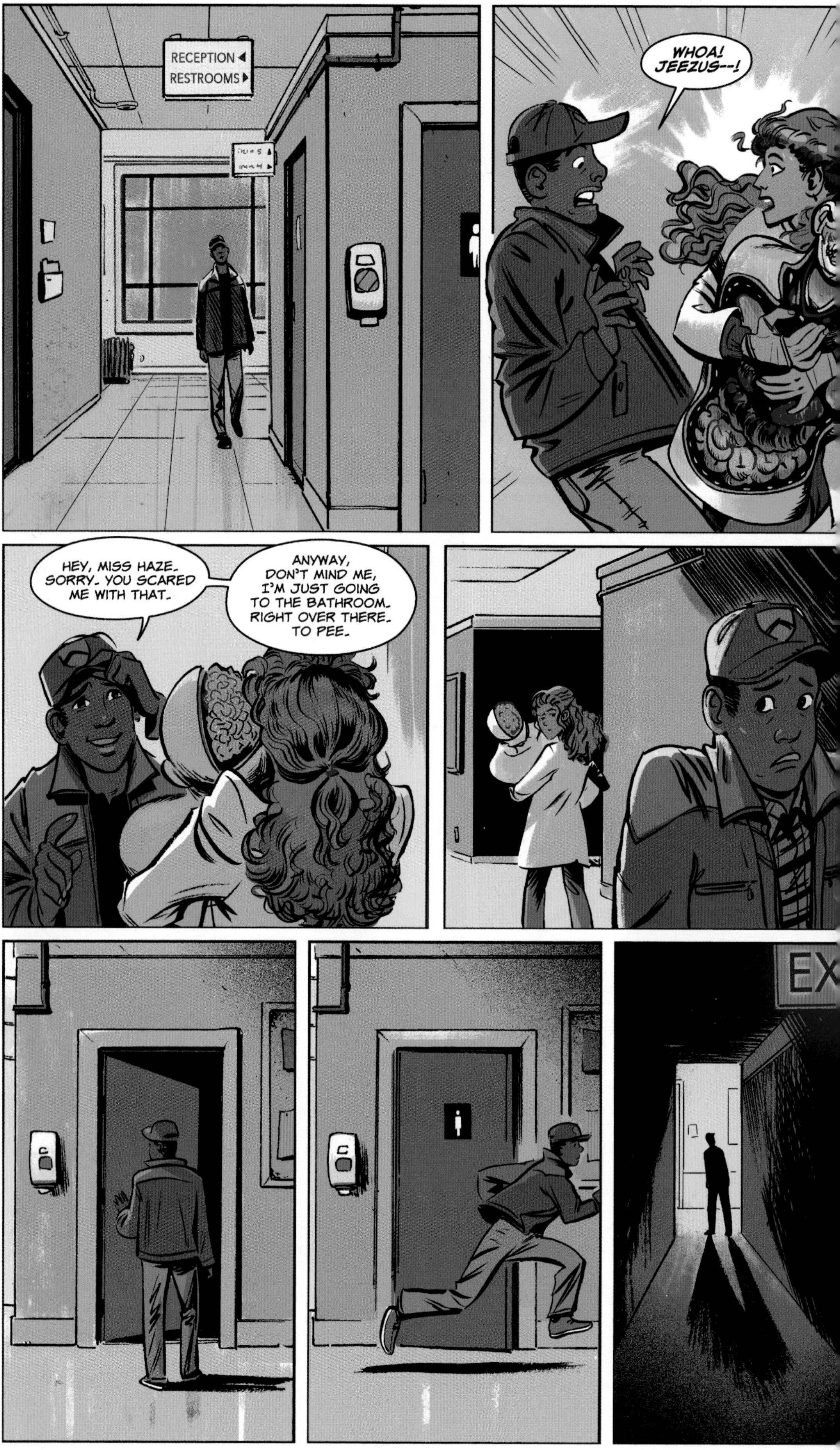
RECEPTION
RESTROOMS
WHOA! JEEZUS--!
HEY, MISS HAZE. SORRY. YOU SCARED ME WITH THAT.
ANYWAY, DON'T MIND ME, I'M JUST GOING TO THE BATHROOM. RIGHT OVER THERE. TO PEE.
EX

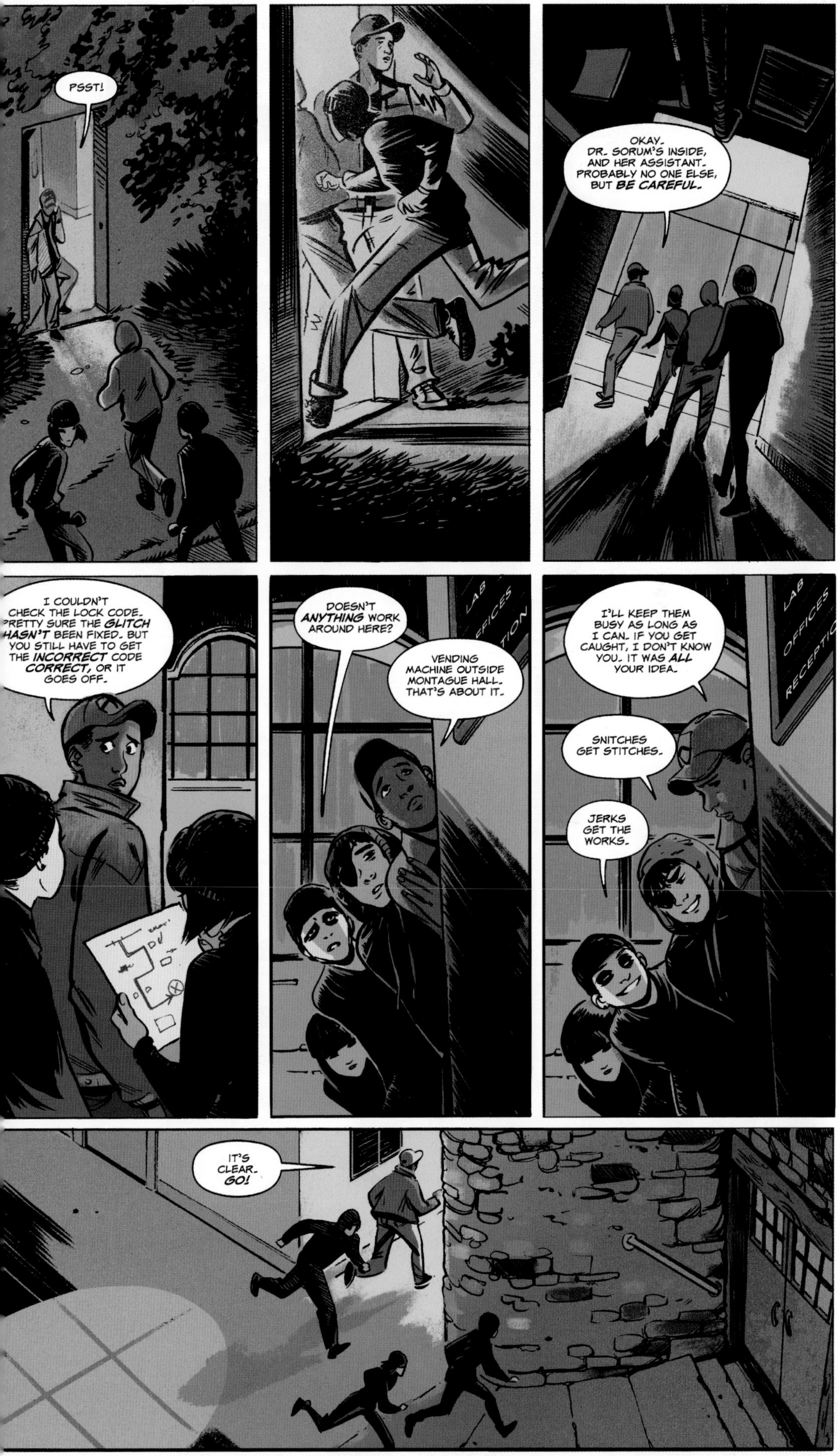
PSST!
OKAY. DR. SORUM'S INSIDE, AND HER ASSISTANT. PROBABLY NO ONE ELSE, BUT BE CAREFUL.
I COULDN'T CHECK THE LOCK CODE. PRETTY SURE THE GLITCH HASN'T BEEN FIXED. BUT YOU STILL HAVE TO GET THE INCORRECT CODE CORRECT, OR IT GOES OFF.
DOESN'T ANYTHING WORK AROUND HERE?
VENDING MACHINE OUTSIDE MONTAGUE HALL. THAT'S ABOUT IT.
I'LL KEEP THEM BUSY AS LONG AS I CAN. IF YOU GET CAUGHT, I DON'T KNOW YOU. IT WAS ALL YOUR IDEA.
SNITCHES GET STITCHES.
JERKS GET THE WORKS.
IT'S CLEAR. GO!

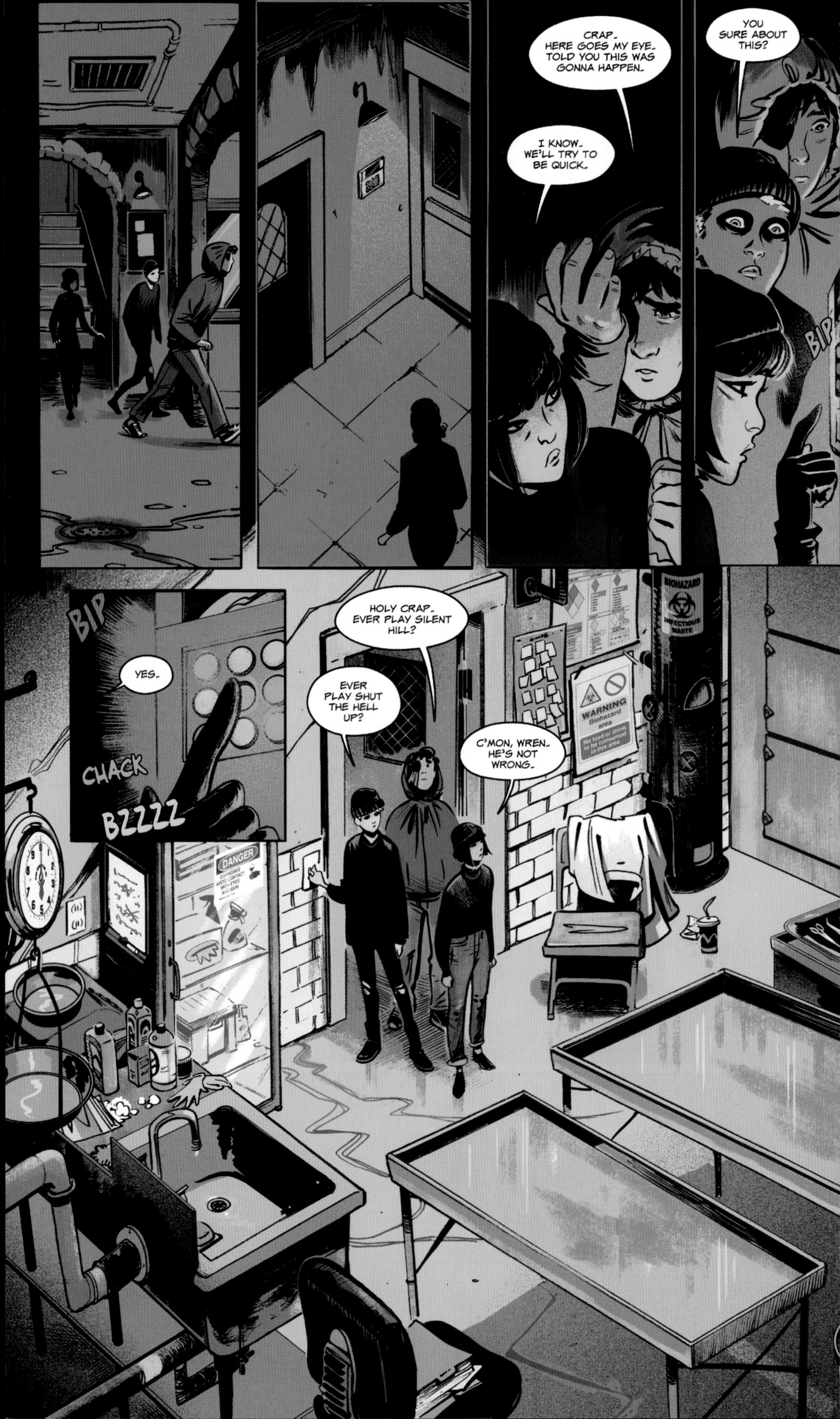
CRAP. HERE GOES MY EYE. TOLD YOU THIS WAS GONNA HAPPEN.
I KNOW. WE'LL TRY TO BE QUICK.
YOU SURE ABOUT THIS?
BIP
BIP
YES.
CHACK
BZZZZ
HOLY CRAP. EVER PLAY SILENT HILL?
EVER PLAY SHUT THE HELL UP?
C'MON, WREN. HE'S NOT WRONG.
WARNING
Biohazard area
No food or drink to be consumed in this area
BIOHAZARD
INFECTIOUS WASTE
DANGER
CORROSIVE
AVOID CONTACT WITH EYES AND SKIN

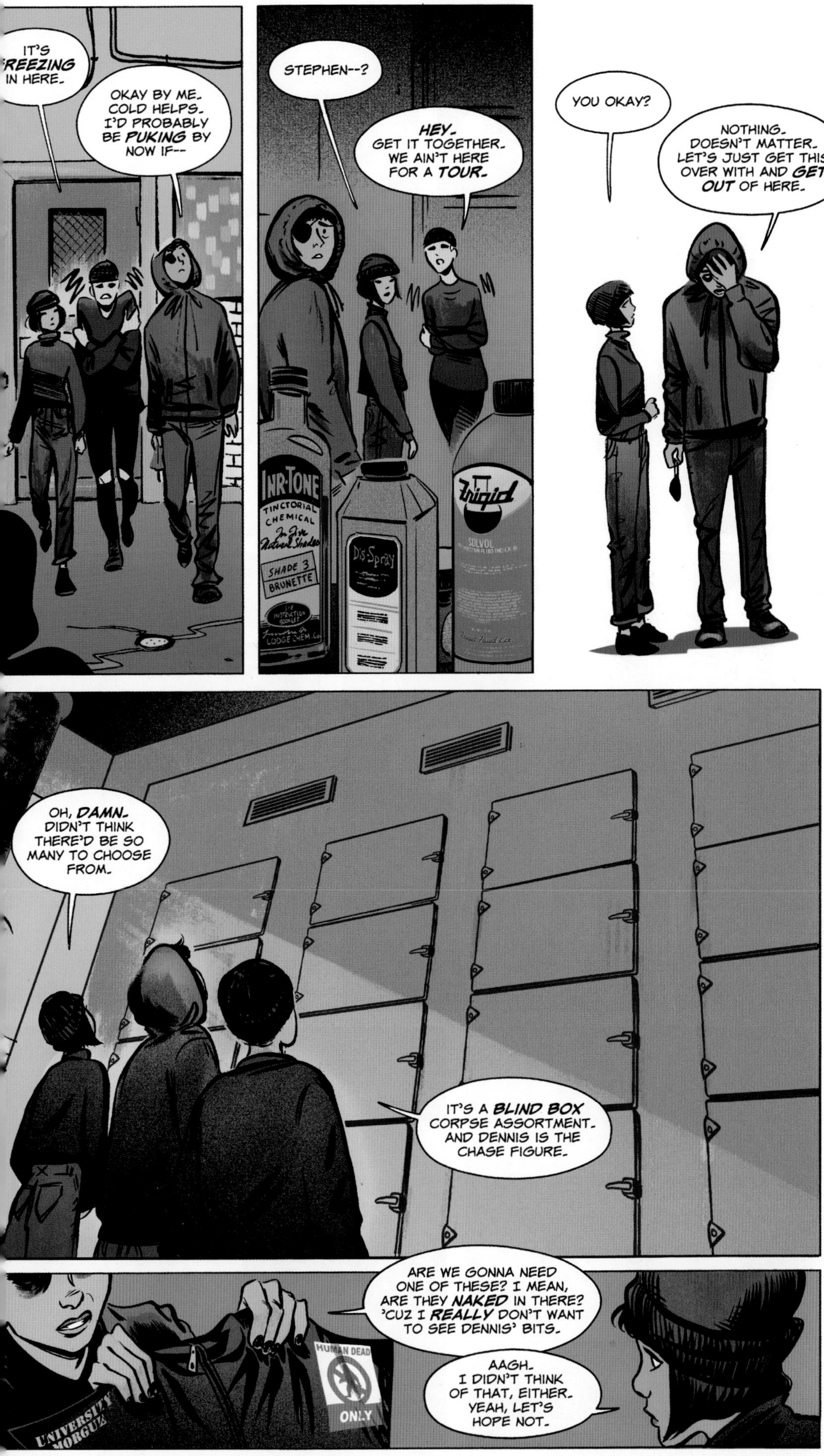

IT'S FREEZING IN HERE.
OKAY BY ME. COLD HELPS. I'D PROBABLY BE PUKING BY NOW IF--
STEPHEN--?
HEY. GET IT TOGETHER. WE AIN'T HERE FOR A TOUR.
INR-TONE
TINCTORIAL CHEMICAL
SHADE 3 BRUNETTE
LODGE CHEM. CO.
Dis-Spray
Frigid
SOLVOL
YOU OKAY?
NOTHING. DOESN'T MATTER. LET'S JUST GET THIS OVER WITH AND GET OUT OF HERE.
OH, DAMN. DIDN'T THINK THERE'D BE SO MANY TO CHOOSE FROM.
IT'S A BLIND BOX CORPSE ASSORTMENT. AND DENNIS IS THE CHASE FIGURE.
ARE WE GONNA NEED ONE OF THESE? I MEAN, ARE THEY NAKED IN THERE? 'CUZ I REALLY DON'T WANT TO SEE DENNIS' BITS.
HUMAN DEAD ONLY
UNIVERSITY MORGUE
AAGH. I DIDN'T THINK OF THAT, EITHER. YEAH, LET'S HOPE NOT.

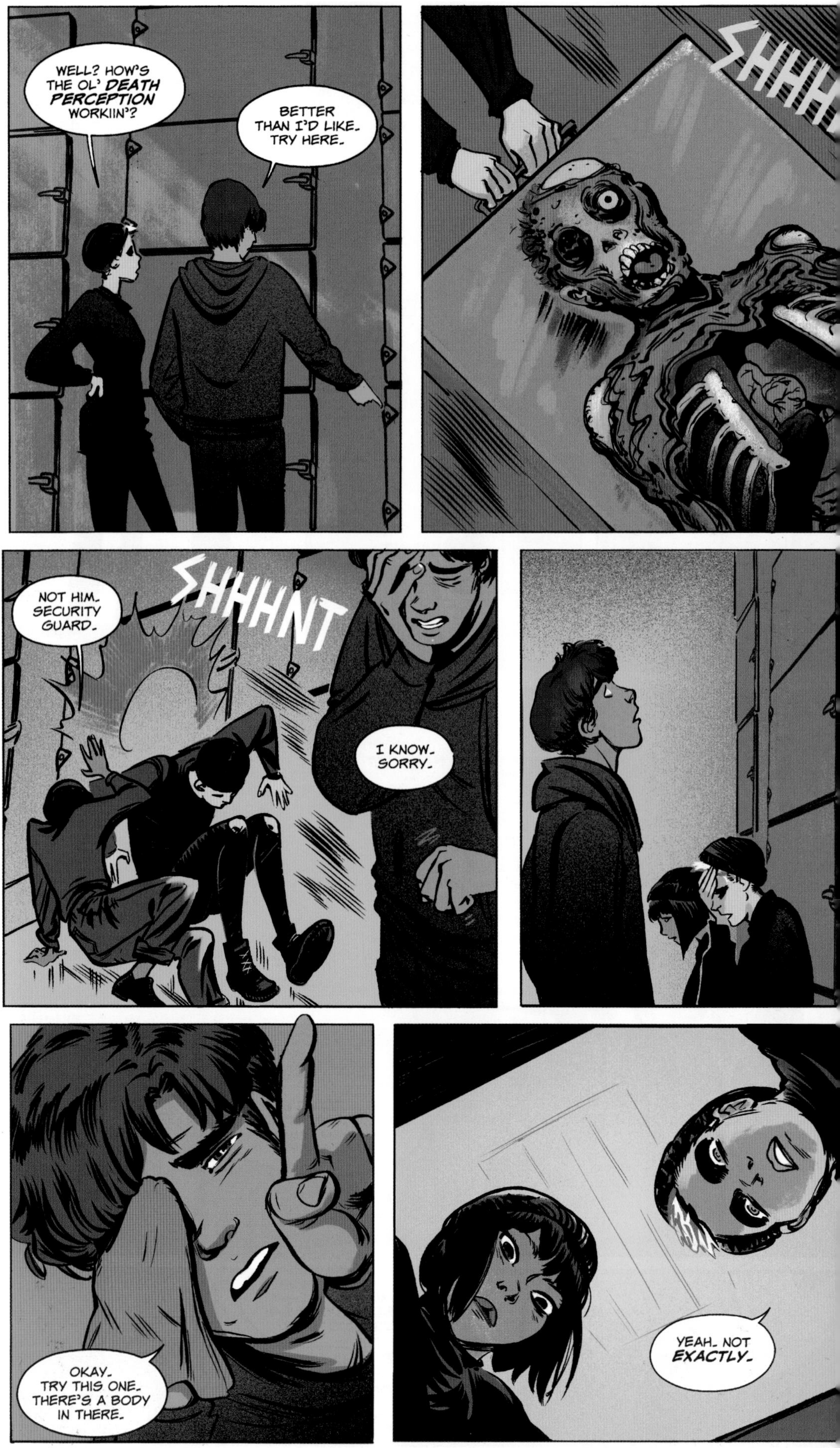
WELL? HOW'S THE OL' *DEATH PERCEPTION* WORKIIN'?
BETTER THAN I'D LIKE. TRY HERE.
SHHH
NOT HIM. SECURITY GUARD.
SHHHNT
I KNOW. SORRY.
OKAY. TRY THIS ONE. THERE'S A BODY IN THERE.
YEAH. NOT *EXACTLY*.

IT'S
GDEN.

HE'S LIKE PART OF SOME KIND OF *SKELETON SALAD--*

CLOSE IT!

P-PLEASE. YOU *GOTTA* CLOSE IT. *NOW.*

HE'S *STRONG.* AND IT'S HURTING ME *BAD.*

JESUS. MAYBE WE SHOULD QUIT, REIKO--

HOLD ON-- LET'S JUST START PULLING THEM ALL, OKAY? STEPHEN CAN STAY OUTSIDE--

HHHN

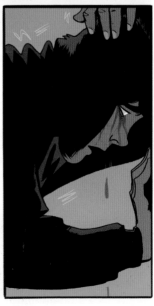

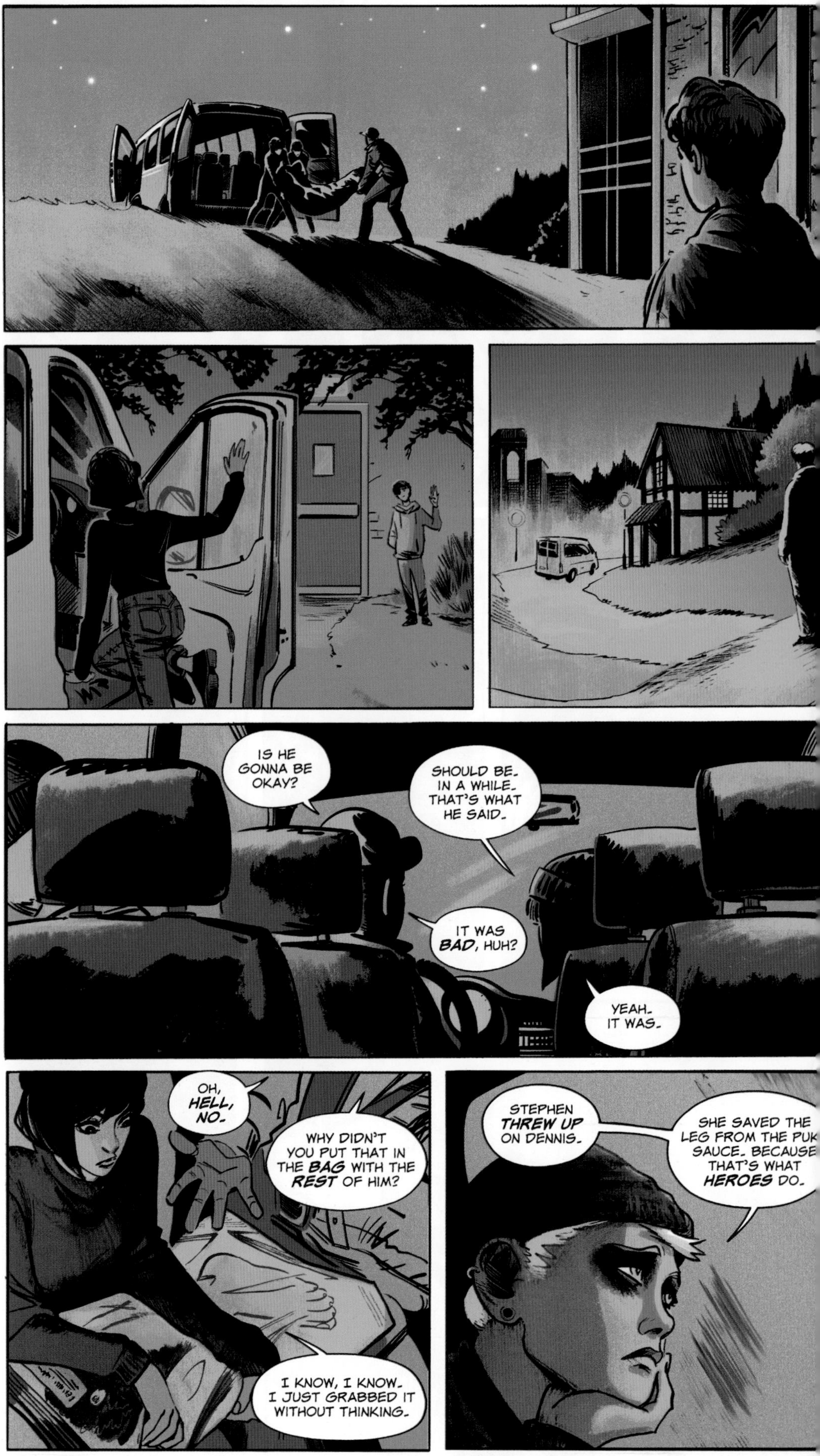
IS HE GONNA BE OKAY?
SHOULD BE. IN A WHILE. THAT'S WHAT HE SAID.
IT WAS BAD, HUH?
YEAH. IT WAS.
OH, HELL, NO.
WHY DIDN'T YOU PUT THAT IN THE BAG WITH THE REST OF HIM?
I KNOW, I KNOW. I JUST GRABBED IT WITHOUT THINKING.
STEPHEN THREW UP ON DENNIS.
SHE SAVED THE LEG FROM THE PUK SAUCE. BECAUSE THAT'S WHAT HEROES DO.

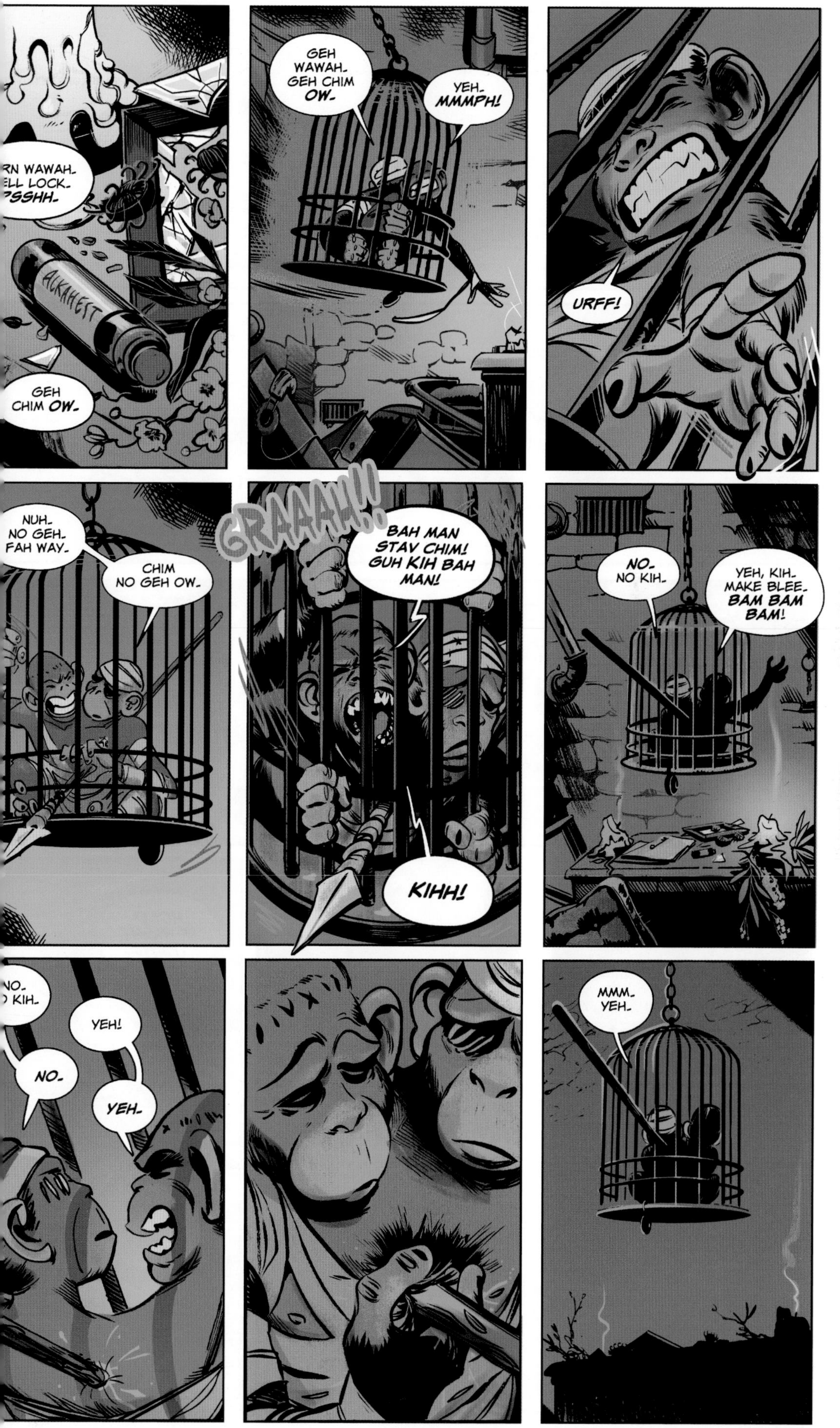

RN WAWAH.
ELL LOCK.
PSSHH.
ALKAHEST
GEH CHIM OW.
GEH WAWAH. GEH CHIM OW.
YEH. MMMPH!
URFF!
NUH. NO GEH. FAH WAY.
CHIM NO GEH OW.
GRAAAH!!
BAH MAN STAV CHIM! GUH KIH BAH MAN!
KIHH!
NO. NO KIH.
YEH, KIH. MAKE BLEE. BAM BAM BAM!
NO. O KIH.
YEH!
NO.
YEH.
MMM. YEH.

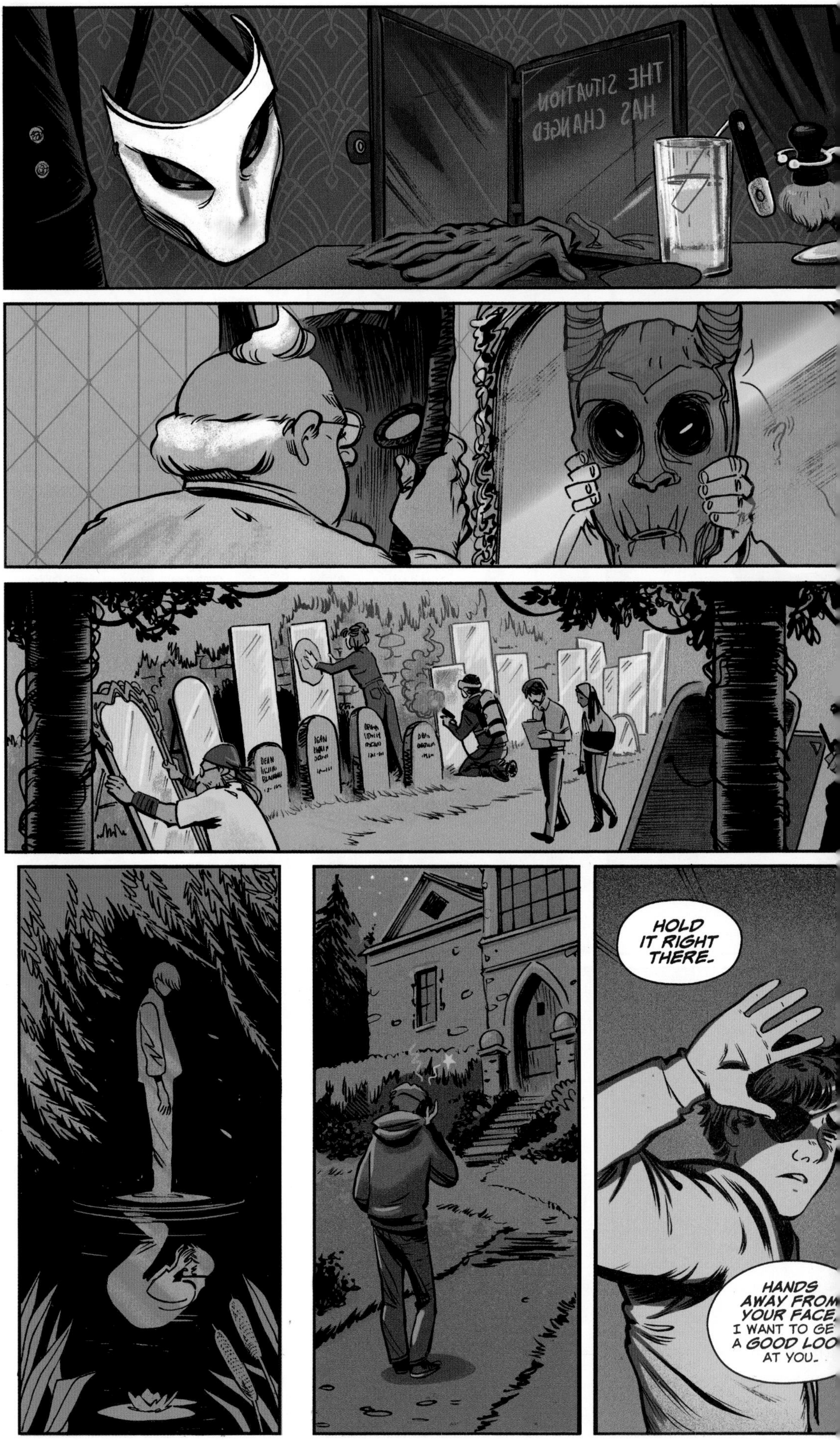
THE SITUATION HAS CHANGED
HOLD IT RIGHT THERE.
HANDS AWAY FROM YOUR FACE. I WANT TO GE A GOOD LOO AT YOU.

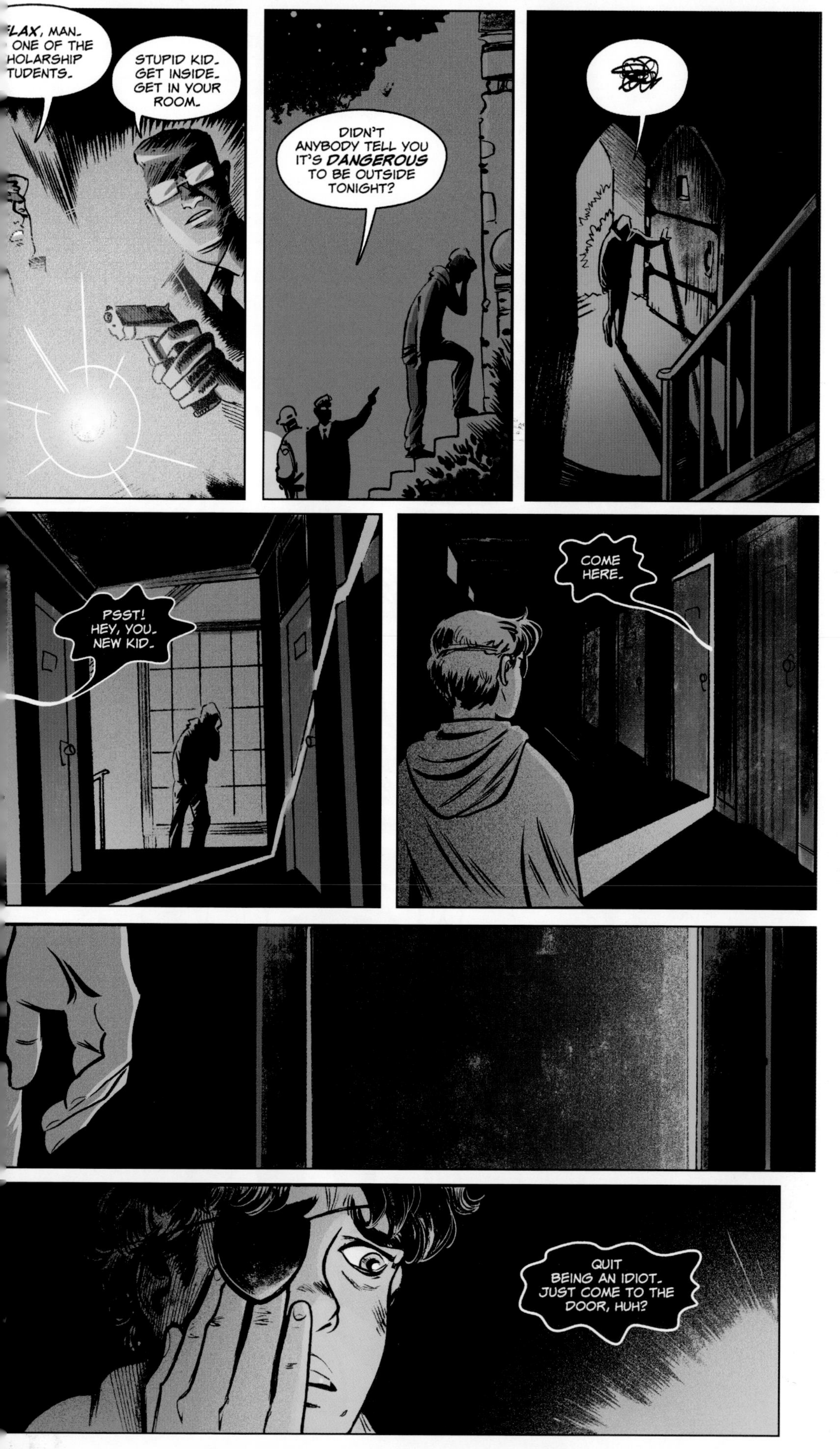

FLAX, MAN. ONE OF THE HOLARSHIP TUDENTS.
STUPID KID. GET INSIDE. GET IN YOUR ROOM.
DIDN'T ANYBODY TELL YOU IT'S DANGEROUS TO BE OUTSIDE TONIGHT?
PSST! HEY, YOU. NEW KID.
COME HERE.
QUIT BEING AN IDIOT. JUST COME TO THE DOOR, HUH?

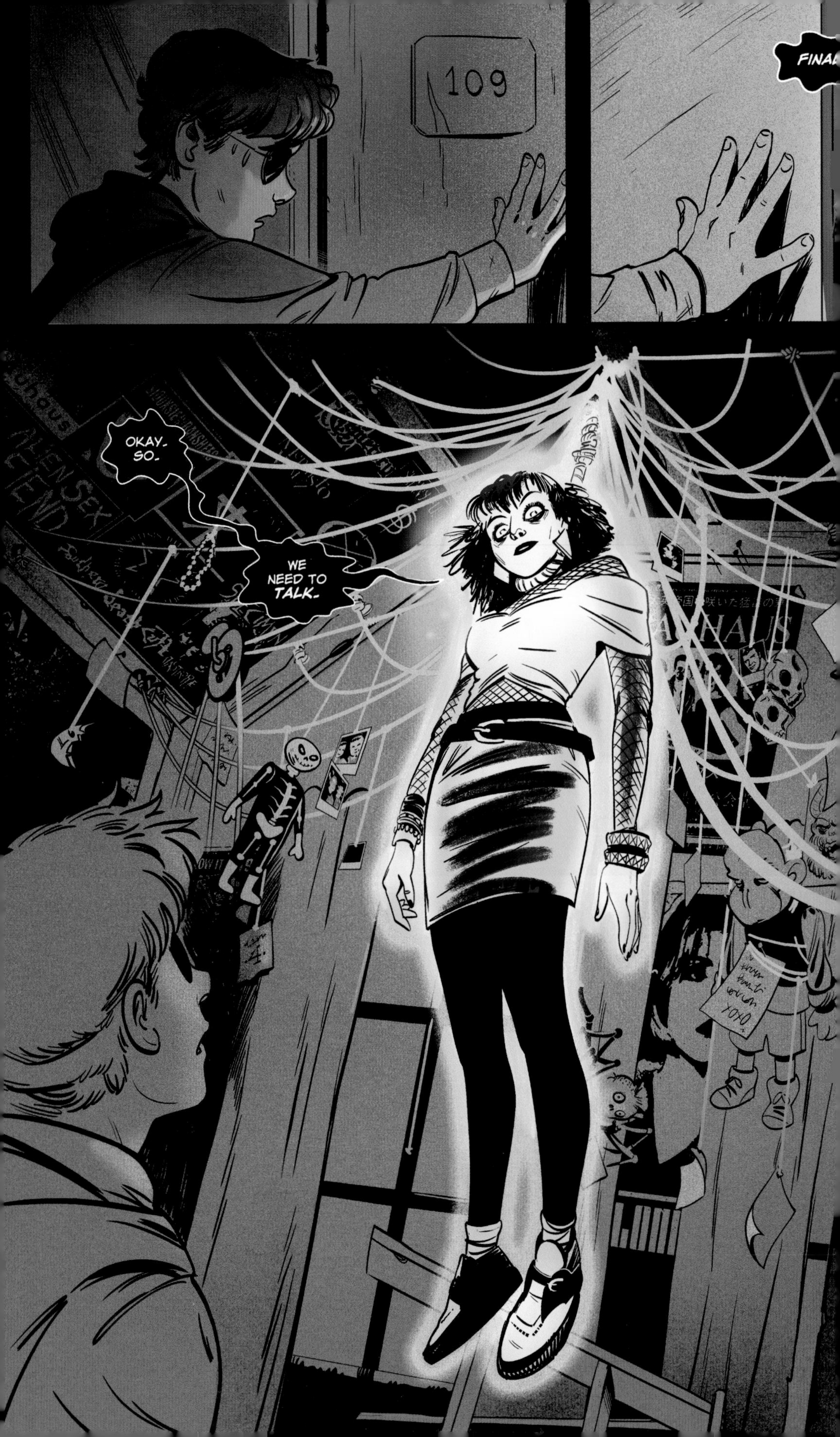
109
OKAY- SO-
WE NEED TO TALK-

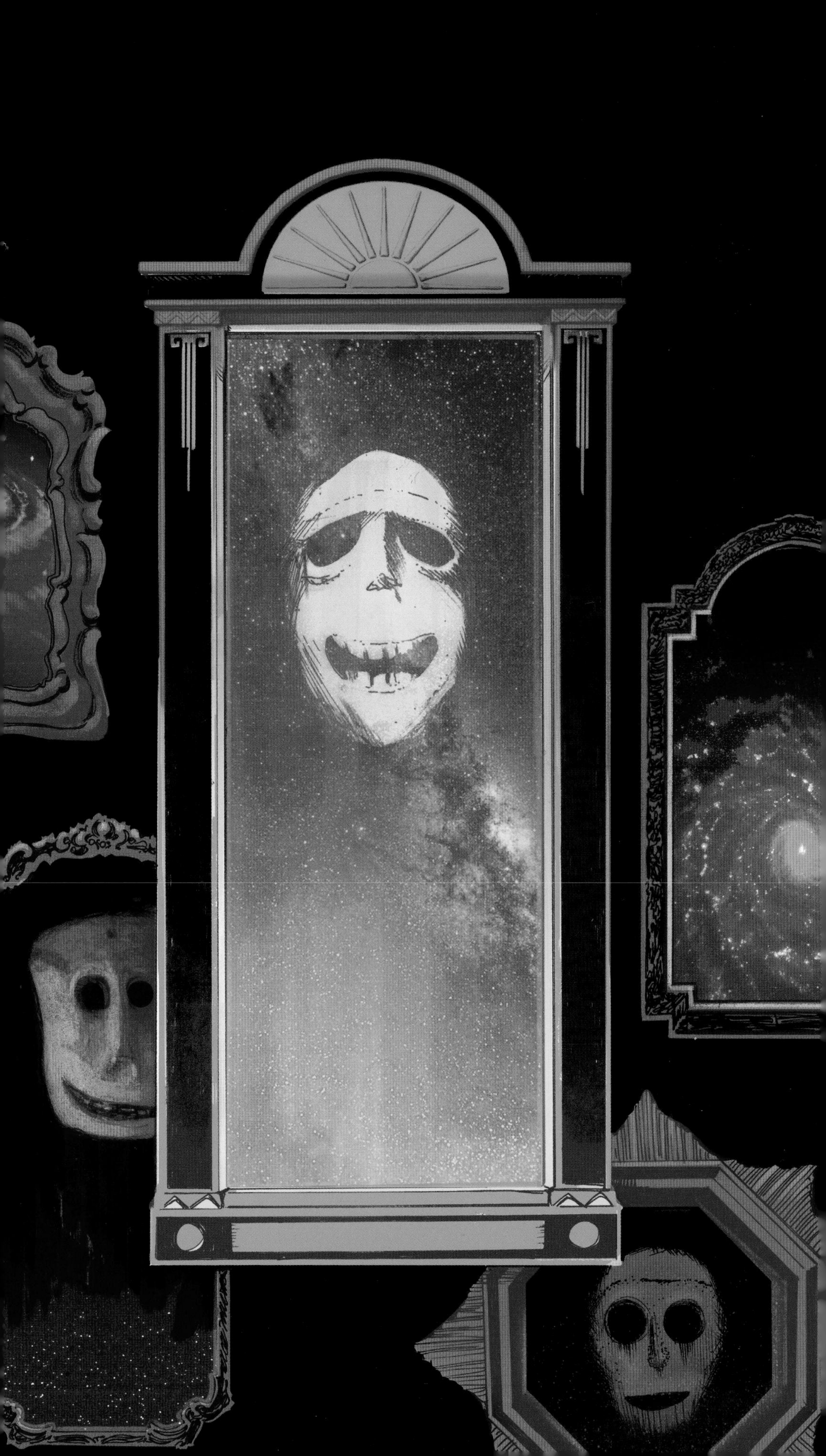

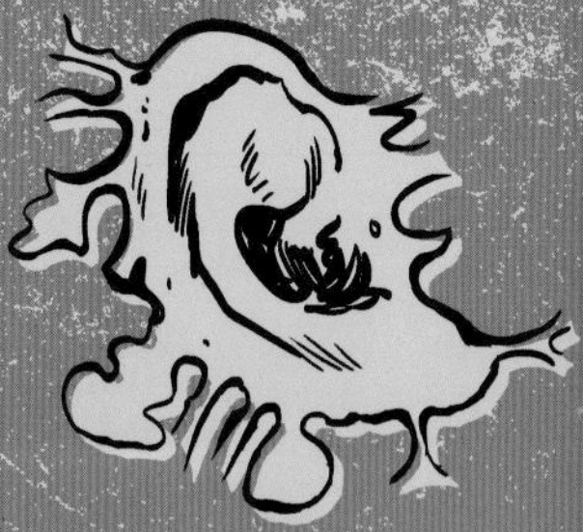

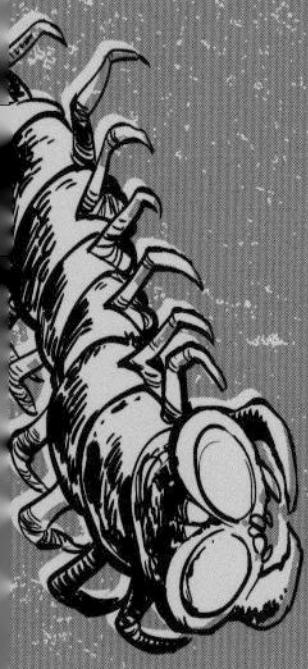

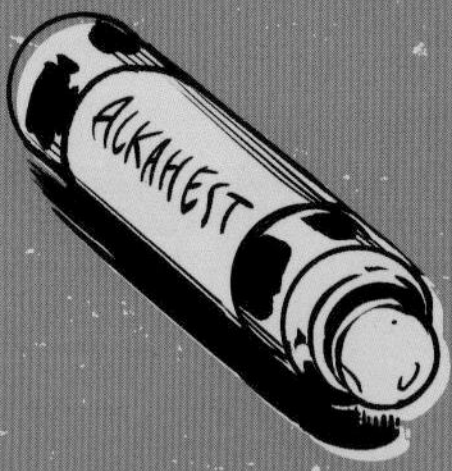
ALKAHEST

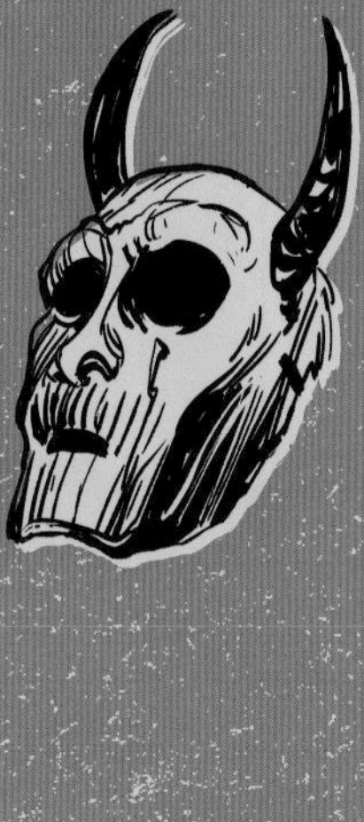

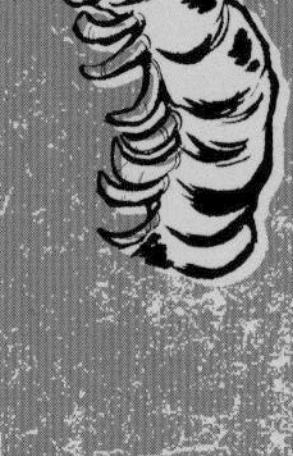

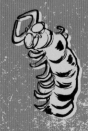

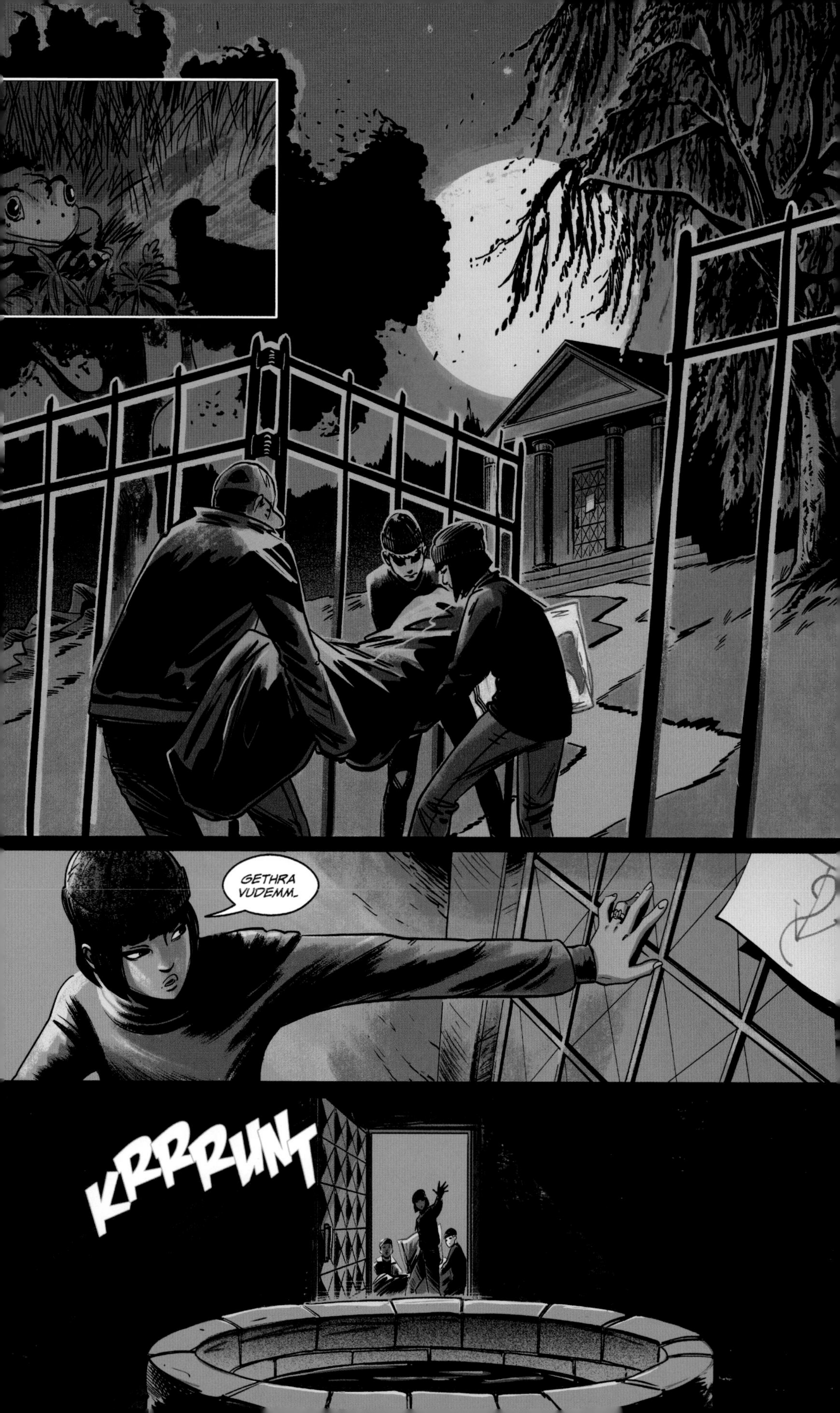
GETHRA VUDEMM_
KRRRUNT

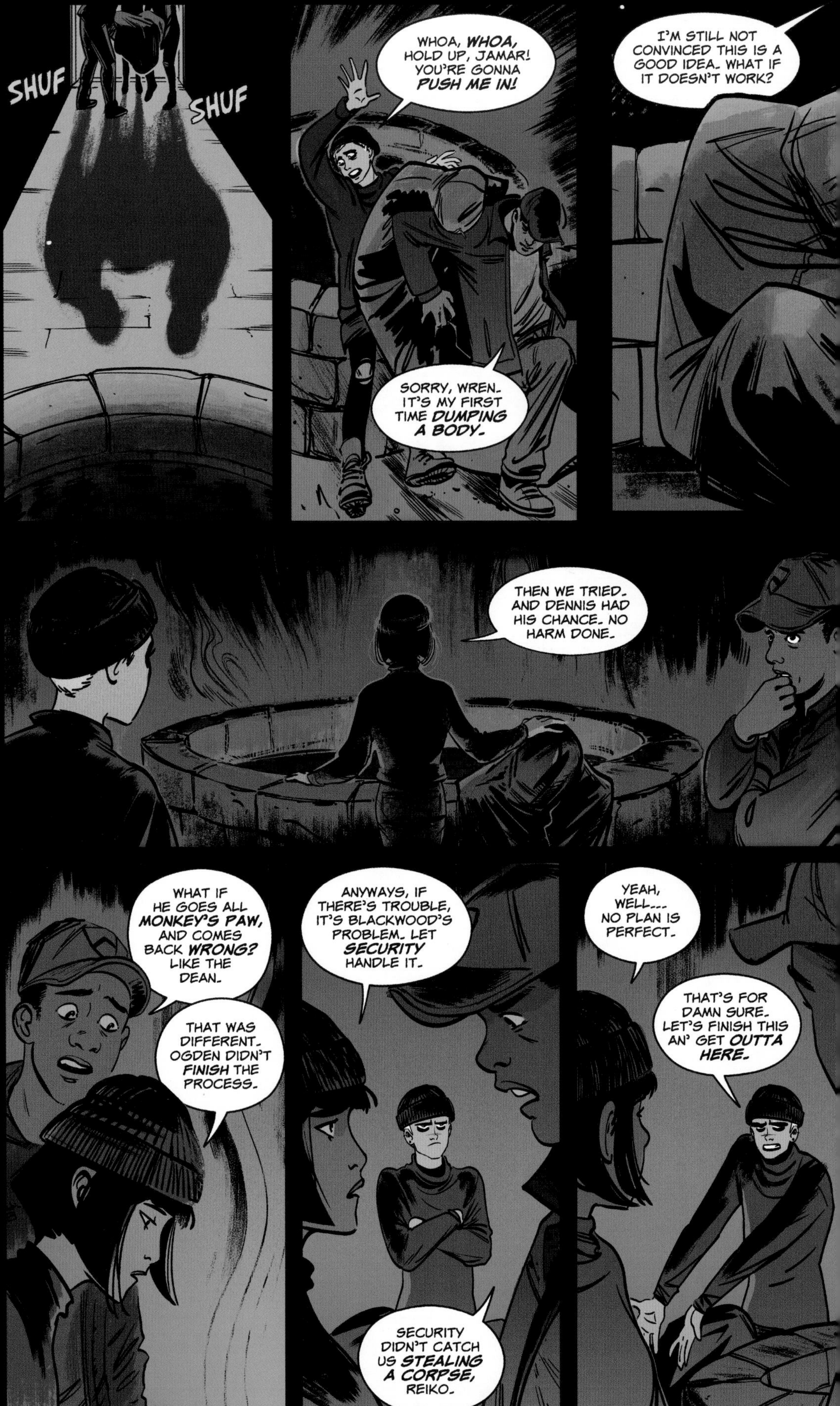
SHUF
SHUF
WHOA, WHOA, HOLD UP, JAMAR! YOU'RE GONNA PUSH ME IN!
SORRY, WREN. IT'S MY FIRST TIME DUMPING A BODY.
I'M STILL NOT CONVINCED THIS IS A GOOD IDEA. WHAT IF IT DOESN'T WORK?
THEN WE TRIED. AND DENNIS HAD HIS CHANCE. NO HARM DONE.
WHAT IF HE GOES ALL MONKEY'S PAW, AND COMES BACK WRONG? LIKE THE DEAN.
THAT WAS DIFFERENT. OGDEN DIDN'T FINISH THE PROCESS.
ANYWAYS, IF THERE'S TROUBLE, IT'S BLACKWOOD'S PROBLEM. LET SECURITY HANDLE IT.
SECURITY DIDN'T CATCH US STEALING A CORPSE, REIKO.
YEAH, WELL... NO PLAN IS PERFECT.
THAT'S FOR DAMN SURE. LET'S FINISH THIS AN' GET OUTTA HERE.

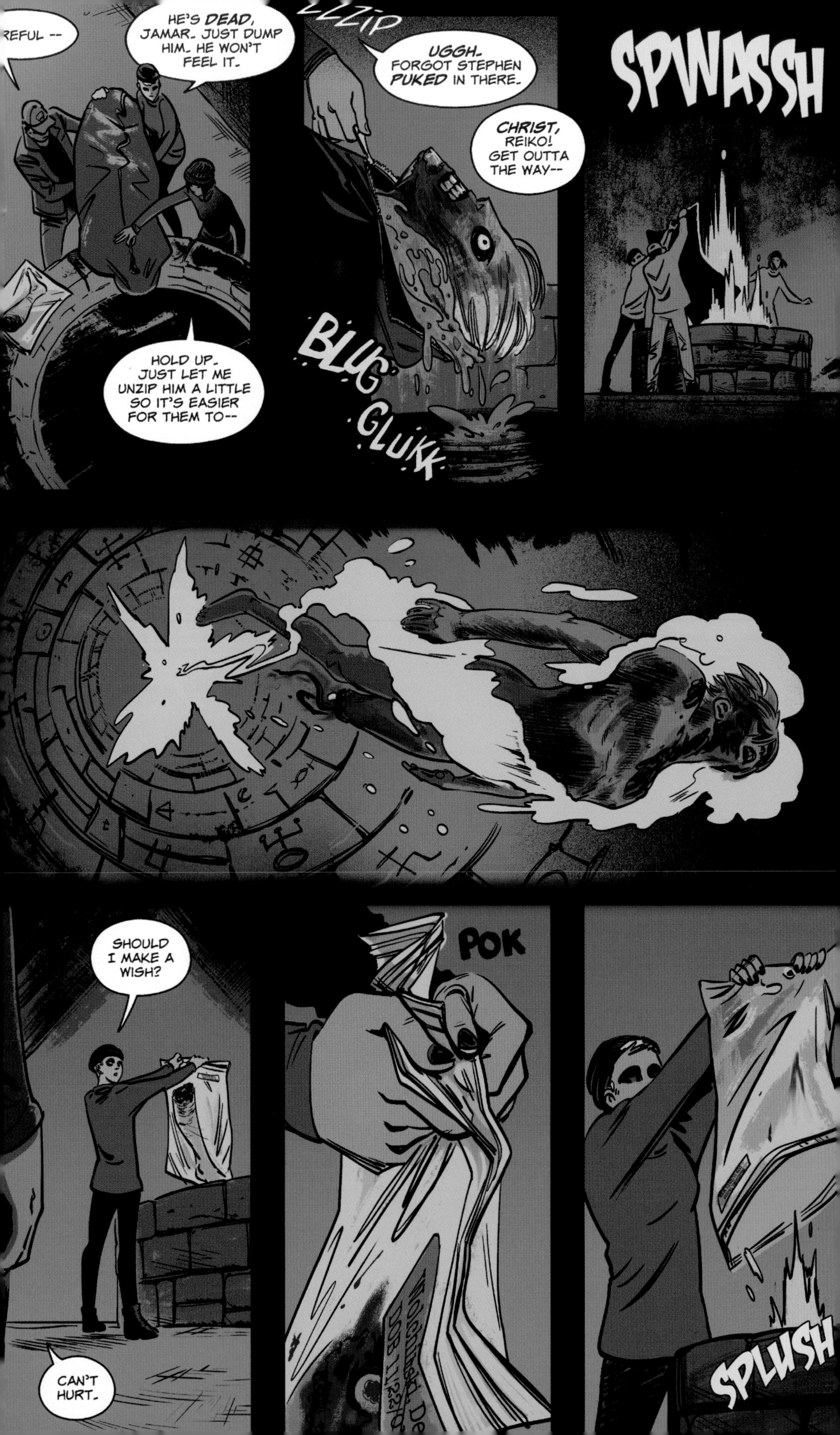
REFUL --
HE'S DEAD, JAMAR. JUST DUMP HIM. HE WON'T FEEL IT.
HOLD UP. JUST LET ME UNZIP HIM A LITTLE SO IT'S EASIER FOR THEM TO--
ZZIP
UGGH. FORGOT STEPHEN PUKED IN THERE.
CHRIST, REIKO! GET OUTTA THE WAY--
BLUG
GLUKK
SPWASSH
SHOULD I MAKE A WISH?
CAN'T HURT.
POK
SPLUSH

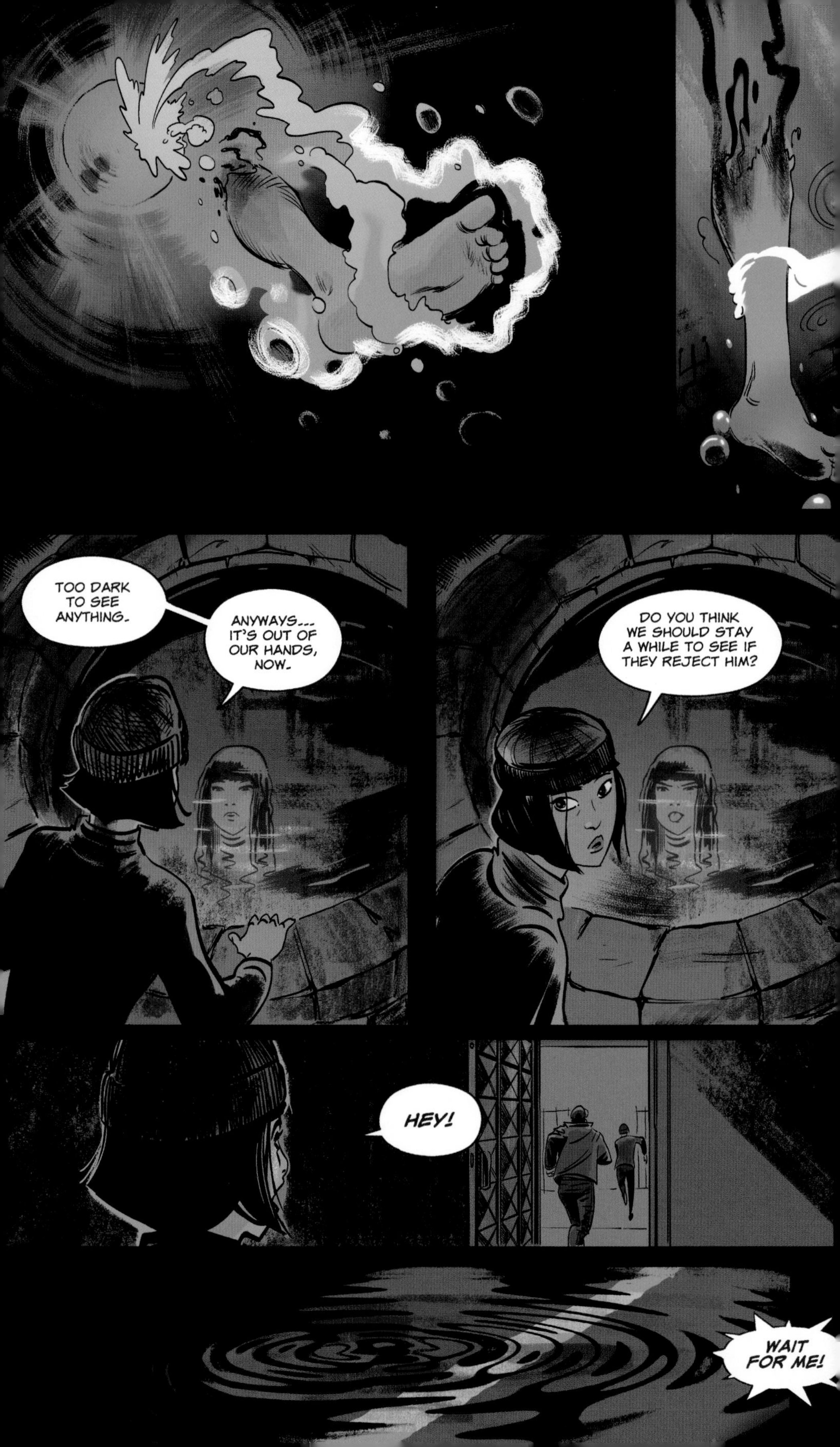
TOO DARK TO SEE ANYTHING.
ANYWAYS... IT'S OUT OF OUR HANDS, NOW.
DO YOU THINK WE SHOULD STAY A WHILE TO SEE IF THEY REJECT HIM?
HEY!
WAIT FOR ME!

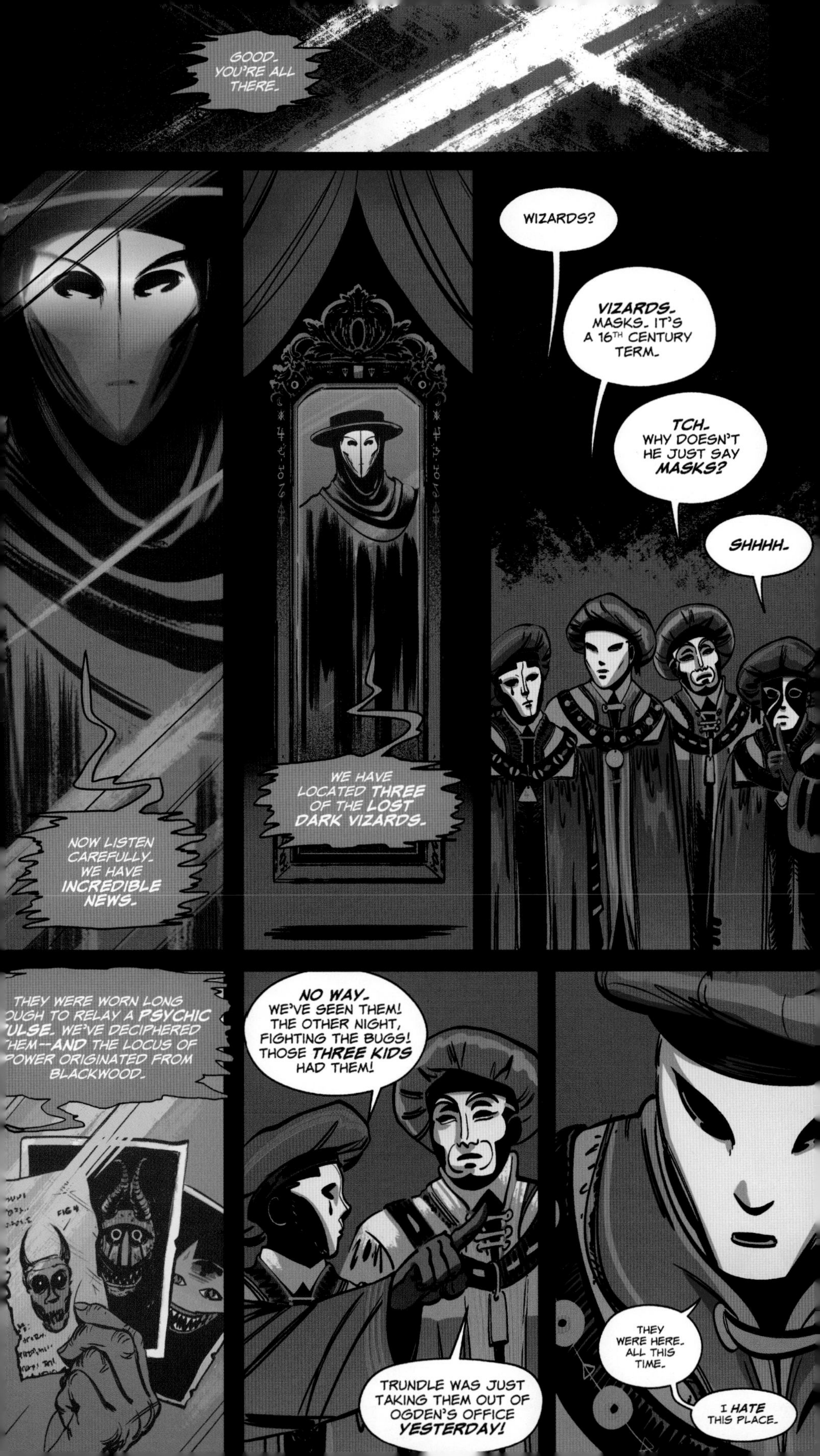
GOOD. YOU'RE ALL THERE.
NOW LISTEN CAREFULLY. WE HAVE INCREDIBLE NEWS.
WE HAVE LOCATED THREE OF THE LOST DARK VIZARDS.
WIZARDS?
VIZARDS. MASKS. IT'S A 16TH CENTURY TERM.
TCH. WHY DOESN'T HE JUST SAY MASKS?
SHHHH.
THEY WERE WORN LONG OUGH TO RELAY A PSYCHIC ULSE. WE'VE DECIPHERED THEM--AND THE LOCUS OF POWER ORIGINATED FROM BLACKWOOD.
NO WAY. WE'VE SEEN THEM! THE OTHER NIGHT, FIGHTING THE BUGS! THOSE THREE KIDS HAD THEM!
TRUNDLE WAS JUST TAKING THEM OUT OF OGDEN'S OFFICE YESTERDAY!
THEY WERE HERE. ALL THIS TIME.
I HATE THIS PLACE.

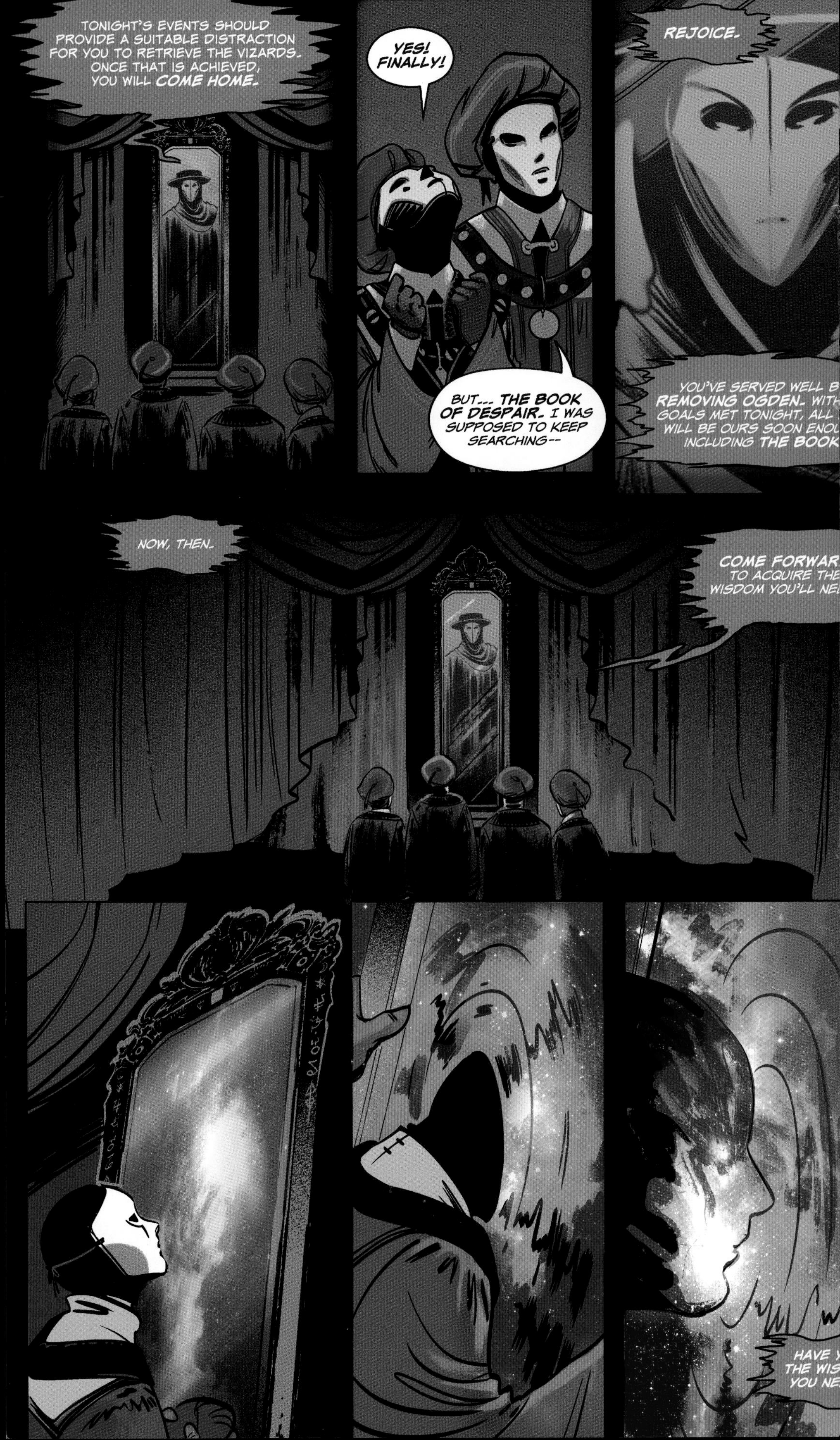

TONIGHT'S EVENTS SHOULD PROVIDE A SUITABLE DISTRACTION FOR YOU TO RETRIEVE THE VIZARDS. ONCE THAT IS ACHIEVED, YOU WILL COME HOME.
YES! FINALLY!
BUT... THE BOOK OF DESPAIR. I WAS SUPPOSED TO KEEP SEARCHING--
REJOICE.
YOU'VE SERVED WELL B
REMOVING OGDEN. WITH
GOALS MET TONIGHT, ALL
WILL BE OURS SOON ENOU
INCLUDING THE BOOK
NOW, THEN.
COME FORWAR
TO ACQUIRE THE
WISDOM YOU'LL NE
HAVE Y
THE WIS
YOU NE

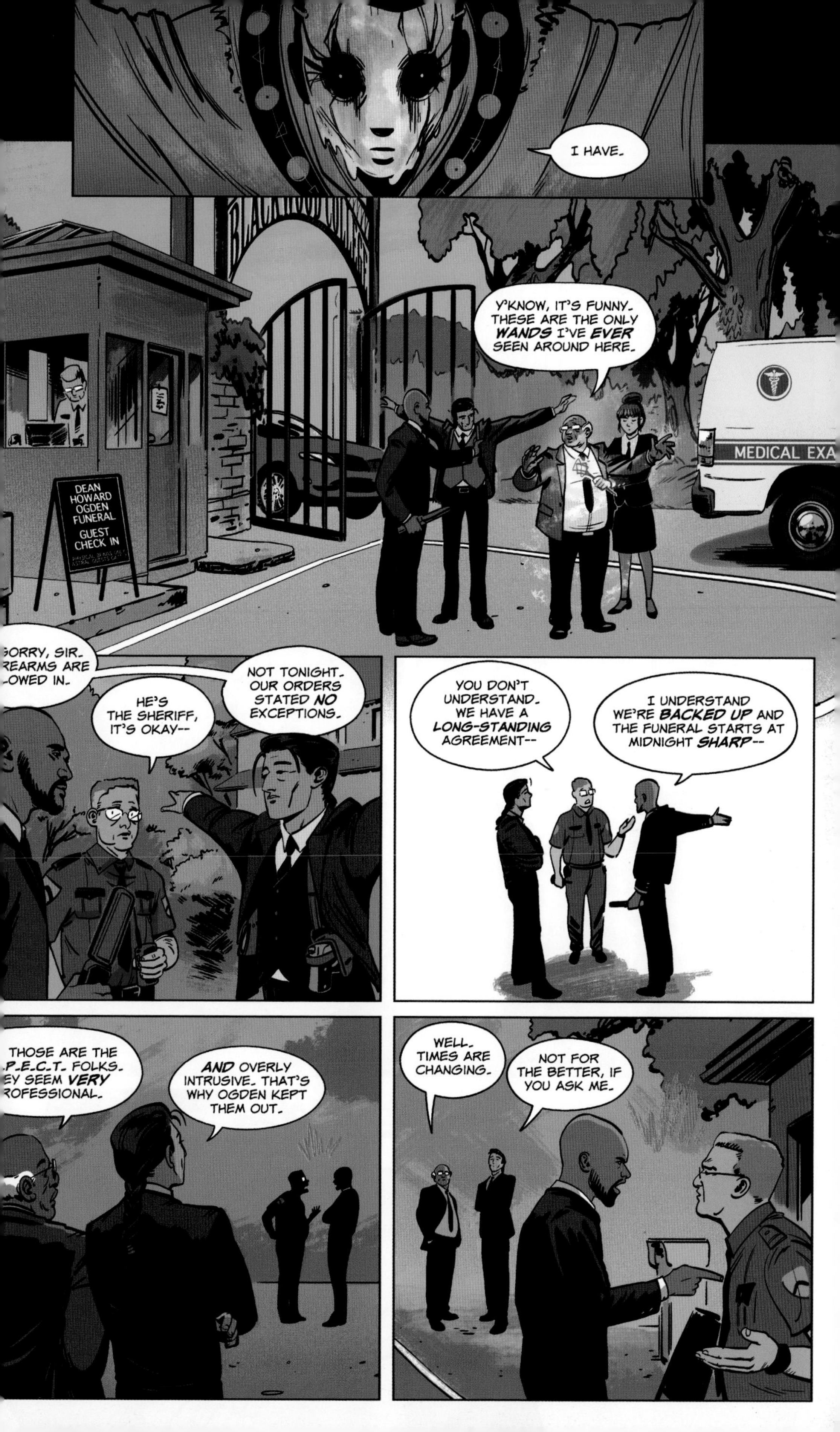
I HAVE.
BLACKWOOD COLLEGE
Y'KNOW, IT'S FUNNY. THESE ARE THE ONLY WANDS I'VE EVER SEEN AROUND HERE.
DEAN HOWARD OGDEN FUNERAL
GUEST CHECK IN
MEDICAL EXA
SORRY, SIR. FIREARMS ARE ...LOWED IN.
HE'S THE SHERIFF, IT'S OKAY--
NOT TONIGHT. OUR ORDERS STATED NO EXCEPTIONS.
YOU DON'T UNDERSTAND. WE HAVE A LONG-STANDING AGREEMENT--
I UNDERSTAND WE'RE BACKED UP AND THE FUNERAL STARTS AT MIDNIGHT SHARP--
THOSE ARE THE .P.E.C.T. FOLKS. ...EY SEEM VERY ...ROFESSIONAL.
AND OVERLY INTRUSIVE. THAT'S WHY OGDEN KEPT THEM OUT.
WELL. TIMES ARE CHANGING.
NOT FOR THE BETTER, IF YOU ASK ME.

DEAN COLBY?

FUNERAL T~
-SET/CLEAN
TREAT MI~
~IGHTS. SEA~
-VIPs, ALUMNI ~
-WAKE UP FRO~
-VOID REMAINS
~G/TREAT GRA~
~VOID WENTWORT~
~SPEECH NOTES ~
-FIND CHIMP
-SPEAKER~

WE'RE *JUST* ABOUT DONE WITH THE LEGACY MIRRORS. GUESTS ARE STARTING TO CHECK IN, NO PROBLEMS *SO FAR.*

GREAT. THANKS, AVERY.

ALL ESSENTIAL AREAS ARE LOCKED DOWN. GUARDS AND PATROLS PLACED. PROTECTION SPELLS, WARDS AND CHARMS SET. AND THE *FRONT GATE'S* UP AND *AWAKE.*

GOOD TO HEAR, SHERRY. THANKS.

IF THE *WORST* HAPPENS, WE'LL HAVE MAGES AND EXTRA FIRE-POWER ON SITE.

I'M NOT MUCH OF A FAN, BUT THE *INS-P-E-C-T.* CREW DEFINITELY CAME TO PLAY *HARDBALL.*

YEAH, WELL, I'M JUST HOPING THE GAME GETS *CALLED.*

AND THE OPPOSING TEAM *GOES HOME.*

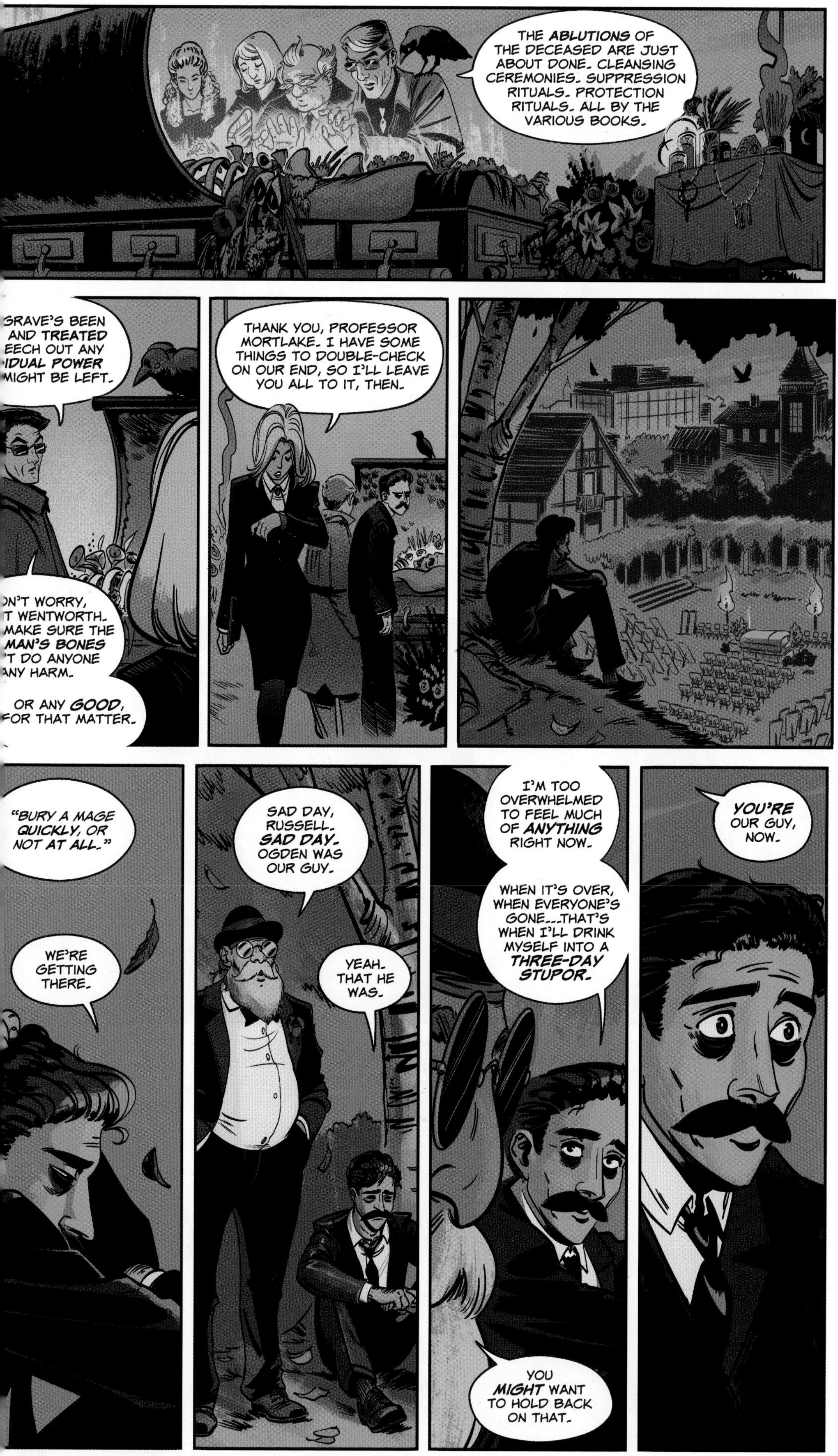
THE ABLUTIONS OF THE DECEASED ARE JUST ABOUT DONE. CLEANSING CEREMONIES. SUPPRESSION RITUALS. PROTECTION RITUALS. ALL BY THE VARIOUS BOOKS.
GRAVE'S BEEN AND TREATED EECH OUT ANY IDUAL POWER MIGHT BE LEFT.
ON'T WORRY, T WENTWORTH. MAKE SURE THE MAN'S BONES 'T DO ANYONE ANY HARM.
OR ANY GOOD, FOR THAT MATTER.
THANK YOU, PROFESSOR MORTLAKE. I HAVE SOME THINGS TO DOUBLE-CHECK ON OUR END, SO I'LL LEAVE YOU ALL TO IT, THEN.
"BURY A MAGE QUICKLY, OR NOT AT ALL."
WE'RE GETTING THERE.
SAD DAY, RUSSELL. SAD DAY. OGDEN WAS OUR GUY.
YEAH. THAT HE WAS.
I'M TOO OVERWHELMED TO FEEL MUCH OF ANYTHING RIGHT NOW.
WHEN IT'S OVER, WHEN EVERYONE'S GONE... THAT'S WHEN I'LL DRINK MYSELF INTO A THREE-DAY STUPOR.
YOU MIGHT WANT TO HOLD BACK ON THAT.
YOU'RE OUR GUY, NOW.

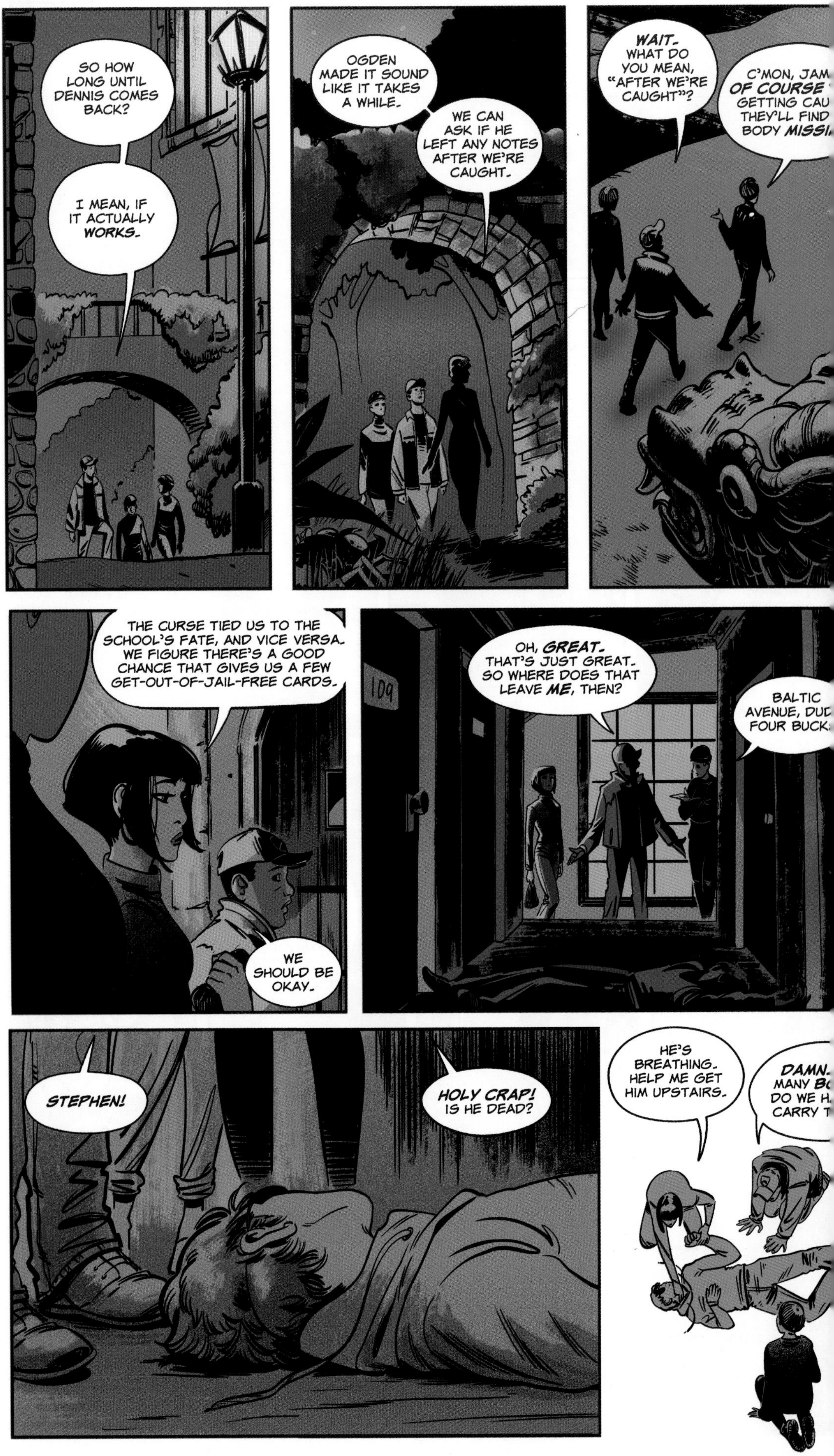
SO HOW LONG UNTIL DENNIS COMES BACK?
I MEAN, IF IT ACTUALLY WORKS.
OGDEN MADE IT SOUND LIKE IT TAKES A WHILE.
WE CAN ASK IF HE LEFT ANY NOTES AFTER WE'RE CAUGHT.
WAIT. WHAT DO YOU MEAN, "AFTER WE'RE CAUGHT"?
C'MON, JAM
OF COURSE
GETTING CAU
THEY'LL FIND
BODY MISSI
THE CURSE TIED US TO THE SCHOOL'S FATE, AND VICE VERSA. WE FIGURE THERE'S A GOOD CHANCE THAT GIVES US A FEW GET-OUT-OF-JAIL-FREE CARDS.
WE SHOULD BE OKAY.
109
OH, GREAT. THAT'S JUST GREAT. SO WHERE DOES THAT LEAVE ME, THEN?
BALTIC AVENUE, DUD
FOUR BUCK
STEPHEN!
HOLY CRAP! IS HE DEAD?
HE'S BREATHING. HELP ME GET HIM UPSTAIRS.
DAMN.
MANY B
DO WE H
CARRY T

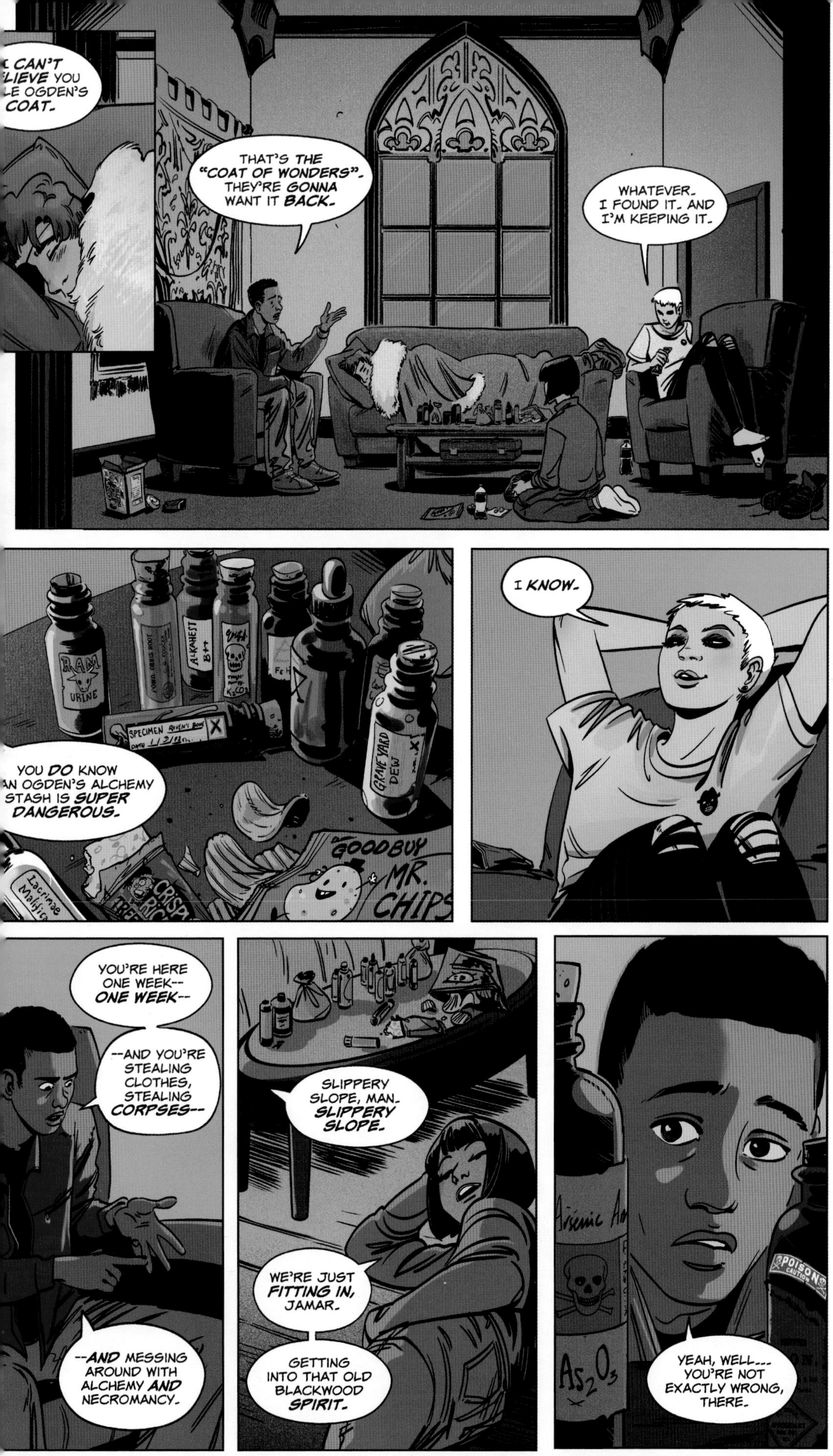
CAN'T LIEVE YOU LE OGDEN'S COAT.
THAT'S THE "COAT OF WONDERS". THEY'RE GONNA WANT IT BACK.
WHATEVER. I FOUND IT. AND I'M KEEPING IT.
RAM URINE
ALKAHEST
SPECIMEN RAVEN'S BONE
GRAVE YARD DEW
YOU DO KNOW AN OGDEN'S ALCHEMY STASH IS SUPER DANGEROUS.
GOODBUY MR. CHIPS
I KNOW.
YOU'RE HERE ONE WEEK-- ONE WEEK--
--AND YOU'RE STEALING CLOTHES, STEALING CORPSES--
--AND MESSING AROUND WITH ALCHEMY AND NECROMANCY.
SLIPPERY SLOPE, MAN. SLIPPERY SLOPE.
WE'RE JUST FITTING IN, JAMAR.
GETTING INTO THAT OLD BLACKWOOD SPIRIT.
POISON
YEAH, WELL... YOU'RE NOT EXACTLY WRONG, THERE.

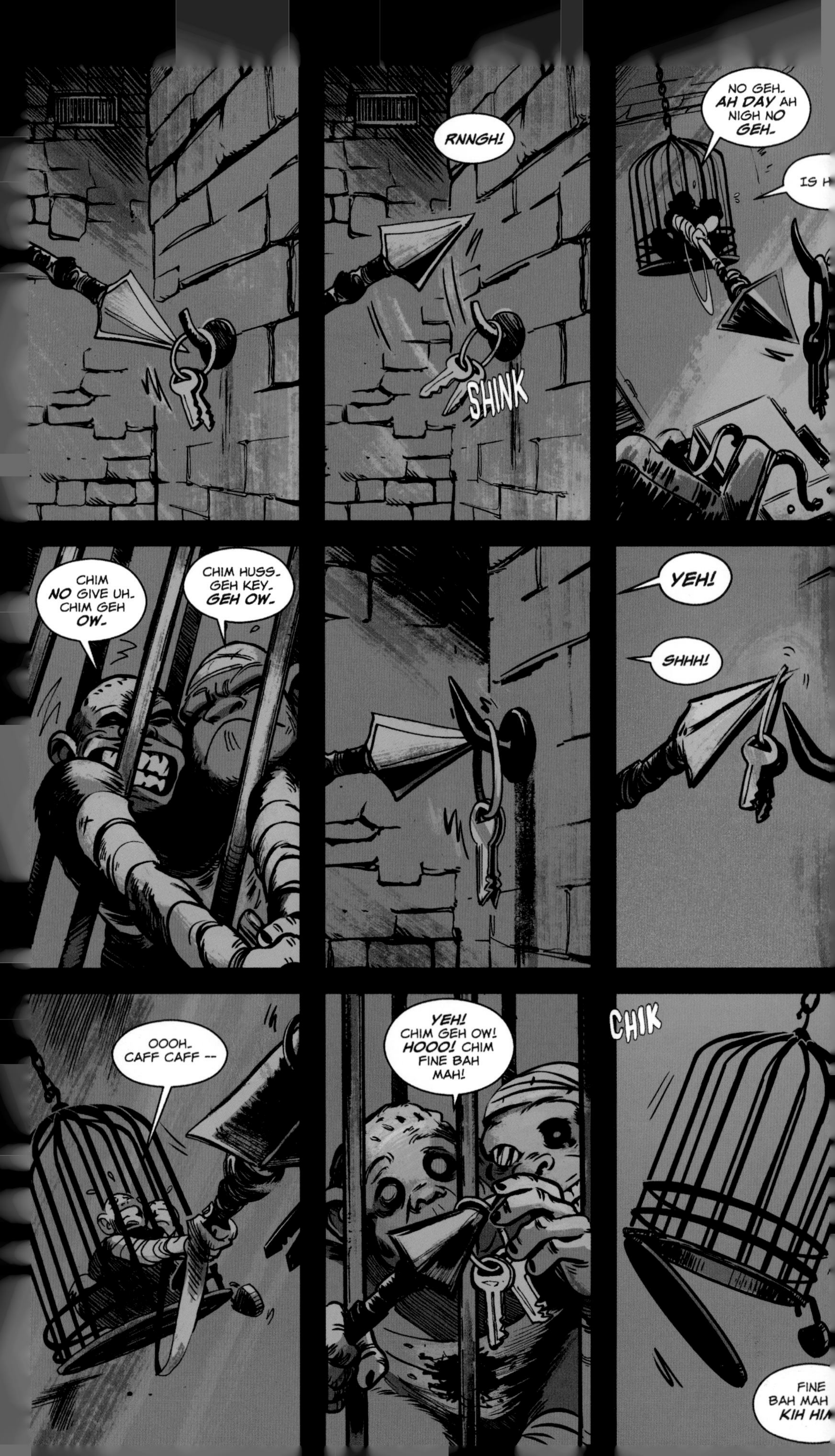
RNNGH!
SHINK
NO GEH. AH DAY AH NIGH NO GEH.
IS H
CHIM NO GIVE UH. CHIM GEH OW.
CHIM HUSS. GEH KEY. GEH OW.
YEH!
SHHH!
OOOH. CAFF CAFF --
YEH! CHIM GEH OW! HOOO! CHIM FINE BAH MAH!
CHIK
FINE BAH MAH KIH HI

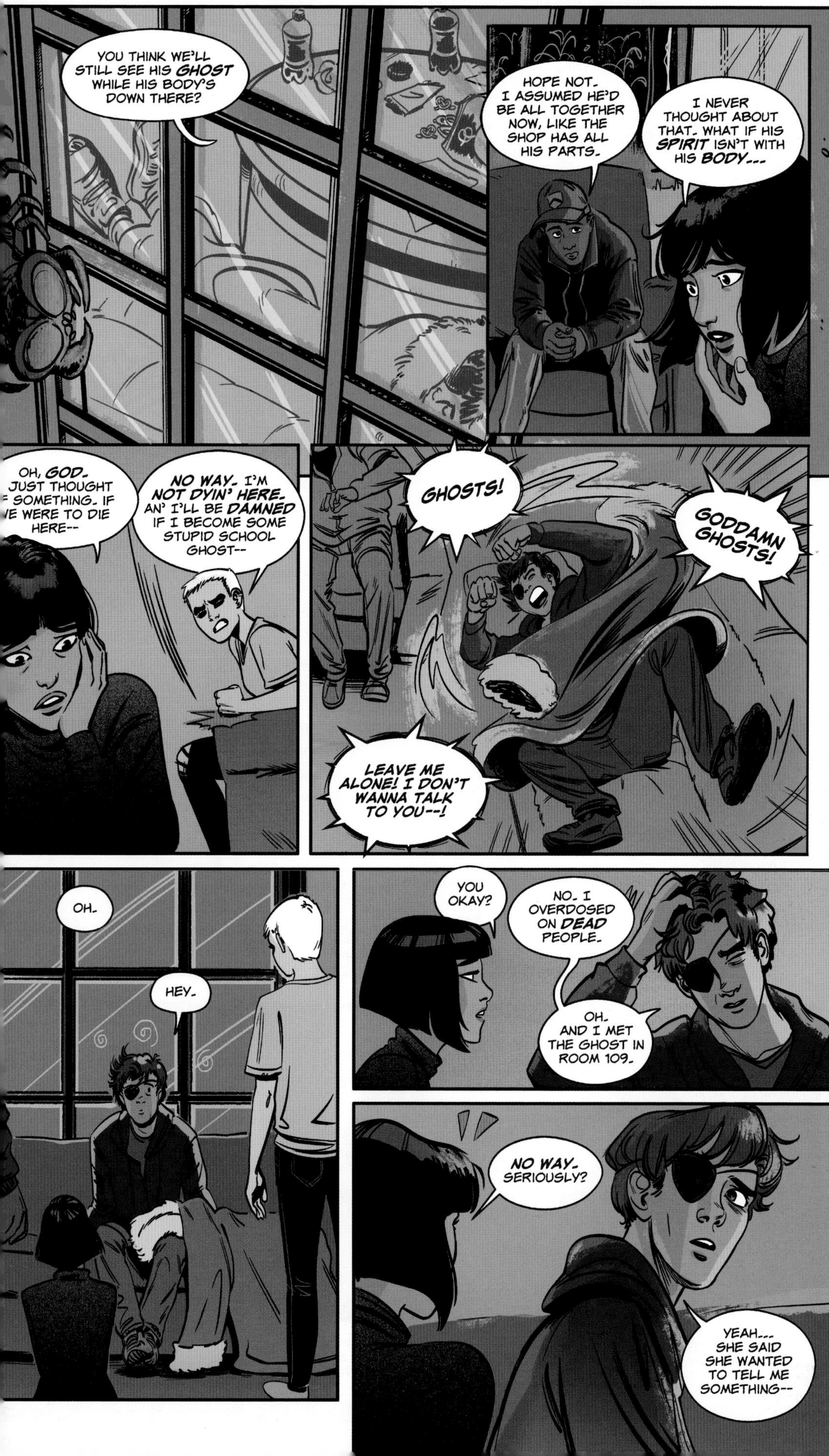
YOU THINK WE'LL STILL SEE HIS GHOST WHILE HIS BODY'S DOWN THERE?
HOPE NOT. I ASSUMED HE'D BE ALL TOGETHER NOW, LIKE THE SHOP HAS ALL HIS PARTS.
I NEVER THOUGHT ABOUT THAT. WHAT IF HIS SPIRIT ISN'T WITH HIS BODY...
OH, GOD. JUST THOUGHT OF SOMETHING. IF WE WERE TO DIE HERE--
NO WAY. I'M NOT DYIN' HERE. AN' I'LL BE DAMNED IF I BECOME SOME STUPID SCHOOL GHOST--
GHOSTS!
GODDAMN GHOSTS!
LEAVE ME ALONE! I DON'T WANNA TALK TO YOU--!
OH.
HEY.
YOU OKAY?
NO. I OVERDOSED ON DEAD PEOPLE.
OH. AND I MET THE GHOST IN ROOM 109.
NO WAY. SERIOUSLY?
YEAH... SHE SAID SHE WANTED TO TELL ME SOMETHING--

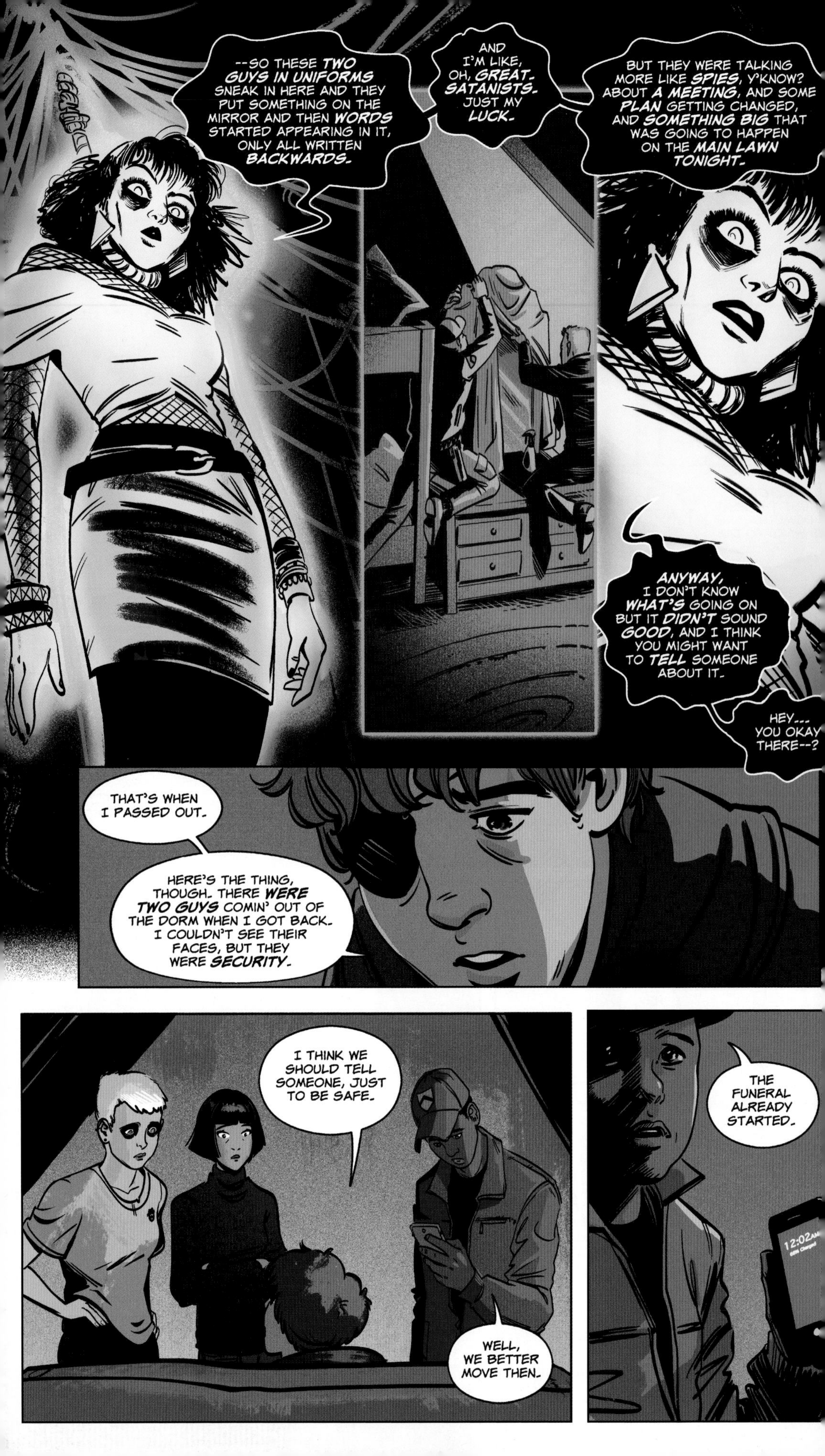
--SO THESE TWO GUYS IN UNIFORMS SNEAK IN HERE AND THEY PUT SOMETHING ON THE MIRROR AND THEN WORDS STARTED APPEARING IN IT, ONLY ALL WRITTEN BACKWARDS.
AND I'M LIKE, OH, GREAT. SATANISTS. JUST MY LUCK.
BUT THEY WERE TALKING MORE LIKE SPIES, Y'KNOW? ABOUT A MEETING, AND SOME PLAN GETTING CHANGED, AND SOMETHING BIG THAT WAS GOING TO HAPPEN ON THE MAIN LAWN TONIGHT.
ANYWAY, I DON'T KNOW WHAT'S GOING ON BUT IT DIDN'T SOUND GOOD, AND I THINK YOU MIGHT WANT TO TELL SOMEONE ABOUT IT.
HEY... YOU OKAY THERE--?
THAT'S WHEN I PASSED OUT.
HERE'S THE THING, THOUGH. THERE WERE TWO GUYS COMIN' OUT OF THE DORM WHEN I GOT BACK. I COULDN'T SEE THEIR FACES, BUT THEY WERE SECURITY.
I THINK WE SHOULD TELL SOMEONE, JUST TO BE SAFE.
WELL, WE BETTER MOVE THEN.
THE FUNERAL ALREADY STARTED.
12:02AM

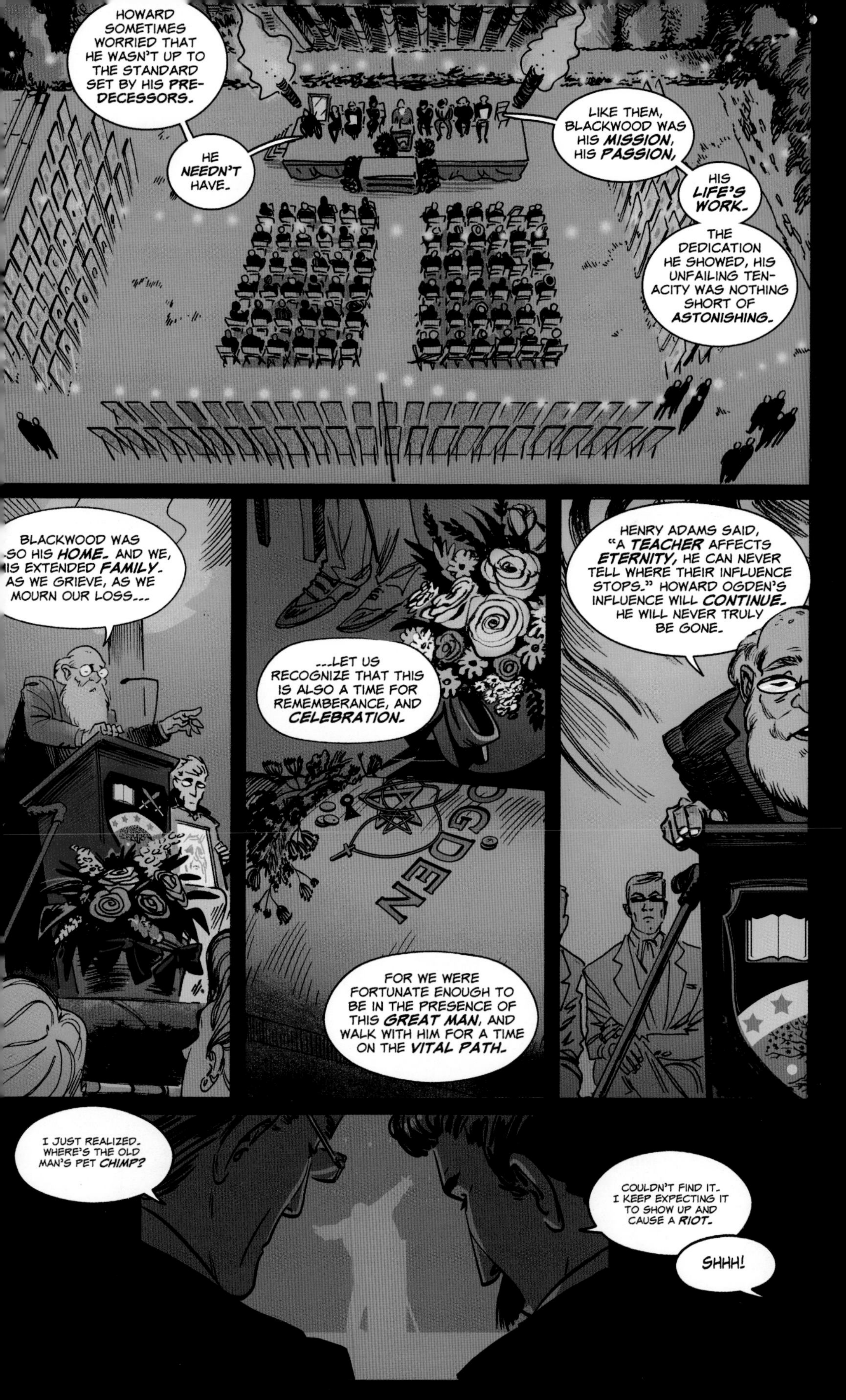
HOWARD SOMETIMES WORRIED THAT HE WASN'T UP TO THE STANDARD SET BY HIS PRE-DECESSORS.
HE NEEDN'T HAVE.
LIKE THEM, BLACKWOOD WAS HIS MISSION, HIS PASSION,
HIS LIFE'S WORK.
THE DEDICATION HE SHOWED, HIS UNFAILING TEN-ACITY WAS NOTHING SHORT OF ASTONISHING.
BLACKWOOD WAS SO HIS HOME. AND WE, IS EXTENDED FAMILY. AS WE GRIEVE, AS WE MOURN OUR LOSS...
...LET US RECOGNIZE THAT THIS IS ALSO A TIME FOR REMEMBERANCE, AND CELEBRATION.
FOR WE WERE FORTUNATE ENOUGH TO BE IN THE PRESENCE OF THIS GREAT MAN, AND WALK WITH HIM FOR A TIME ON THE VITAL PATH.
HENRY ADAMS SAID, "A TEACHER AFFECTS ETERNITY, HE CAN NEVER TELL WHERE THEIR INFLUENCE STOPS." HOWARD OGDEN'S INFLUENCE WILL CONTINUE. HE WILL NEVER TRULY BE GONE.
OGDEN
I JUST REALIZED. WHERE'S THE OLD MAN'S PET CHIMP?
COULDN'T FIND IT. I KEEP EXPECTING IT TO SHOW UP AND CAUSE A RIOT.
SHHH!

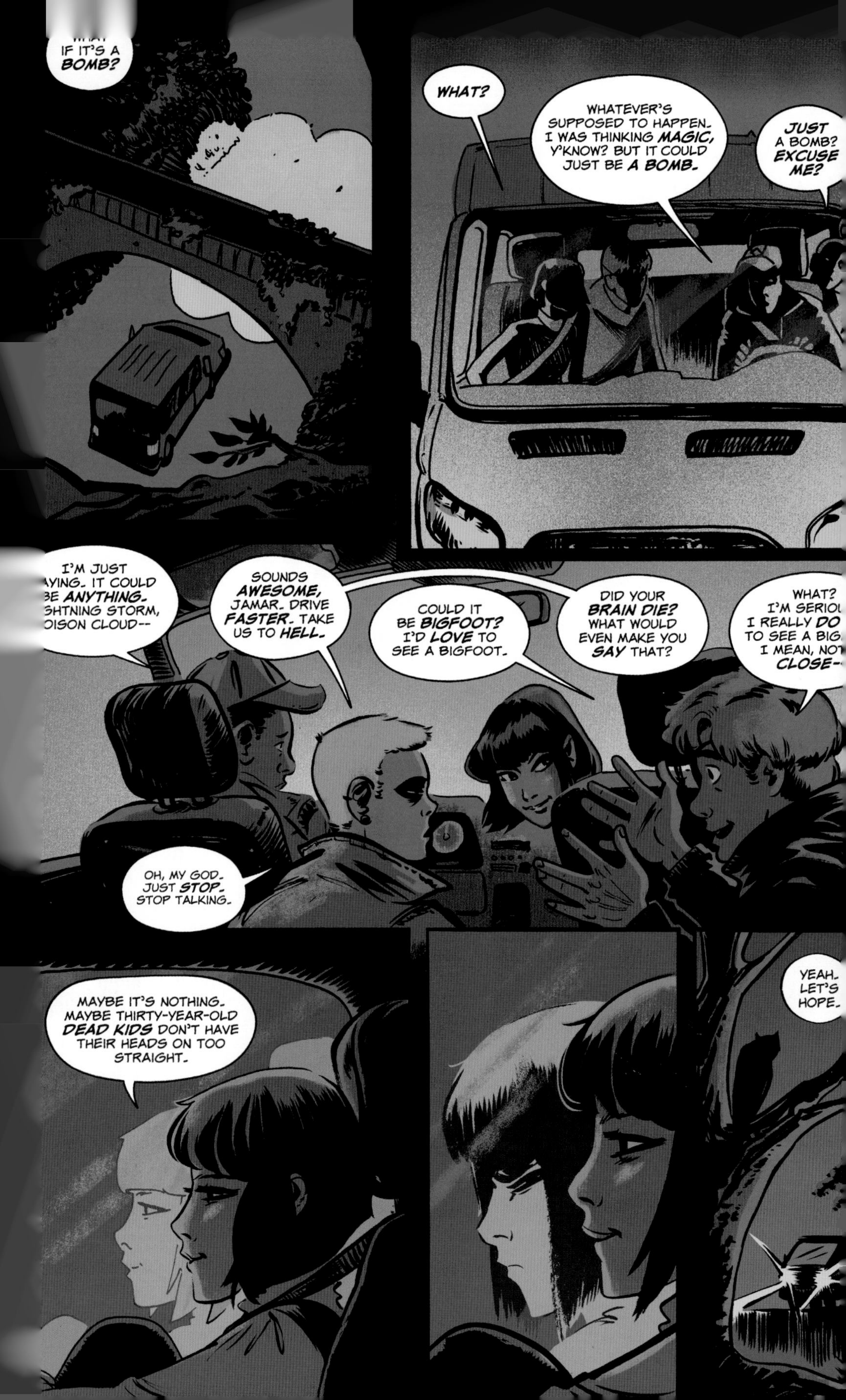
IF IT'S A BOMB?
WHAT?
WHATEVER'S SUPPOSED TO HAPPEN. I WAS THINKING MAGIC, Y'KNOW? BUT IT COULD JUST BE A BOMB.
JUST A BOMB? EXCUSE ME?
I'M JUST AYING. IT COULD BE ANYTHING. GHTNING STORM, OISON CLOUD--
SOUNDS AWESOME, JAMAR. DRIVE FASTER. TAKE US TO HELL.
COULD IT BE BIGFOOT? I'D LOVE TO SEE A BIGFOOT.
DID YOUR BRAIN DIE? WHAT WOULD EVEN MAKE YOU SAY THAT?
WHAT? I'M SERIOU I REALLY DO TO SEE A BIG I MEAN, NOT CLOSE--
OH, MY GOD. JUST STOP. STOP TALKING.
MAYBE IT'S NOTHING. MAYBE THIRTY-YEAR-OLD DEAD KIDS DON'T HAVE THEIR HEADS ON TOO STRAIGHT.
YEAH. LET'S HOPE.

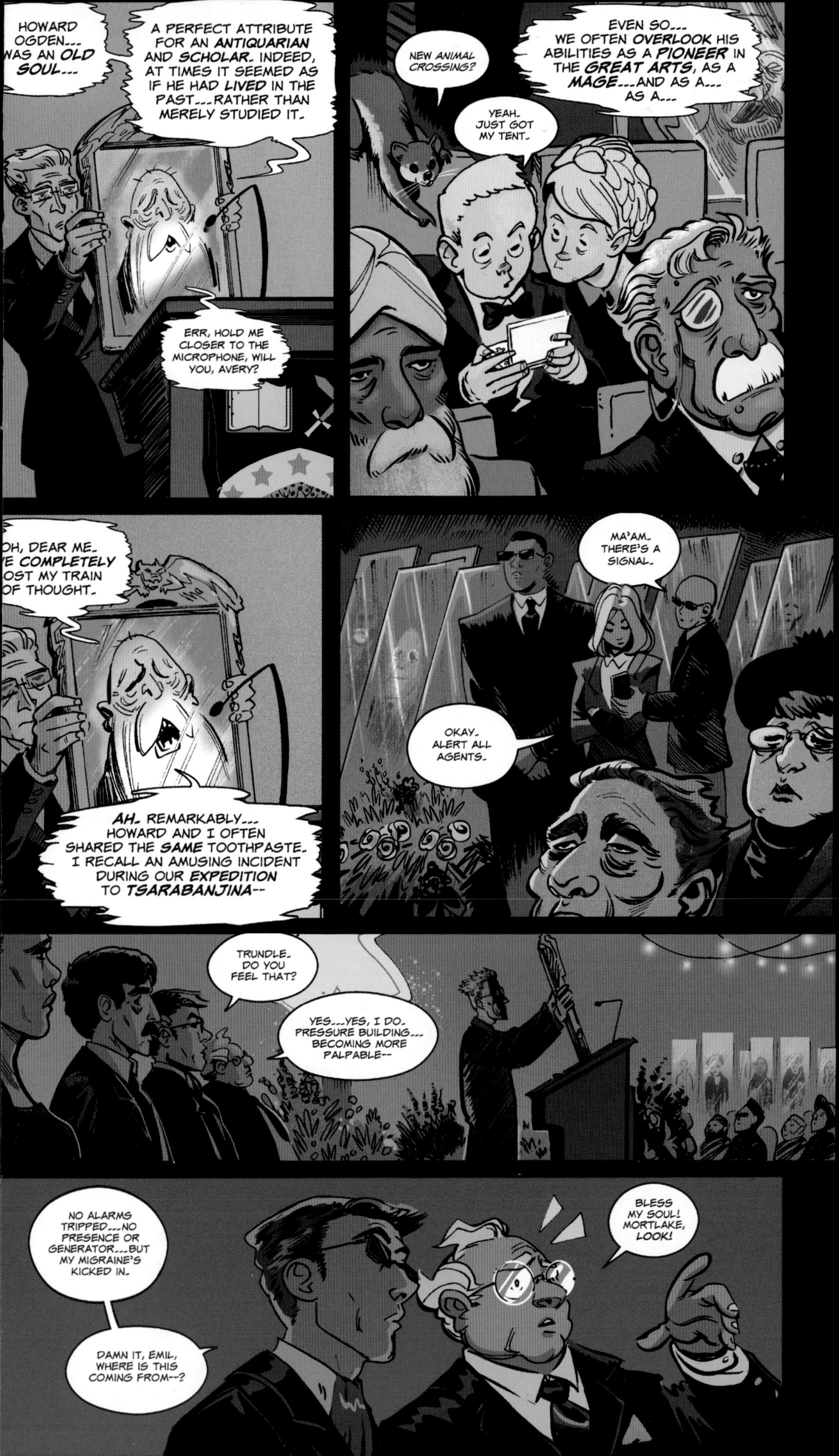

HOWARD OGDEN... WAS AN OLD SOUL...
A PERFECT ATTRIBUTE FOR AN ANTIQUARIAN AND SCHOLAR. INDEED, AT TIMES IT SEEMED AS IF HE HAD LIVED IN THE PAST... RATHER THAN MERELY STUDIED IT.
ERR, HOLD ME CLOSER TO THE MICROPHONE, WILL YOU, AVERY?
NEW ANIMAL CROSSING?
YEAH. JUST GOT MY TENT.
EVEN SO... WE OFTEN OVERLOOK HIS ABILITIES AS A PIONEER IN THE GREAT ARTS, AS A MAGE... AND AS A... AS A...
OH, DEAR ME. I'VE COMPLETELY LOST MY TRAIN OF THOUGHT.
AH. REMARKABLY... HOWARD AND I OFTEN SHARED THE SAME TOOTHPASTE. I RECALL AN AMUSING INCIDENT DURING OUR EXPEDITION TO TSARABANJINA--
MA'AM. THERE'S A SIGNAL.
OKAY. ALERT ALL AGENTS.
TRUNDLE. DO YOU FEEL THAT?
YES... YES, I DO. PRESSURE BUILDING... BECOMING MORE PALPABLE--
NO ALARMS TRIPPED... NO PRESENCE OR GENERATOR... BUT MY MIGRAINE'S KICKED IN.
DAMN IT, EMIL, WHERE IS THIS COMING FROM--?
BLESS MY SOUL! MORTLAKE, LOOK!

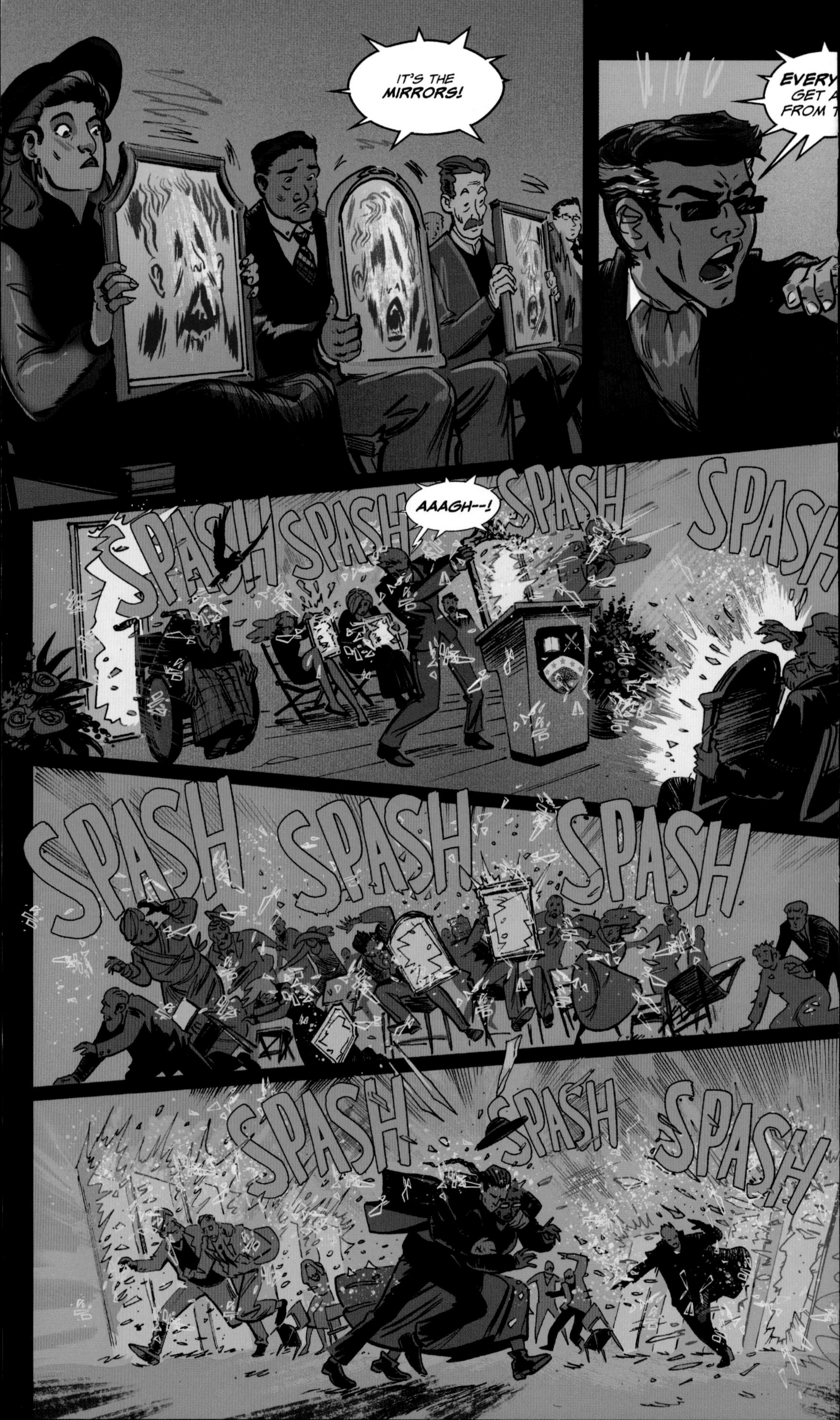
IT'S THE MIRRORS!
EVERY
GET A
FROM T
SPASH
SPASH
AAAGH--!
SPASH
SPASH
SPASH
SPASH
SPASH
SPASH
SPASH
SPASH

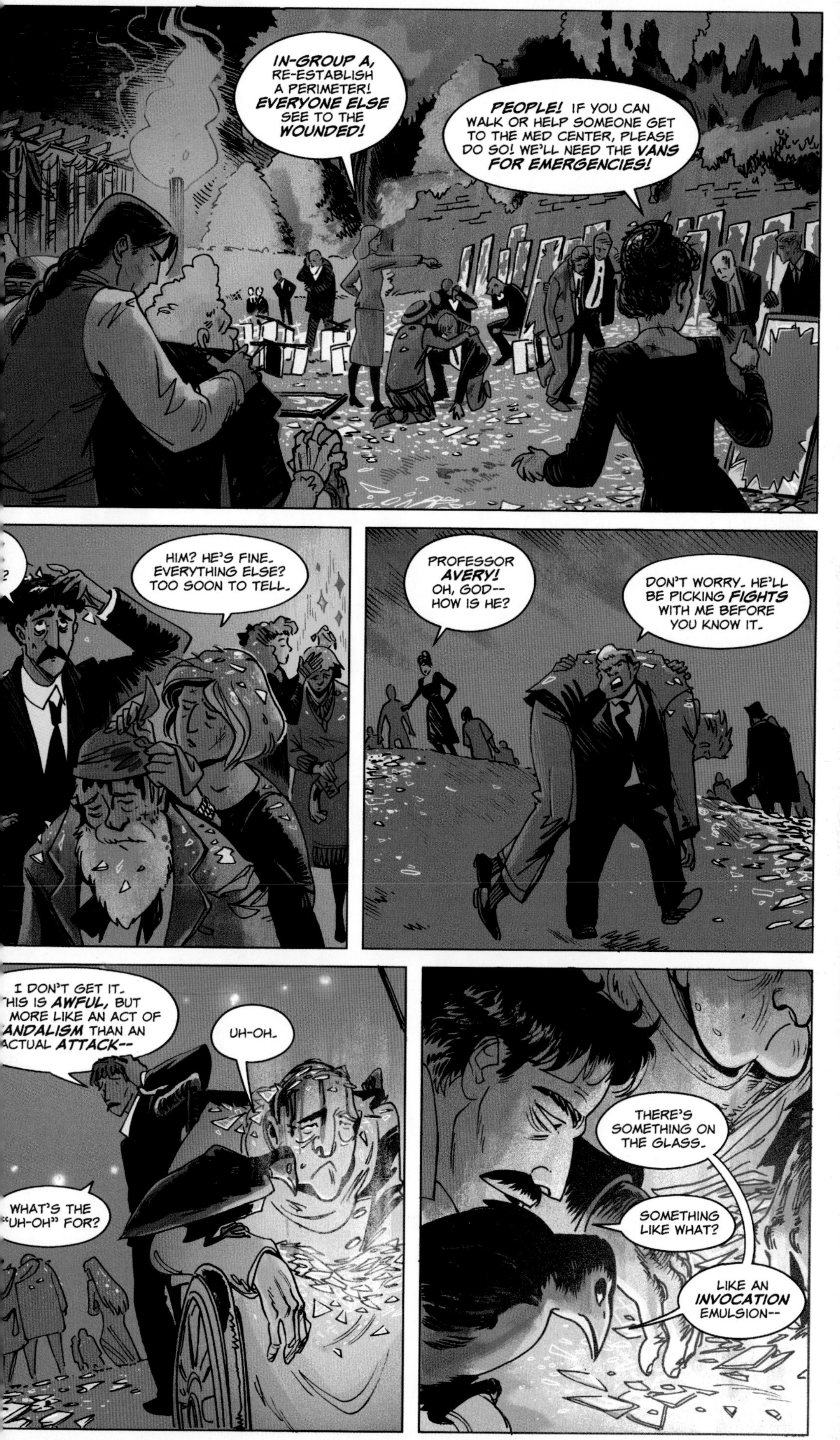
IN-GROUP A, RE-ESTABLISH A PERIMETER! EVERYONE ELSE SEE TO THE WOUNDED!
PEOPLE! IF YOU CAN WALK OR HELP SOMEONE GET TO THE MED CENTER, PLEASE DO SO! WE'LL NEED THE VANS FOR EMERGENCIES!
HIM? HE'S FINE. EVERYTHING ELSE? TOO SOON TO TELL.
PROFESSOR AVERY! OH, GOD-- HOW IS HE?
DON'T WORRY. HE'LL BE PICKING FIGHTS WITH ME BEFORE YOU KNOW IT.
I DON'T GET IT. THIS IS AWFUL, BUT MORE LIKE AN ACT OF ANDALISM THAN AN ACTUAL ATTACK--
UH-OH.
WHAT'S THE "UH-OH" FOR?
THERE'S SOMETHING ON THE GLASS.
SOMETHING LIKE WHAT?
LIKE AN INVOCATION EMULSION--

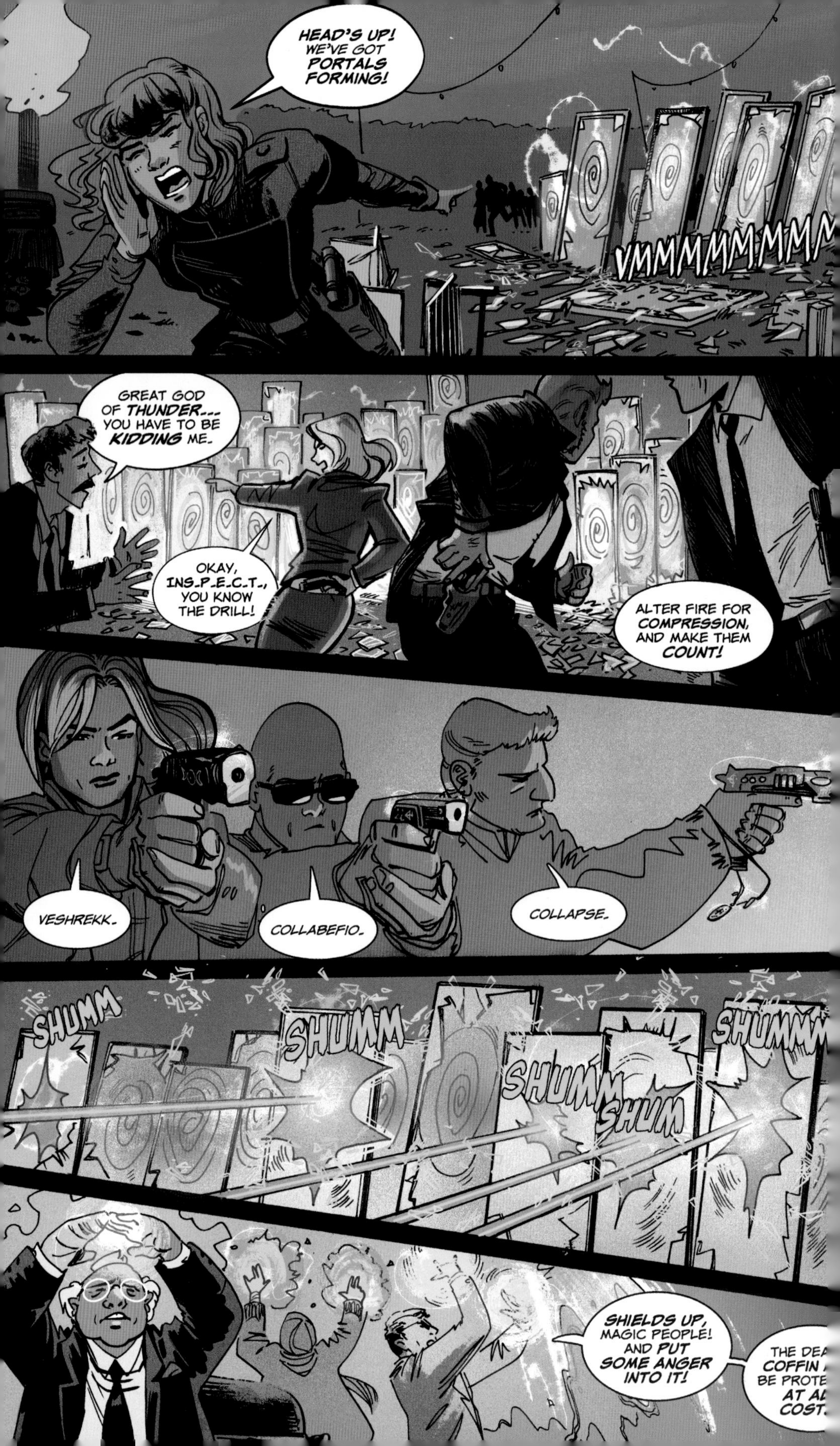
HEAD'S UP! WE'VE GOT PORTALS FORMING!
VMMMMMMMMM
GREAT GOD OF THUNDER... YOU HAVE TO BE KIDDING ME.
OKAY, INS.P.E.C.T., YOU KNOW THE DRILL!
ALTER FIRE FOR COMPRESSION, AND MAKE THEM COUNT!
VESHREKK.
COLLABEFIO.
COLLAPSE.
SHUMM
SHUMM
SHUMM
SHUM
SHUMMM
SHIELDS UP, MAGIC PEOPLE! AND PUT SOME ANGER INTO IT!

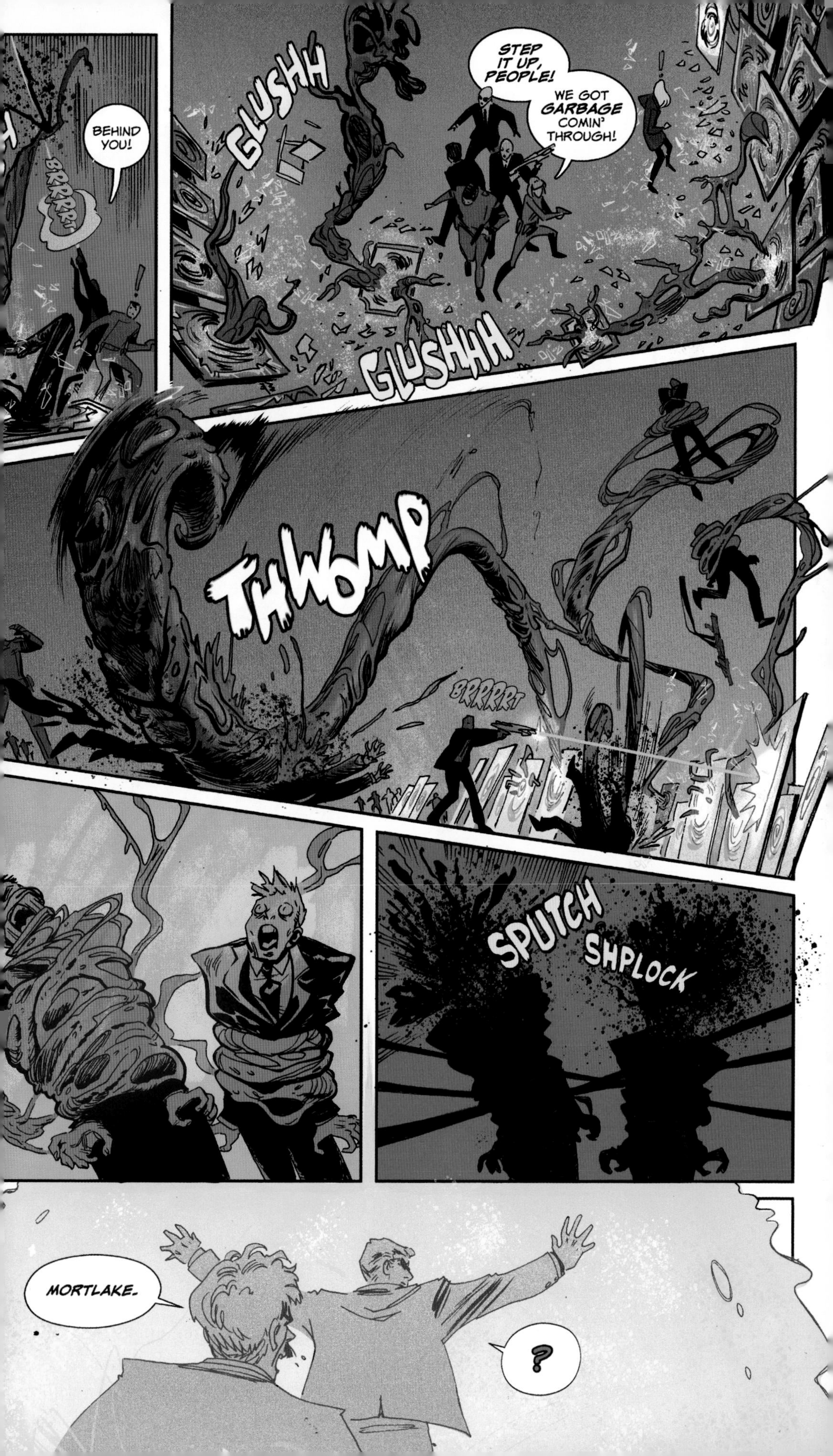
BEHIND YOU!
BRRRRT
GLUSHH
STEP IT UP, PEOPLE!
WE GOT GARBAGE COMIN' THROUGH!
GLUSHHH
THWOMP
BRRRRT
SPUTCH
SHPLOCK
MORTLAKE.
?

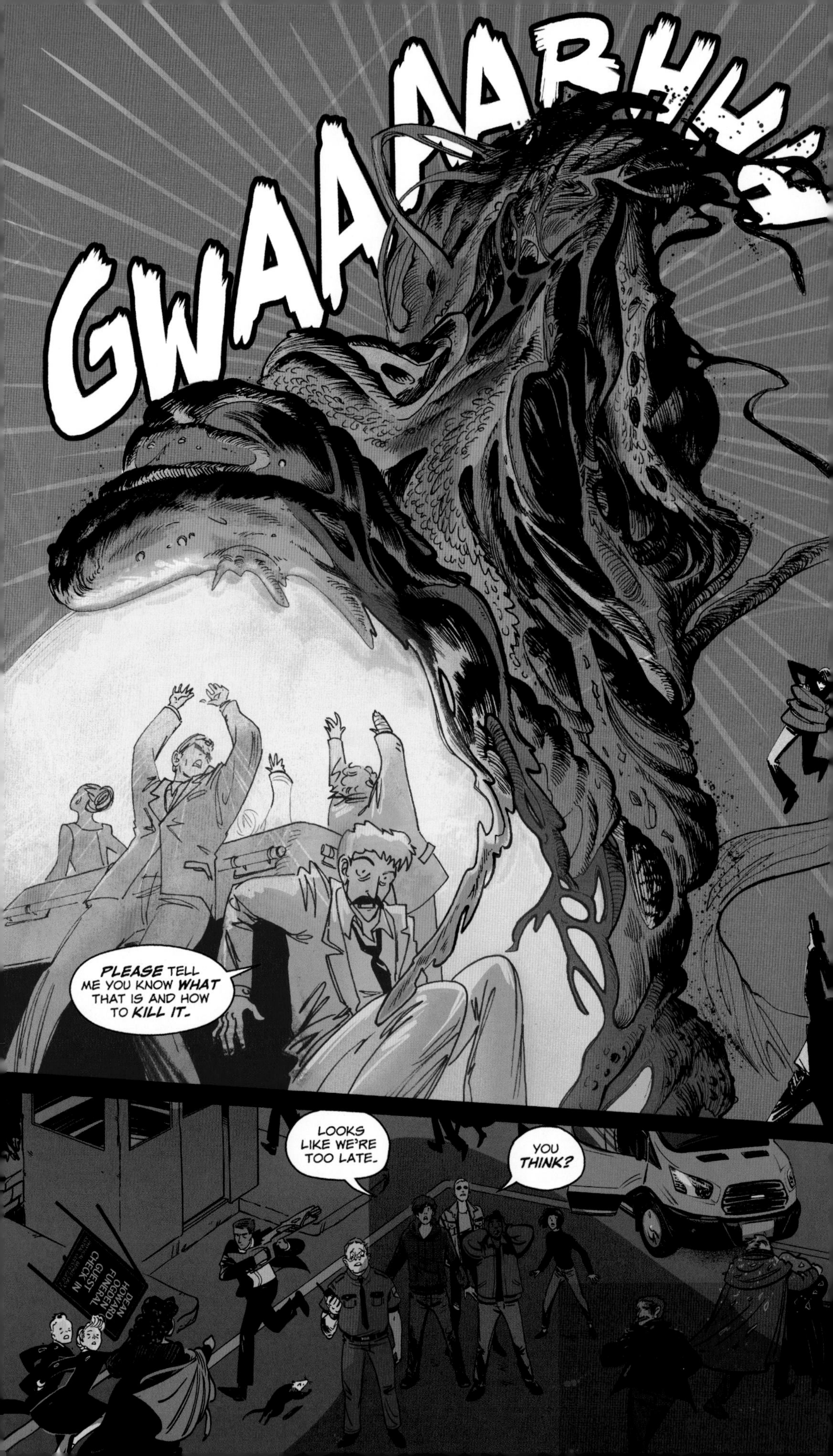
GWAAAARHH
PLEASE TELL ME YOU KNOW WHAT THAT IS AND HOW TO KILL IT.
LOOKS LIKE WE'RE TOO LATE.
YOU THINK?
DEAN HOWARD OGDEN FUNERAL GUEST CHECK IN

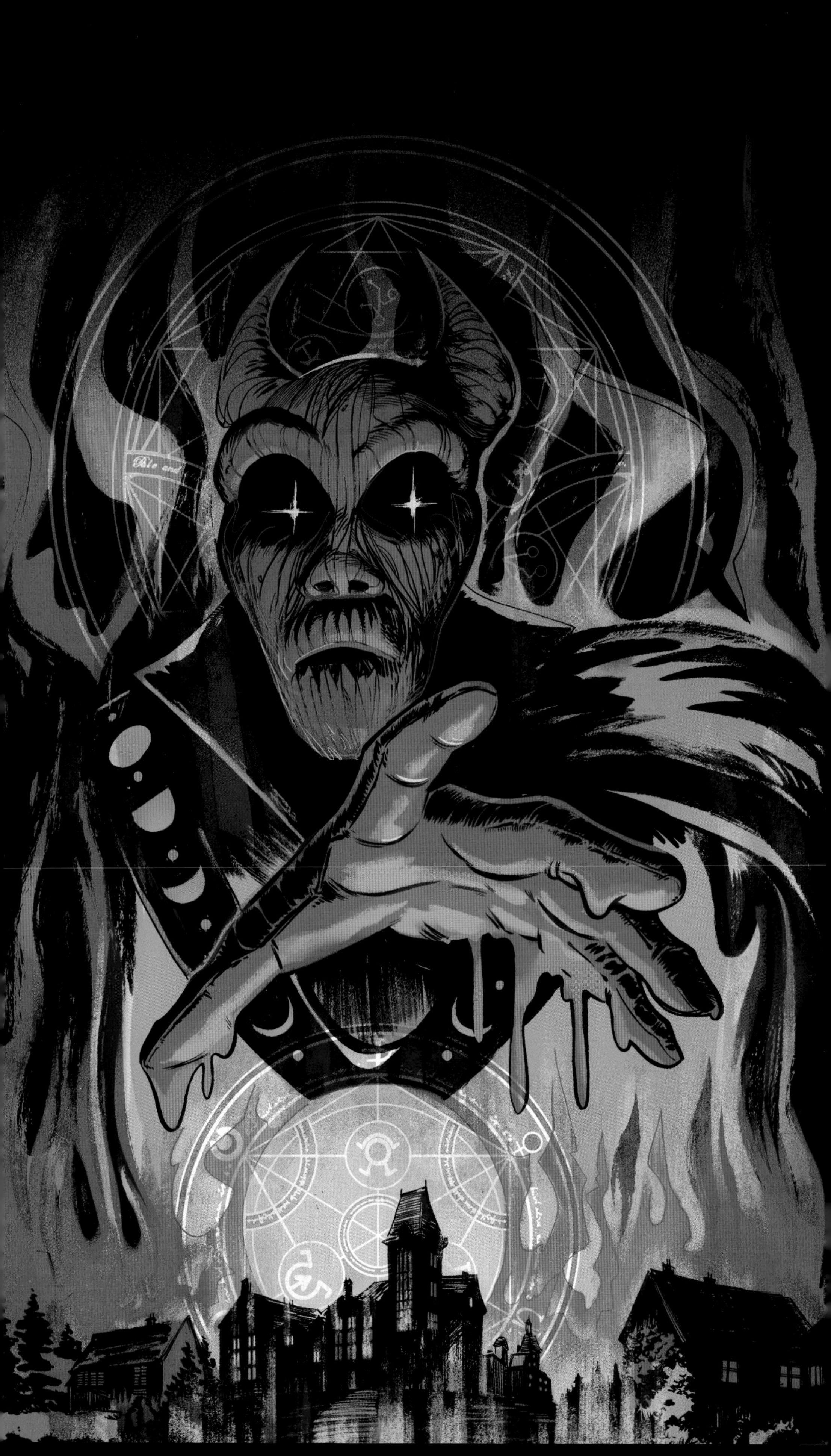

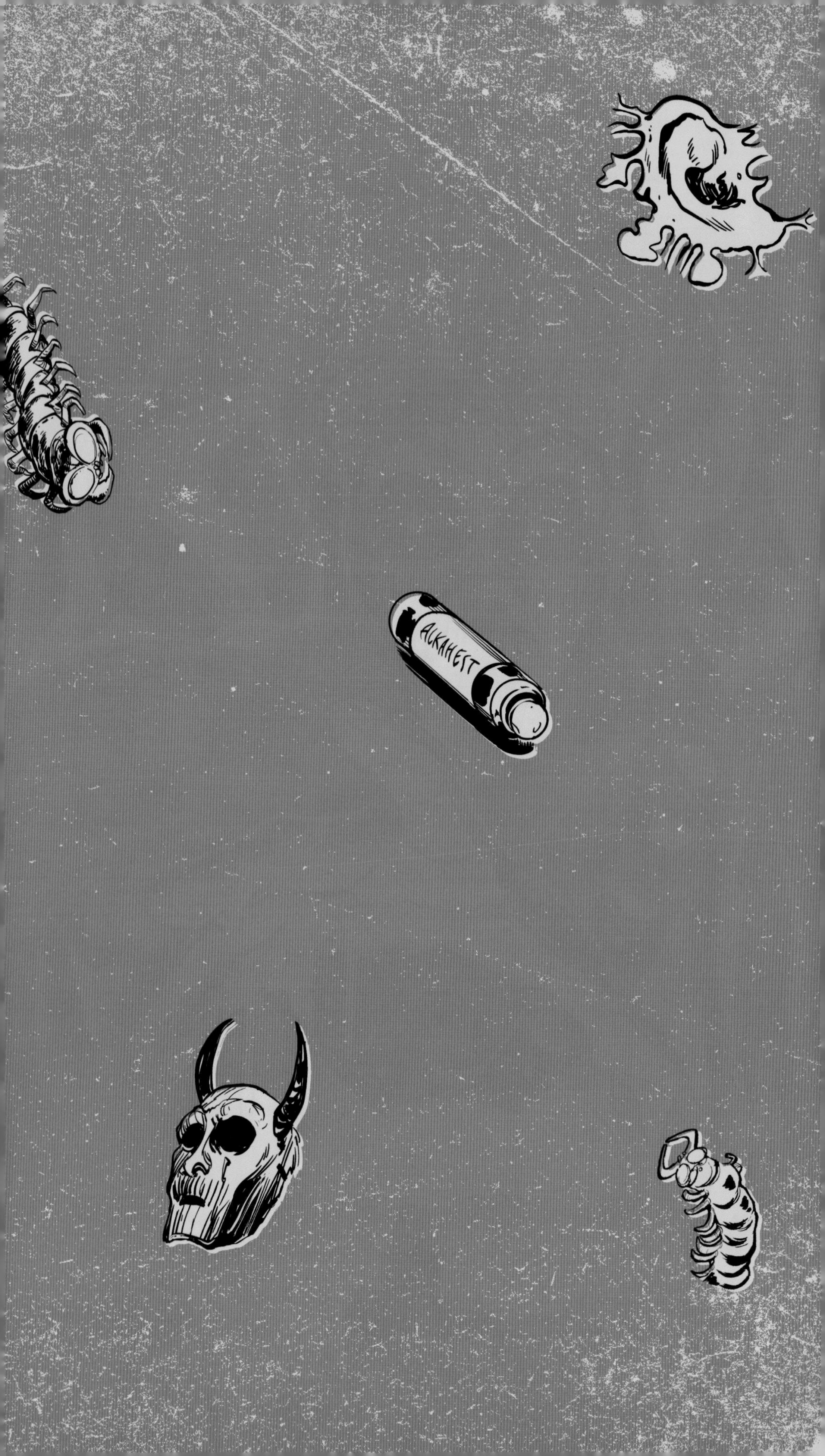
ALKAHEST

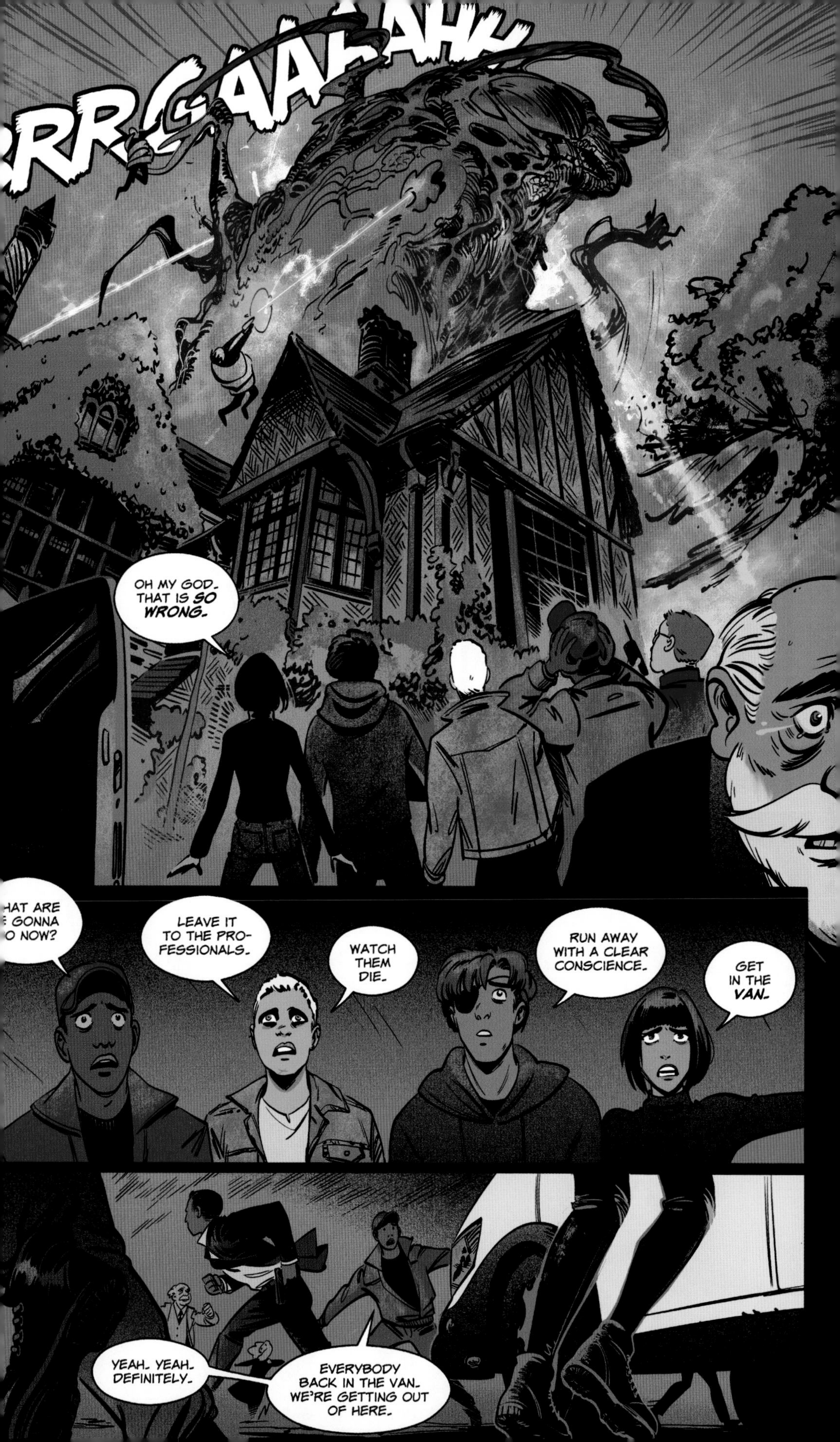
RRRGAAAAHK
OH MY GOD. THAT IS SO WRONG.
HAT ARE E GONNA O NOW?
LEAVE IT TO THE PRO- FESSIONALS.
WATCH THEM DIE.
RUN AWAY WITH A CLEAR CONSCIENCE.
GET IN THE VAN.
YEAH. YEAH. DEFINITELY.
EVERYBODY BACK IN THE VAN. WE'RE GETTING OUT OF HERE.

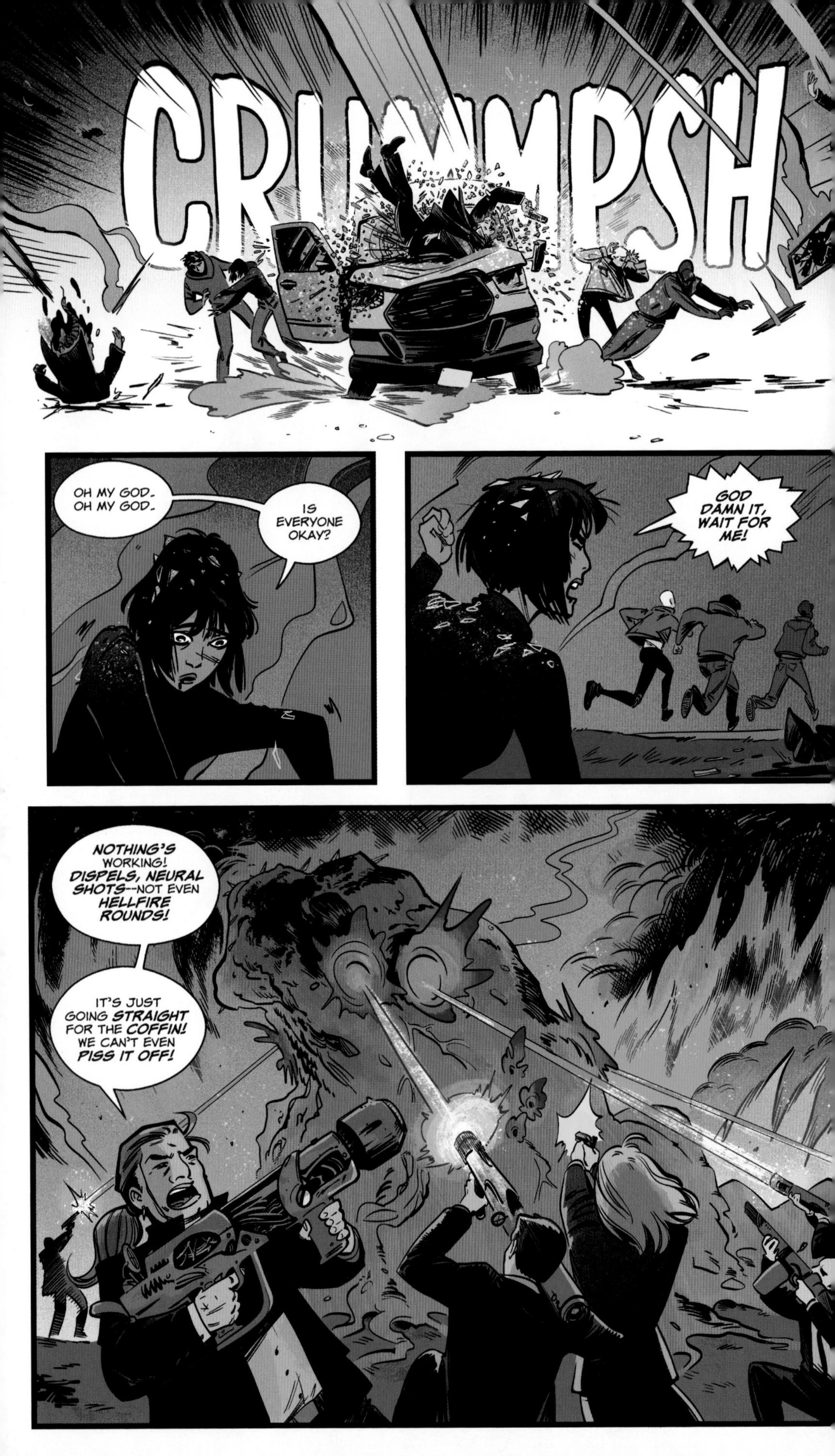

CRUMMPSH
OH MY GOD. OH MY GOD.
IS EVERYONE OKAY?
GOD DAMN IT, WAIT FOR ME!
NOTHING'S WORKING! DISPELS, NEURAL SHOTS--NOT EVEN HELLFIRE ROUNDS!
IT'S JUST GOING STRAIGHT FOR THE COFFIN! WE CAN'T EVEN PISS IT OFF!

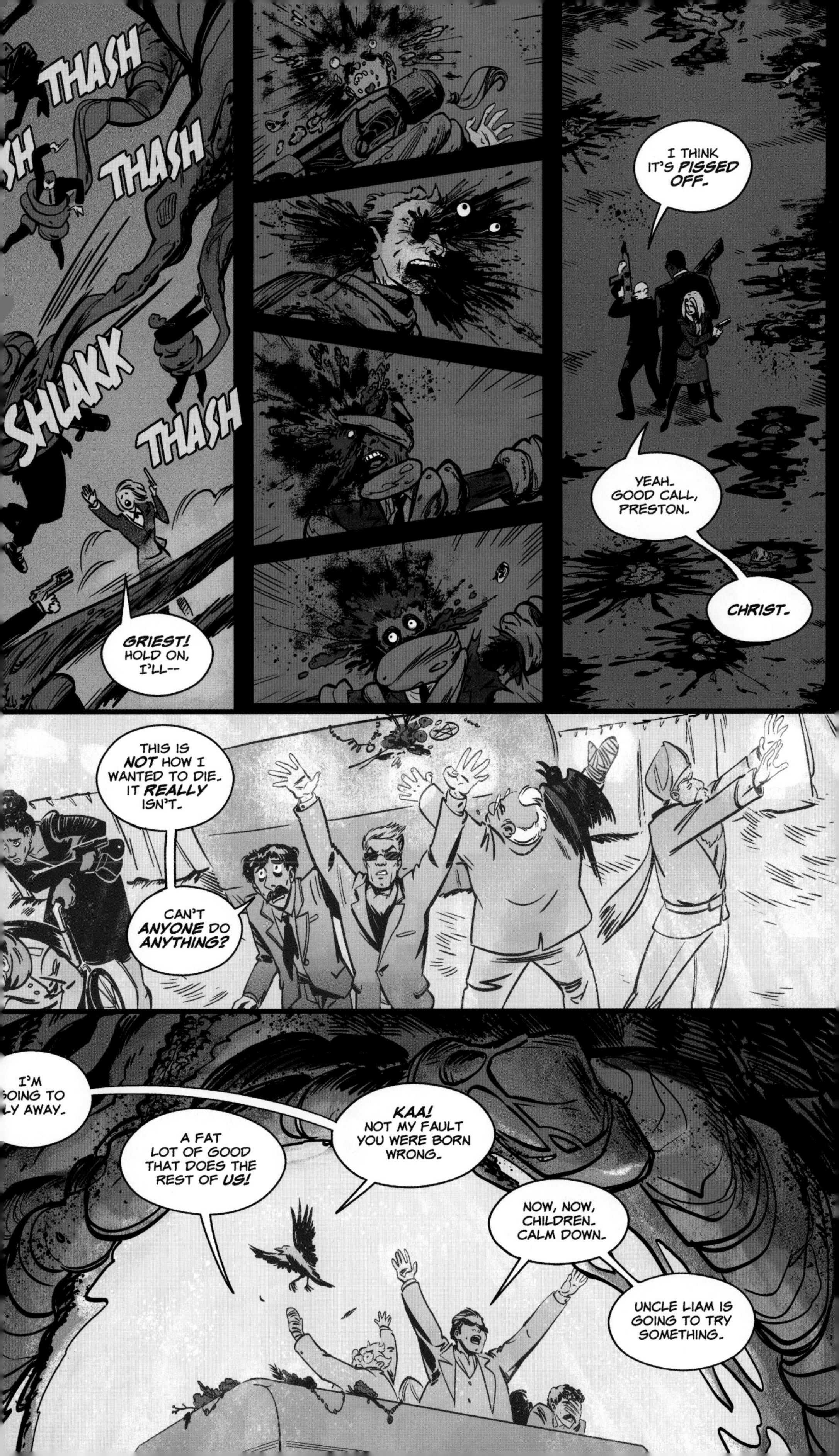
THASH
SH
THASH
SHLAKK
THASH
GRIEST! HOLD ON, I'LL--
I THINK IT'S PISSED OFF.
YEAH. GOOD CALL, PRESTON.
CHRIST.
THIS IS NOT HOW I WANTED TO DIE. IT REALLY ISN'T.
CAN'T ANYONE DO ANYTHING?
I'M GOING TO LY AWAY.
A FAT LOT OF GOOD THAT DOES THE REST OF US!
KAA! NOT MY FAULT YOU WERE BORN WRONG.
NOW, NOW, CHILDREN. CALM DOWN.
UNCLE LIAM IS GOING TO TRY SOMETHING.

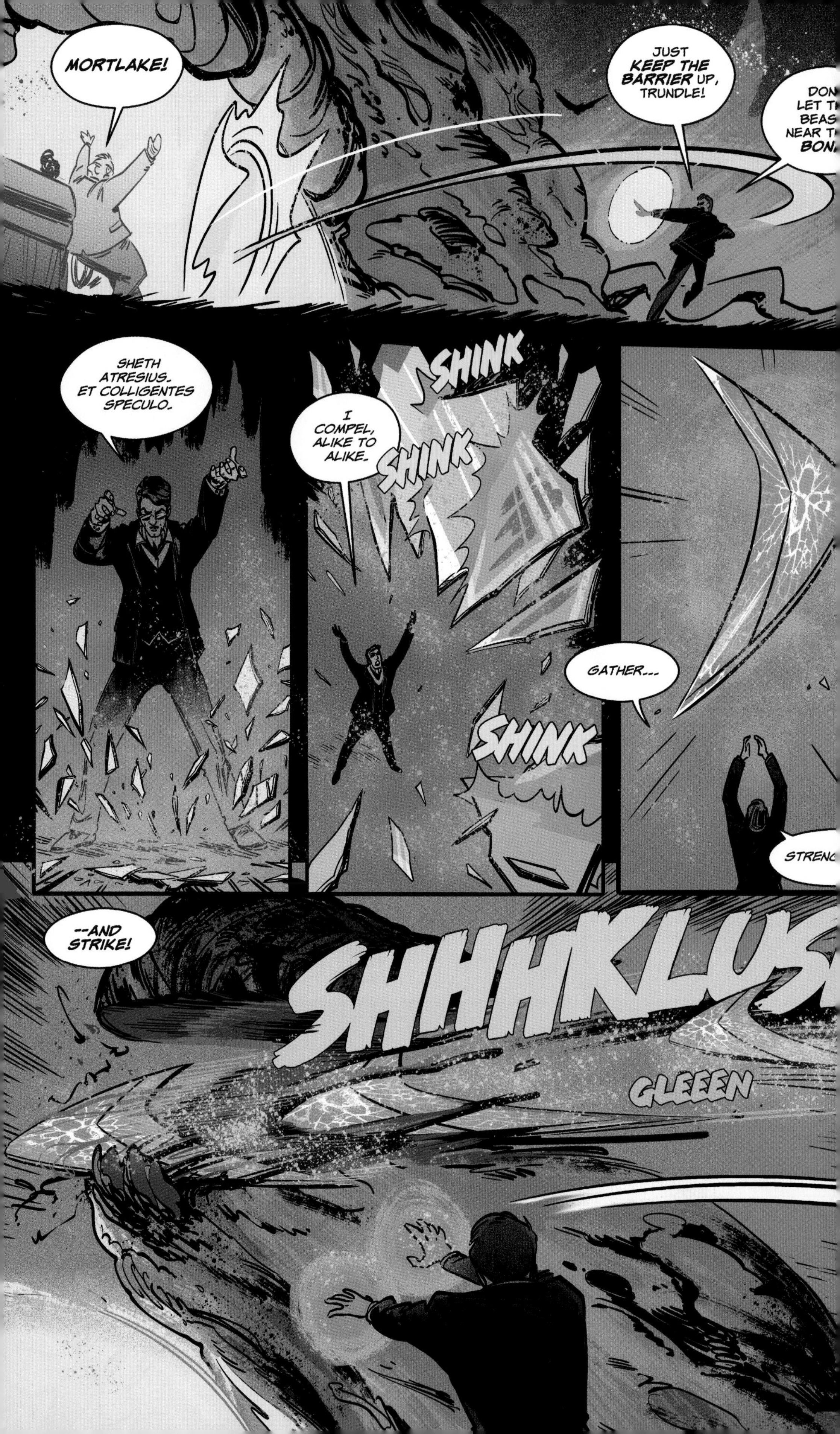
MORTLAKE!
JUST KEEP THE BARRIER UP, TRUNDLE!
DON LET T BEAS NEAR T BON
SHETH ATRESIUS. ET COLLIGENTES SPECULO.
SHINK
I COMPEL, ALIKE TO ALIKE.
SHINK
SHINK
GATHER...
STRENG
--AND STRIKE!
SHHHKLUS
GLEEEN

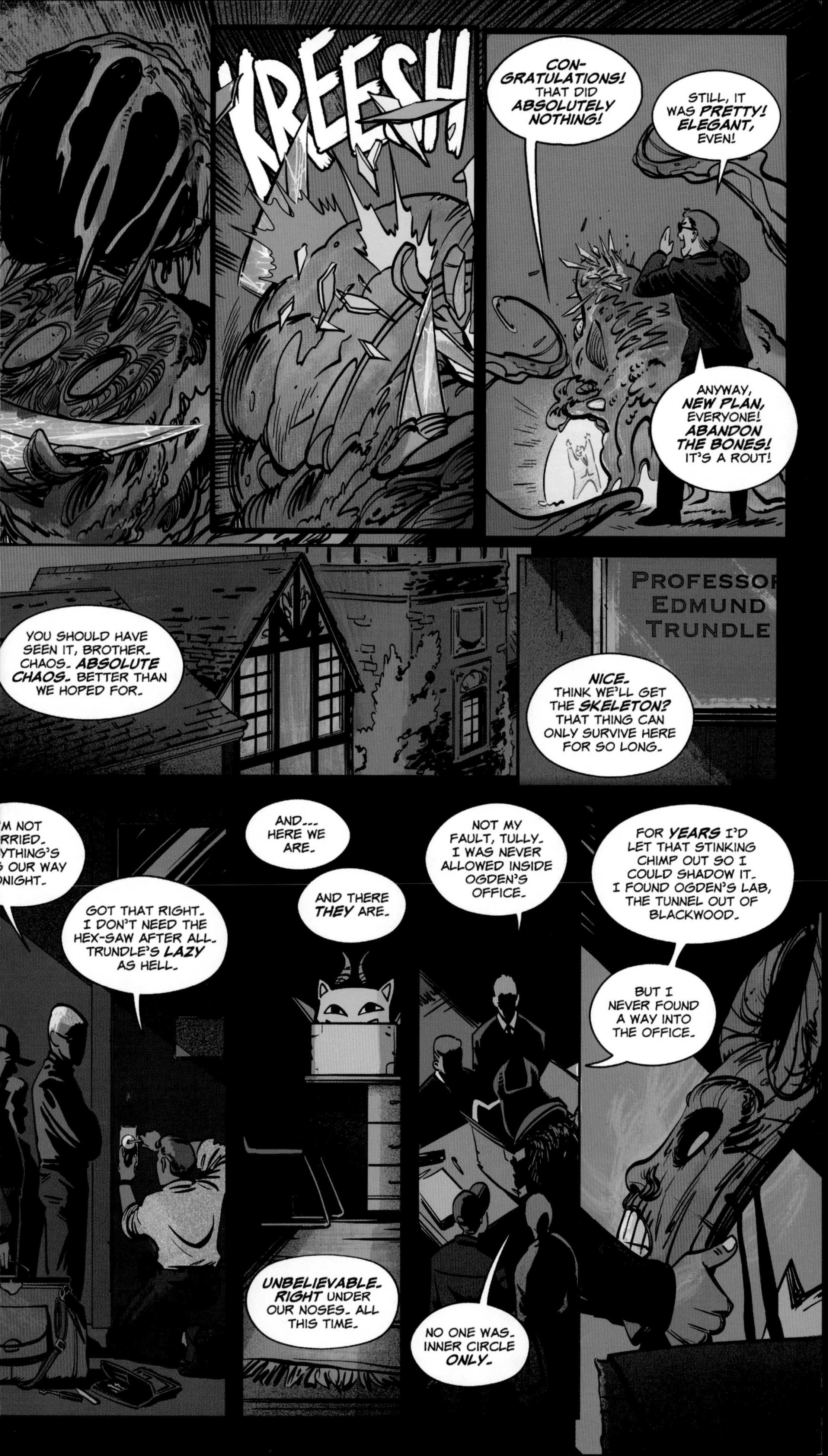
KREESH
CON-GRATULATIONS! THAT DID ABSOLUTELY NOTHING!
STILL, IT WAS PRETTY! ELEGANT, EVEN!
ANYWAY, NEW PLAN, EVERYONE! ABANDON THE BONES! IT'S A ROUT!
YOU SHOULD HAVE SEEN IT, BROTHER. CHAOS. ABSOLUTE CHAOS. BETTER THAN WE HOPED FOR.
PROFESSOR EDMUND TRUNDLE
NICE. THINK WE'LL GET THE SKELETON? THAT THING CAN ONLY SURVIVE HERE FOR SO LONG.
GOT THAT RIGHT. I DON'T NEED THE HEX-SAW AFTER ALL. TRUNDLE'S LAZY AS HELL.
AND... HERE WE ARE.
AND THERE THEY ARE.
UNBELIEVABLE. RIGHT UNDER OUR NOSES. ALL THIS TIME.
NOT MY FAULT, TULLY. I WAS NEVER ALLOWED INSIDE OGDEN'S OFFICE.
NO ONE WAS. INNER CIRCLE ONLY.
FOR YEARS I'D LET THAT STINKING CHIMP OUT SO I COULD SHADOW IT. I FOUND OGDEN'S LAB, THE TUNNEL OUT OF BLACKWOOD.
BUT I NEVER FOUND A WAY INTO THE OFFICE.

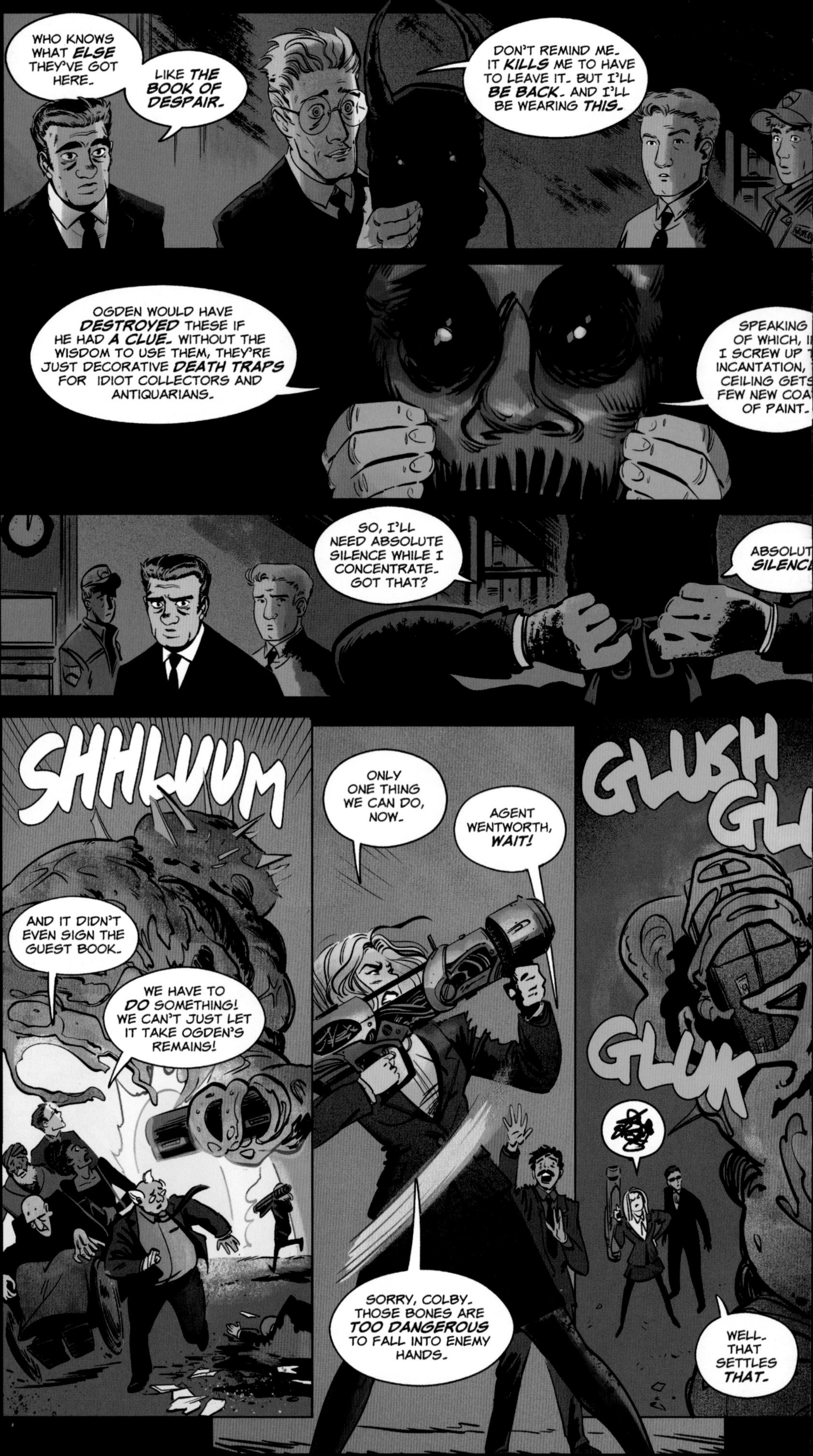
WHO KNOWS WHAT ELSE THEY'VE GOT HERE.
LIKE THE BOOK OF DESPAIR.
DON'T REMIND ME. IT KILLS ME TO HAVE TO LEAVE IT. BUT I'LL BE BACK. AND I'LL BE WEARING THIS.
OGDEN WOULD HAVE DESTROYED THESE IF HE HAD A CLUE. WITHOUT THE WISDOM TO USE THEM, THEY'RE JUST DECORATIVE DEATH TRAPS FOR IDIOT COLLECTORS AND ANTIQUARIANS.
SPEAKING OF WHICH, I I SCREW UP INCANTATION, CEILING GETS FEW NEW COA OF PAINT.
SO, I'LL NEED ABSOLUTE SILENCE WHILE I CONCENTRATE. GOT THAT?
ABSOLUT SILENCE
SHHLUUM
AND IT DIDN'T EVEN SIGN THE GUEST BOOK.
WE HAVE TO DO SOMETHING! WE CAN'T JUST LET IT TAKE OGDEN'S REMAINS!
ONLY ONE THING WE CAN DO, NOW.
AGENT WENTWORTH, WAIT!
SORRY, COLBY. THOSE BONES ARE TOO DANGEROUS TO FALL INTO ENEMY HANDS.
GLUSH
GL
GLUK
WELL. THAT SETTLES THAT.

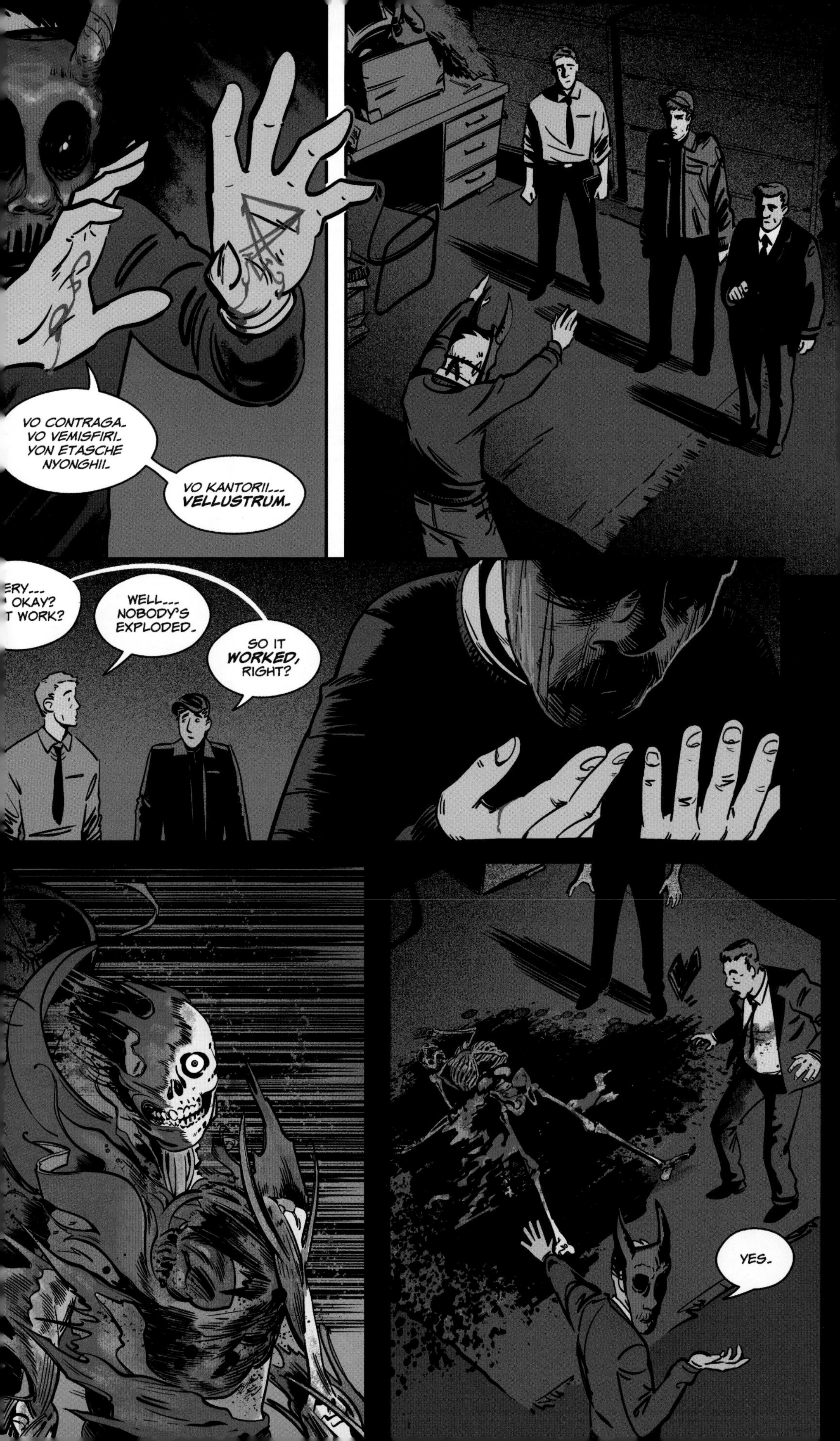
VO CONTRAGA. VO VEMISFIRI. YON ETASCHE NYONGHII.
VO KANTORII... **VELLUSTRUM.**
ERY... OKAY? T WORK?
WELL... NOBODY'S EXPLODED.
SO IT **WORKED,** RIGHT?
YES.

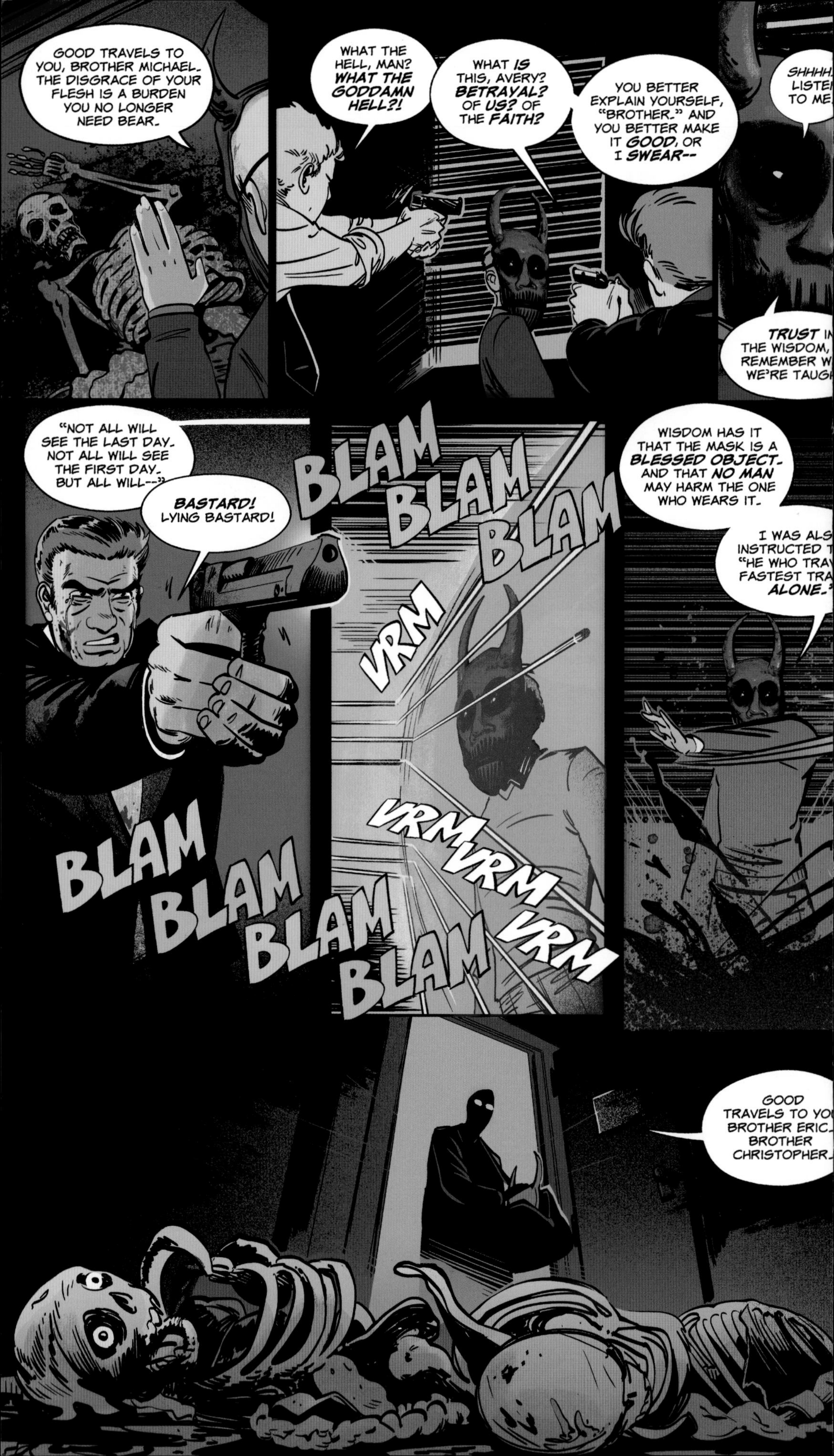
GOOD TRAVELS TO YOU, BROTHER MICHAEL. THE DISGRACE OF YOUR FLESH IS A BURDEN YOU NO LONGER NEED BEAR.
WHAT THE HELL, MAN? WHAT THE GODDAMN HELL?!
WHAT IS THIS, AVERY? BETRAYAL? OF US? OF THE FAITH?
YOU BETTER EXPLAIN YOURSELF, "BROTHER." AND YOU BETTER MAKE IT GOOD, OR I SWEAR--
SHHHH. LISTEN TO ME.
TRUST IN THE WISDOM, REMEMBER W WE'RE TAUG
"NOT ALL WILL SEE THE LAST DAY. NOT ALL WILL SEE THE FIRST DAY. BUT ALL WILL--"
BASTARD! LYING BASTARD!
BLAM BLAM BLAM
VRM
WISDOM HAS IT THAT THE MASK IS A BLESSED OBJECT. AND THAT NO MAN MAY HARM THE ONE WHO WEARS IT.
I WAS ALS INSTRUCTED T "HE WHO TRAV FASTEST TRA ALONE."
BLAM BLAM BLAM BLAM
VRM VRM VRM VRM
GOOD TRAVELS TO YO BROTHER ERIC. BROTHER CHRISTOPHER.

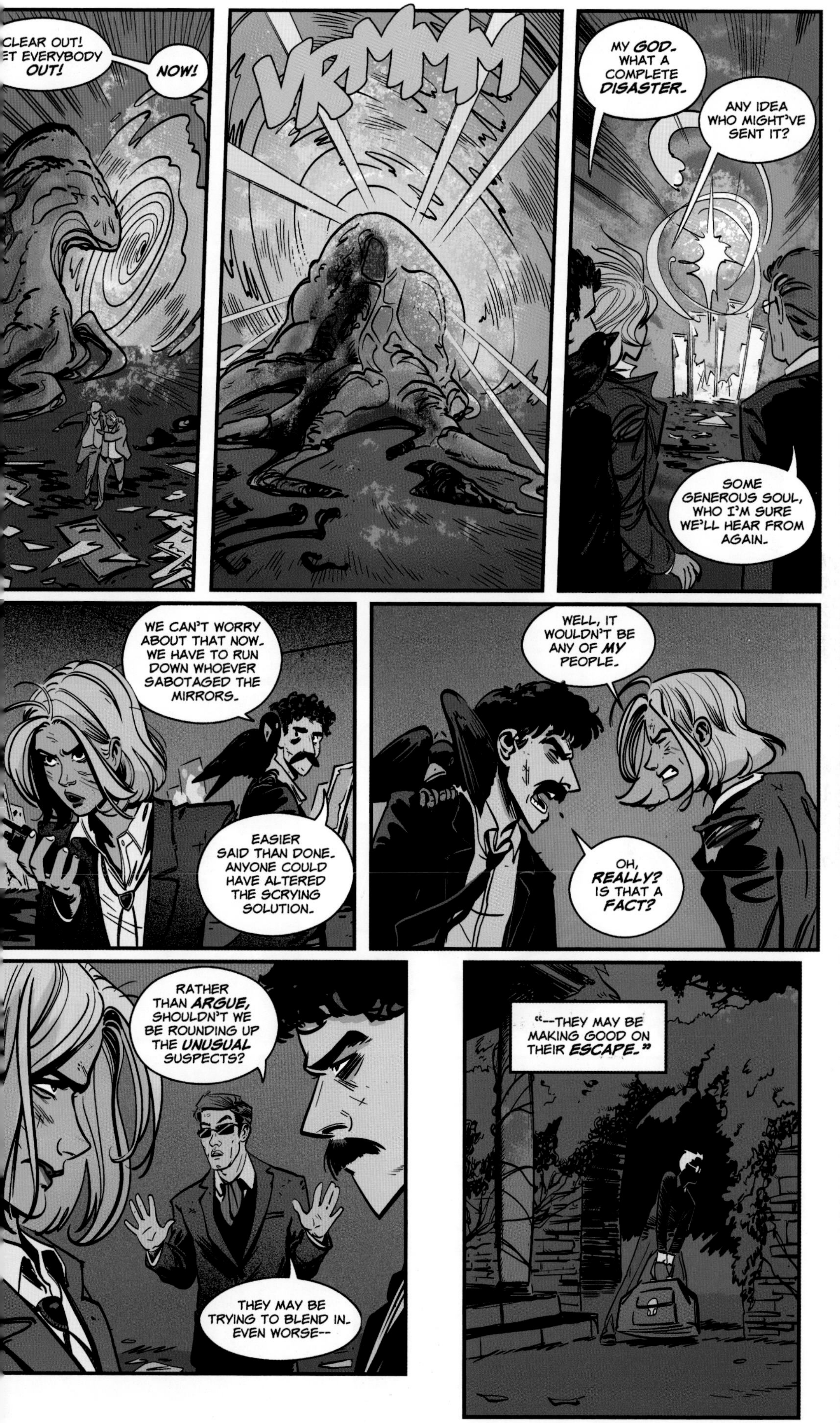
CLEAR OUT! ET EVERYBODY OUT!
NOW!
VRMMMM
MY GOD. WHAT A COMPLETE DISASTER.
ANY IDEA WHO MIGHT'VE SENT IT?
SOME GENEROUS SOUL, WHO I'M SURE WE'LL HEAR FROM AGAIN.
WE CAN'T WORRY ABOUT THAT NOW. WE HAVE TO RUN DOWN WHOEVER SABOTAGED THE MIRRORS.
EASIER SAID THAN DONE. ANYONE COULD HAVE ALTERED THE SCRYING SOLUTION.
WELL, IT WOULDN'T BE ANY OF MY PEOPLE.
OH, REALLY? IS THAT A FACT?
RATHER THAN ARGUE, SHOULDN'T WE BE ROUNDING UP THE UNUSUAL SUSPECTS?
THEY MAY BE TRYING TO BLEND IN. EVEN WORSE--
"--THEY MAY BE MAKING GOOD ON THEIR ESCAPE."

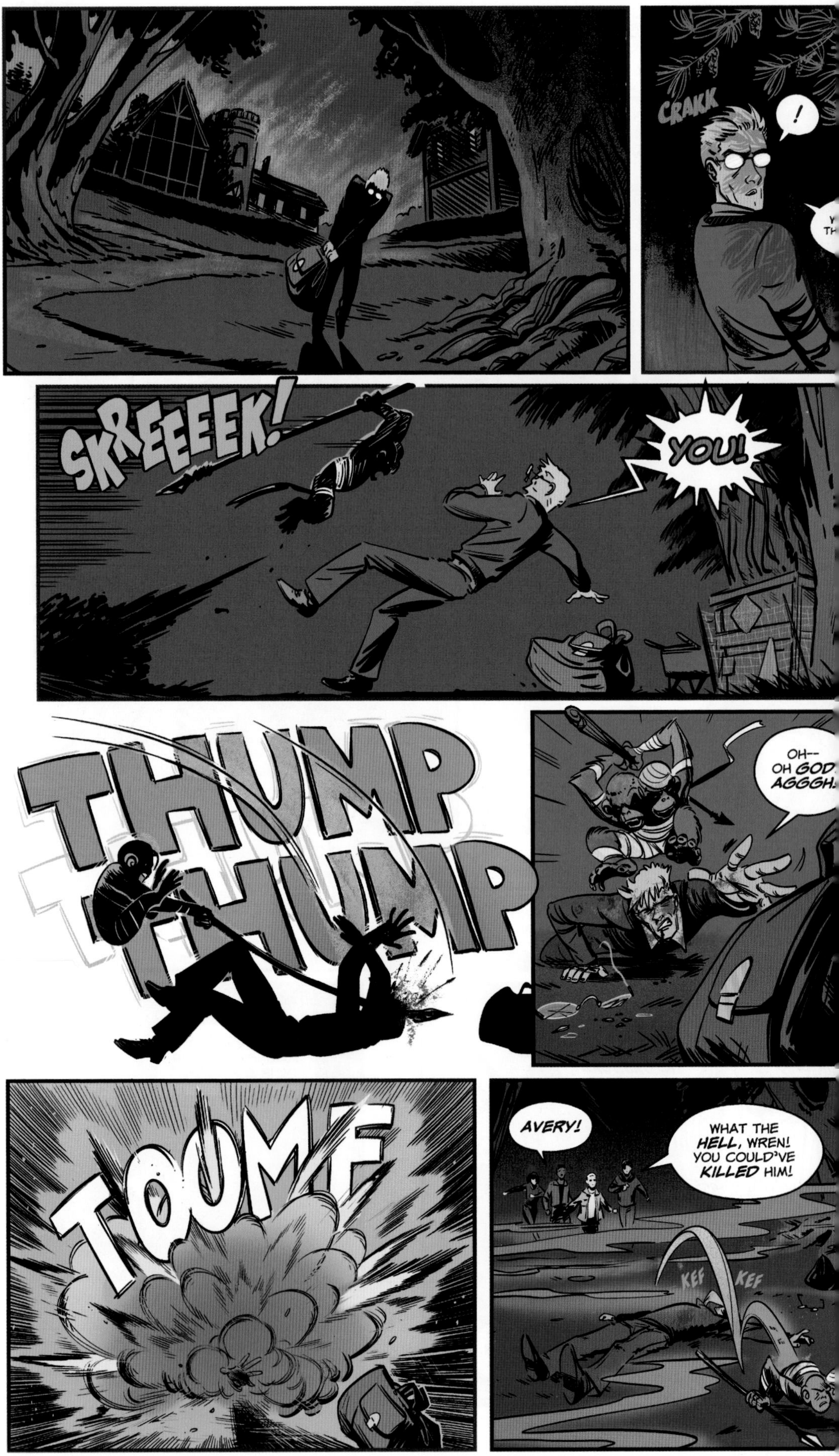
CRAKK
!
SKREEEEK!
YOU!
THUMP
THUMP
OH--
OH GOD.
AGGGH...
TOOMF
AVERY!
WHAT THE HELL, WREN! YOU COULD'VE KILLED HIM!
KEF KEF

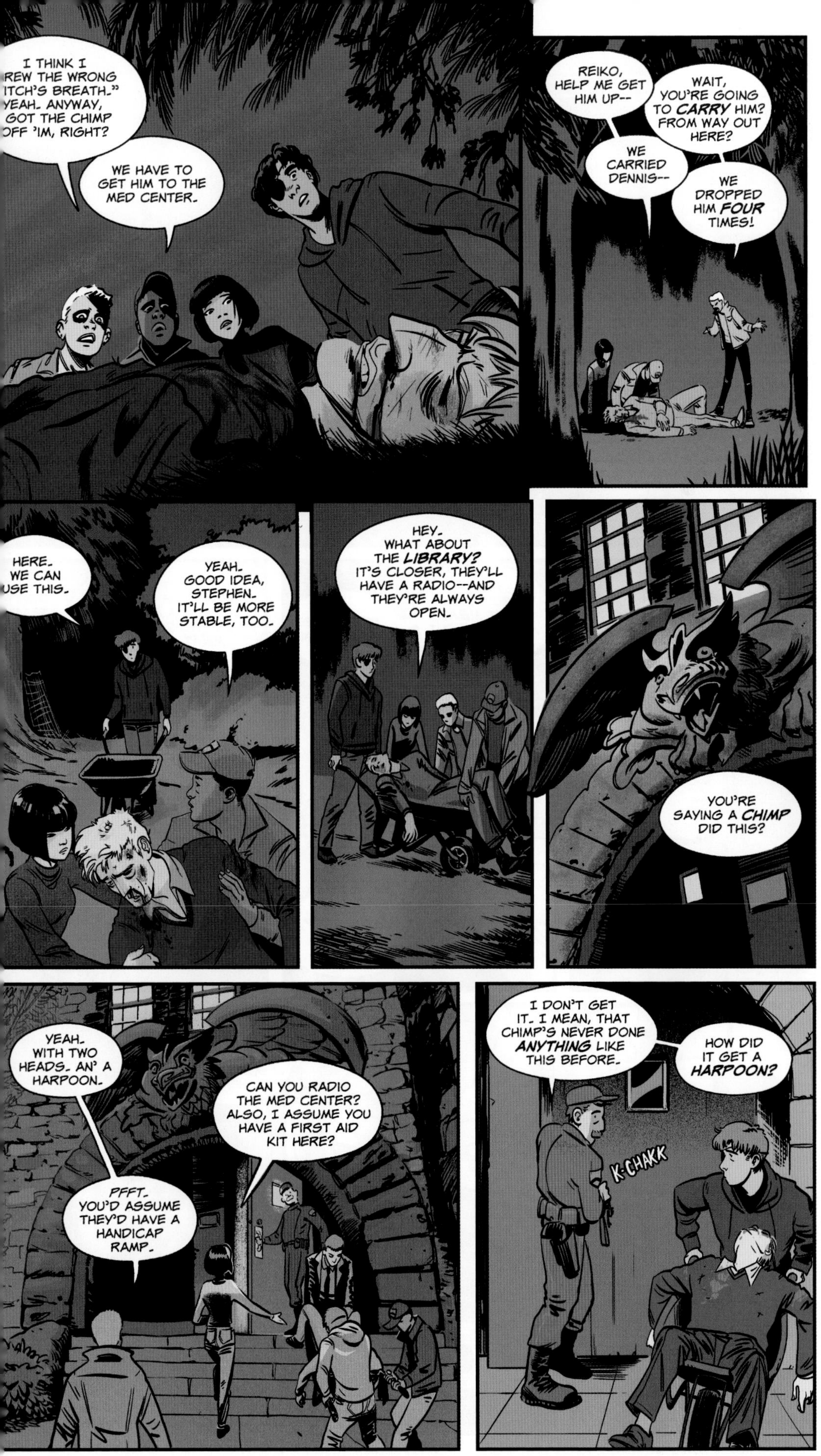
I THINK I REW THE WRONG ITCH'S BREATH." YEAH. ANYWAY, GOT THE CHIMP OFF 'IM, RIGHT?
WE HAVE TO GET HIM TO THE MED CENTER.
REIKO, HELP ME GET HIM UP--
WAIT, YOU'RE GOING TO *CARRY* HIM? FROM WAY OUT HERE?
WE CARRIED DENNIS--
WE DROPPED HIM *FOUR* TIMES!
HERE. WE CAN USE THIS.
YEAH. GOOD IDEA, STEPHEN. IT'LL BE MORE STABLE, TOO.
HEY. WHAT ABOUT THE *LIBRARY?* IT'S CLOSER, THEY'LL HAVE A RADIO--AND THEY'RE ALWAYS OPEN.
YOU'RE SAYING A *CHIMP* DID THIS?
YEAH. WITH TWO HEADS. AN' A HARPOON.
CAN YOU RADIO THE MED CENTER? ALSO, I ASSUME YOU HAVE A FIRST AID KIT HERE?
PFFT. YOU'D ASSUME THEY'D HAVE A HANDICAP RAMP.
I DON'T GET IT. I MEAN, THAT CHIMP'S NEVER DONE *ANYTHING* LIKE THIS BEFORE.
HOW DID IT GET A *HARPOON?*
K-CHAKK

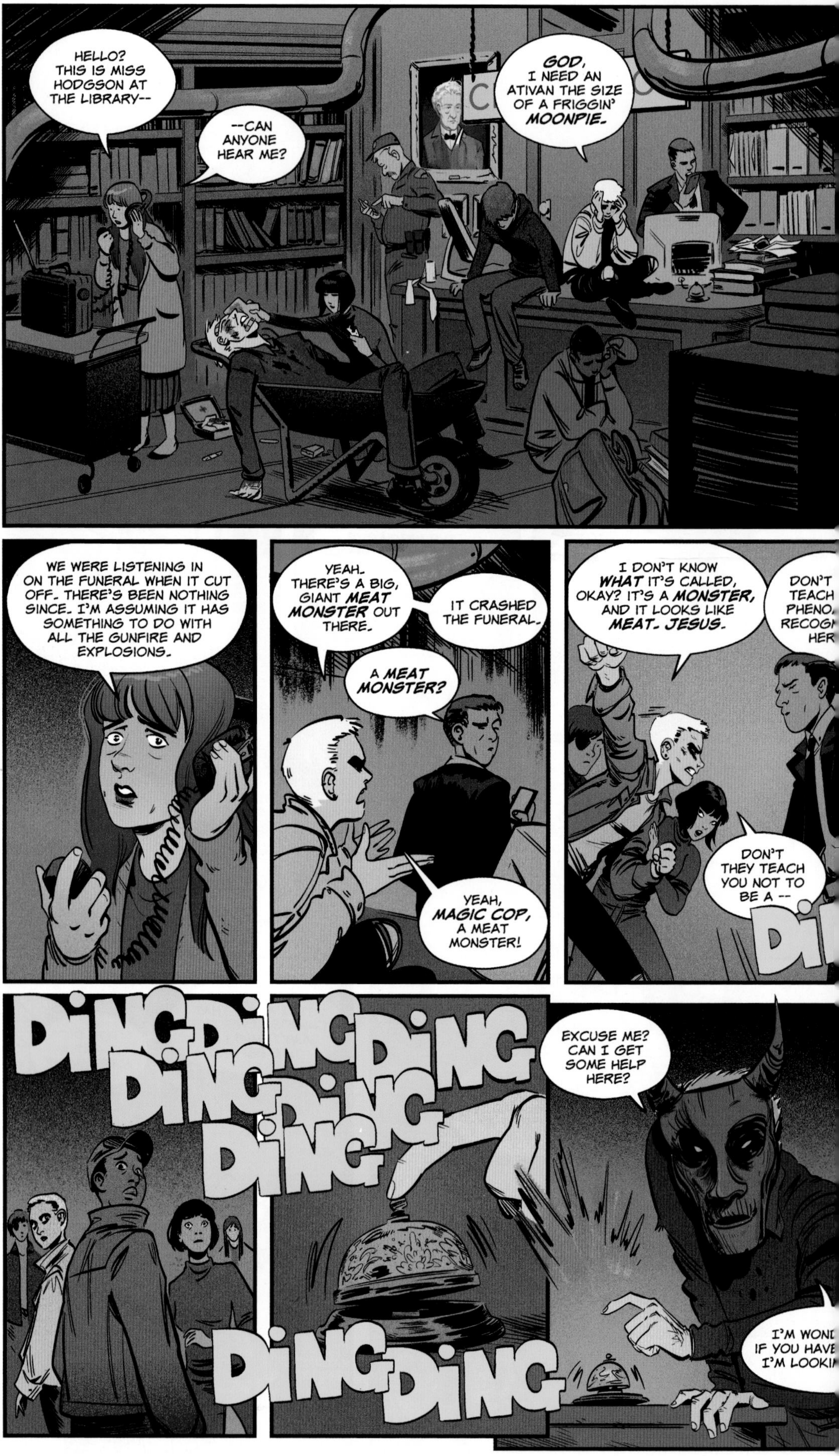
HELLO? THIS IS MISS HODGSON AT THE LIBRARY--
--CAN ANYONE HEAR ME?
GOD, I NEED AN ATIVAN THE SIZE OF A FRIGGIN' MOONPIE.
WE WERE LISTENING IN ON THE FUNERAL WHEN IT CUT OFF. THERE'S BEEN NOTHING SINCE. I'M ASSUMING IT HAS SOMETHING TO DO WITH ALL THE GUNFIRE AND EXPLOSIONS.
YEAH. THERE'S A BIG, GIANT MEAT MONSTER OUT THERE.
IT CRASHED THE FUNERAL.
A MEAT MONSTER?
YEAH, MAGIC COP, A MEAT MONSTER!
I DON'T KNOW WHAT IT'S CALLED, OKAY? IT'S A MONSTER, AND IT LOOKS LIKE MEAT- JESUS.
DON'T TEACH PHENO RECOG HER
DON'T THEY TEACH YOU NOT TO BE A --
DINGDINGDINGDINGDINGDINGDING
EXCUSE ME? CAN I GET SOME HELP HERE?
DINGDING
I'M WOND IF YOU HAVE I'M LOOKI

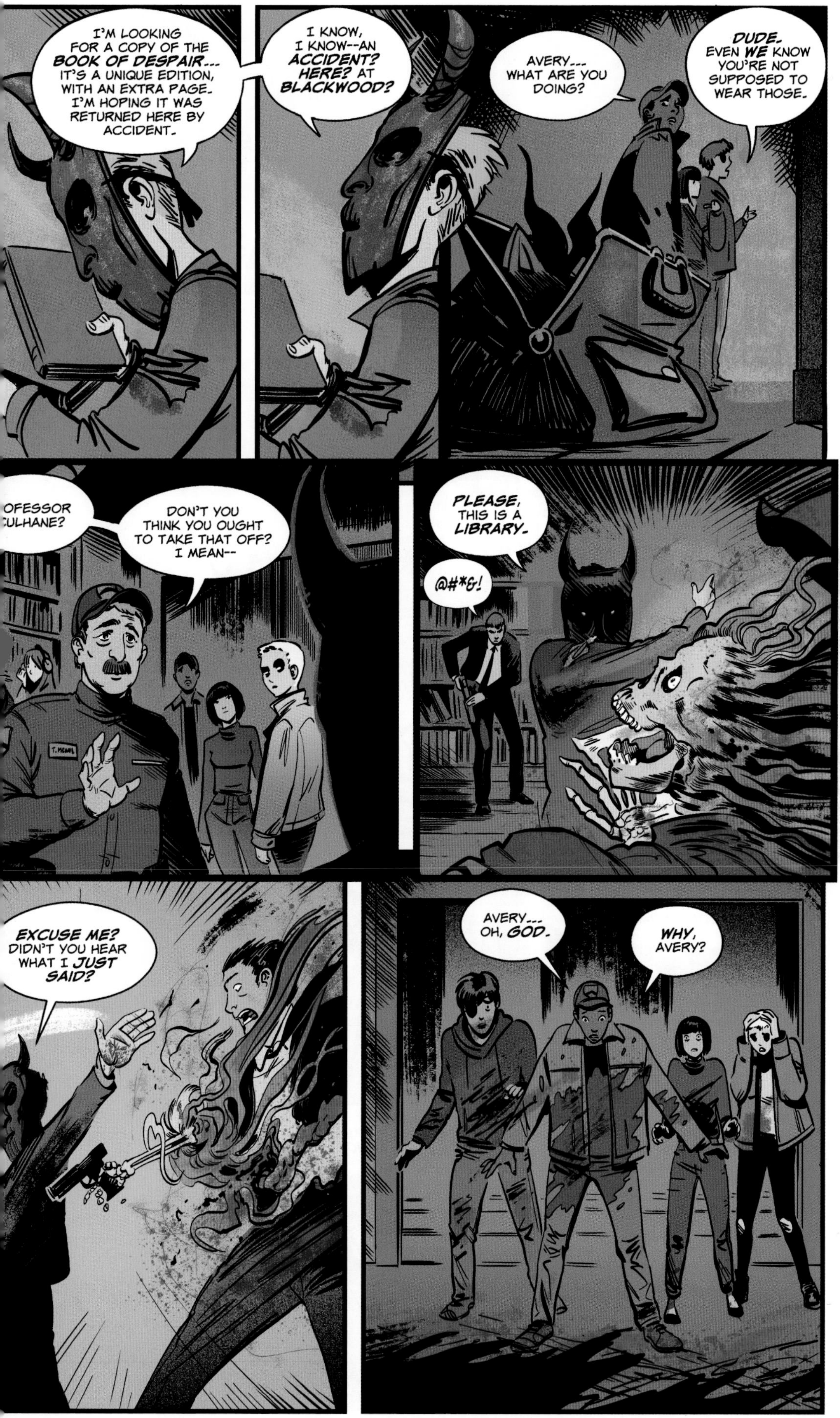
I'M LOOKING FOR A COPY OF THE BOOK OF DESPAIR... IT'S A UNIQUE EDITION, WITH AN EXTRA PAGE. I'M HOPING IT WAS RETURNED HERE BY ACCIDENT.
I KNOW, I KNOW--AN ACCIDENT? HERE? AT BLACKWOOD?
AVERY... WHAT ARE YOU DOING?
DUDE. EVEN WE KNOW YOU'RE NOT SUPPOSED TO WEAR THOSE.
OFESSOR CULHANE?
DON'T YOU THINK YOU OUGHT TO TAKE THAT OFF? I MEAN--
PLEASE, THIS IS A LIBRARY.
@#*&!
EXCUSE ME? DIDN'T YOU HEAR WHAT I JUST SAID?
AVERY... OH, GOD.
WHY, AVERY?

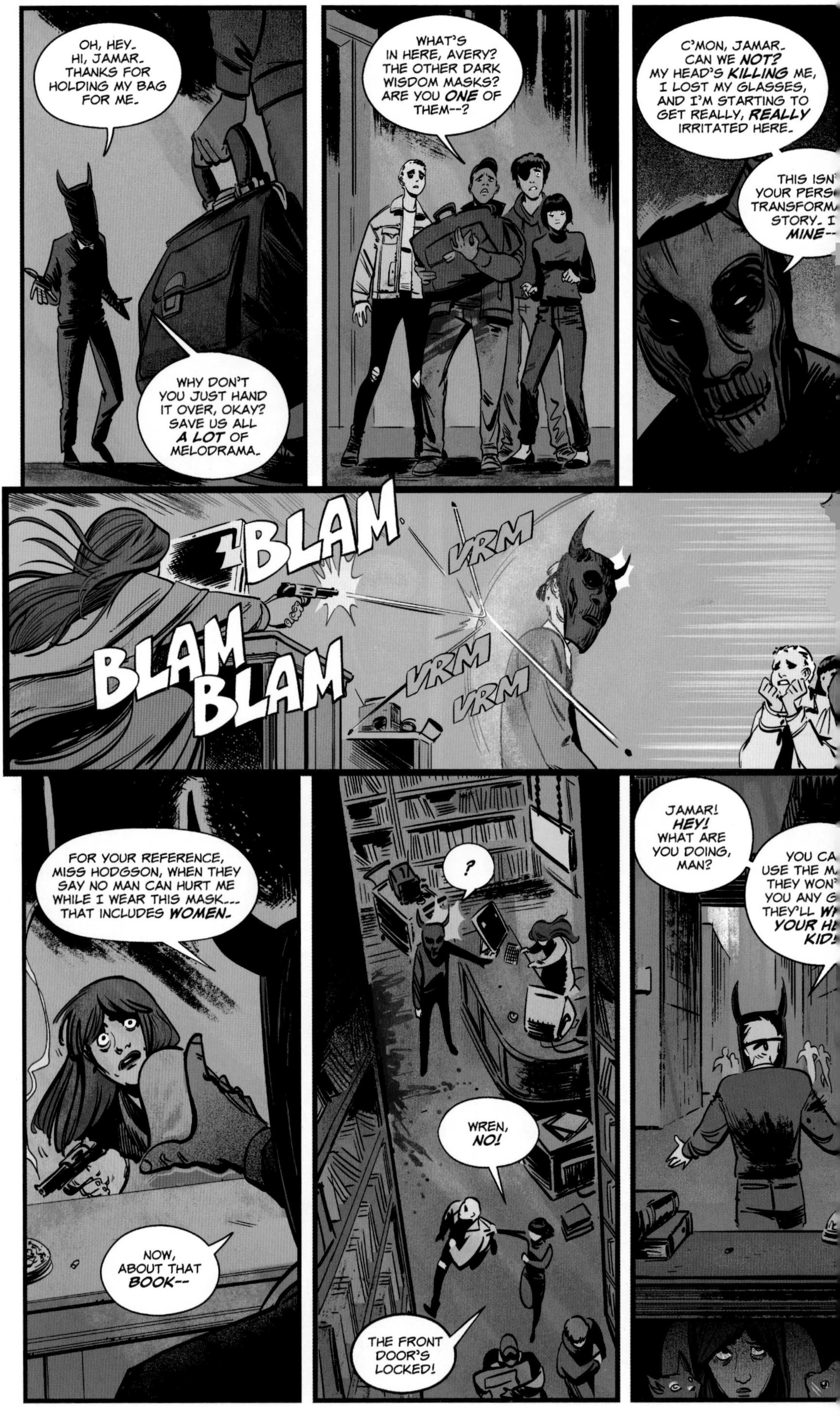
OH, HEY. HI, JAMAR. THANKS FOR HOLDING MY BAG FOR ME.
WHY DON'T YOU JUST HAND IT OVER, OKAY? SAVE US ALL A LOT OF MELODRAMA.
WHAT'S IN HERE, AVERY? THE OTHER DARK WISDOM MASKS? ARE YOU ONE OF THEM--?
C'MON, JAMAR. CAN WE NOT? MY HEAD'S KILLING ME, I LOST MY GLASSES, AND I'M STARTING TO GET REALLY, REALLY IRRITATED HERE.
THIS ISN YOUR PERS TRANSFORM STORY. I MINE--
BLAM
VRM
BLAM BLAM
VRM
VRM
FOR YOUR REFERENCE, MISS HODGSON, WHEN THEY SAY NO MAN CAN HURT ME WHILE I WEAR THIS MASK... THAT INCLUDES WOMEN.
NOW, ABOUT THAT BOOK--
?
WREN, NO!
THE FRONT DOOR'S LOCKED!
JAMAR! HEY! WHAT ARE YOU DOING, MAN?
YOU CA USE THE M THEY WON YOU ANY G THEY'LL W YOUR H KID!

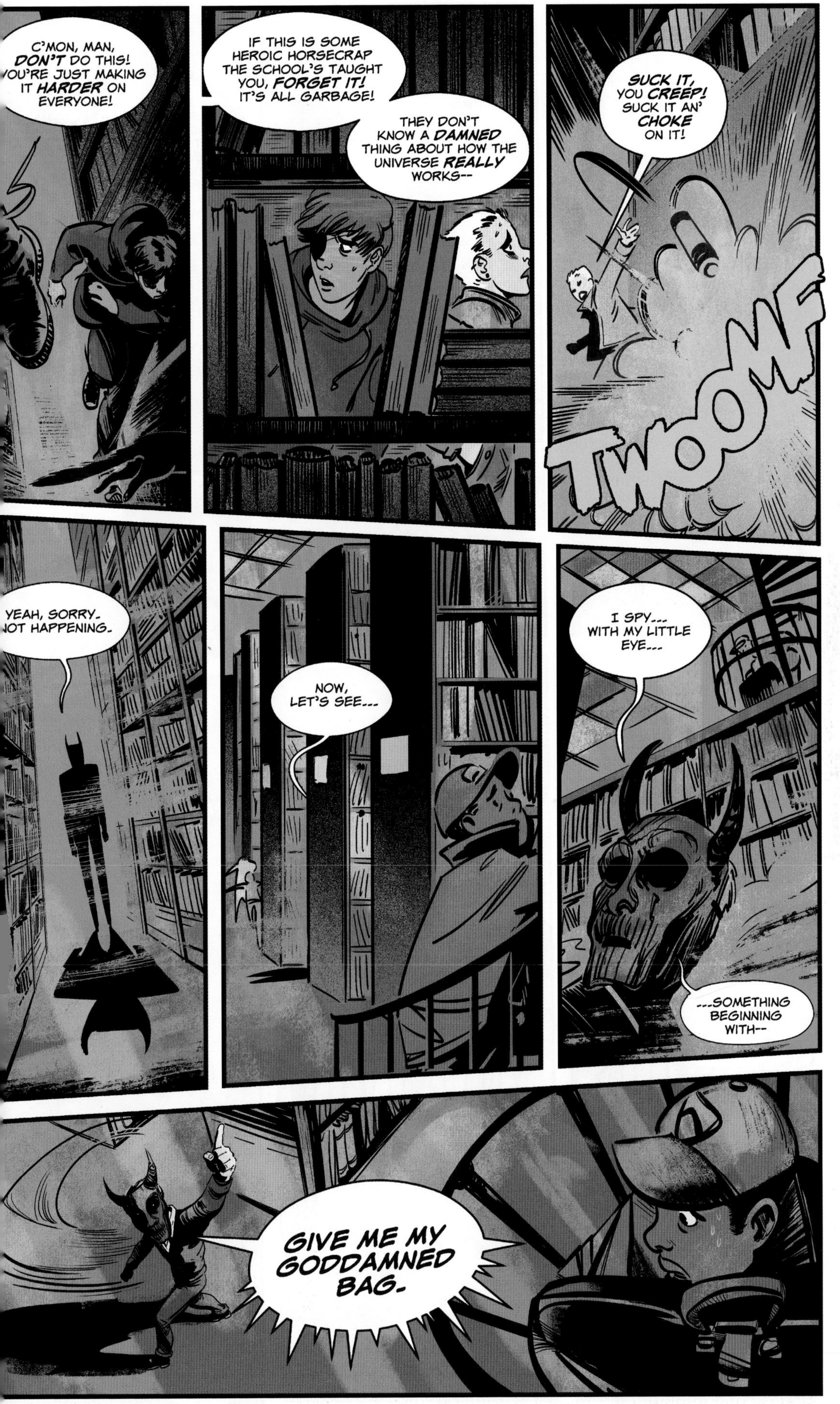
C'MON, MAN, DON'T DO THIS! YOU'RE JUST MAKING IT HARDER ON EVERYONE!
IF THIS IS SOME HEROIC HORSECRAP THE SCHOOL'S TAUGHT YOU, FORGET IT! IT'S ALL GARBAGE!
THEY DON'T KNOW A DAMNED THING ABOUT HOW THE UNIVERSE REALLY WORKS--
SUCK IT, YOU CREEP! SUCK IT AN' CHOKE ON IT!
TWOOMF
YEAH, SORRY. NOT HAPPENING.
NOW, LET'S SEE...
I SPY... WITH MY LITTLE EYE...
...SOMETHING BEGINNING WITH--
GIVE ME MY GODDAMNED BAG.

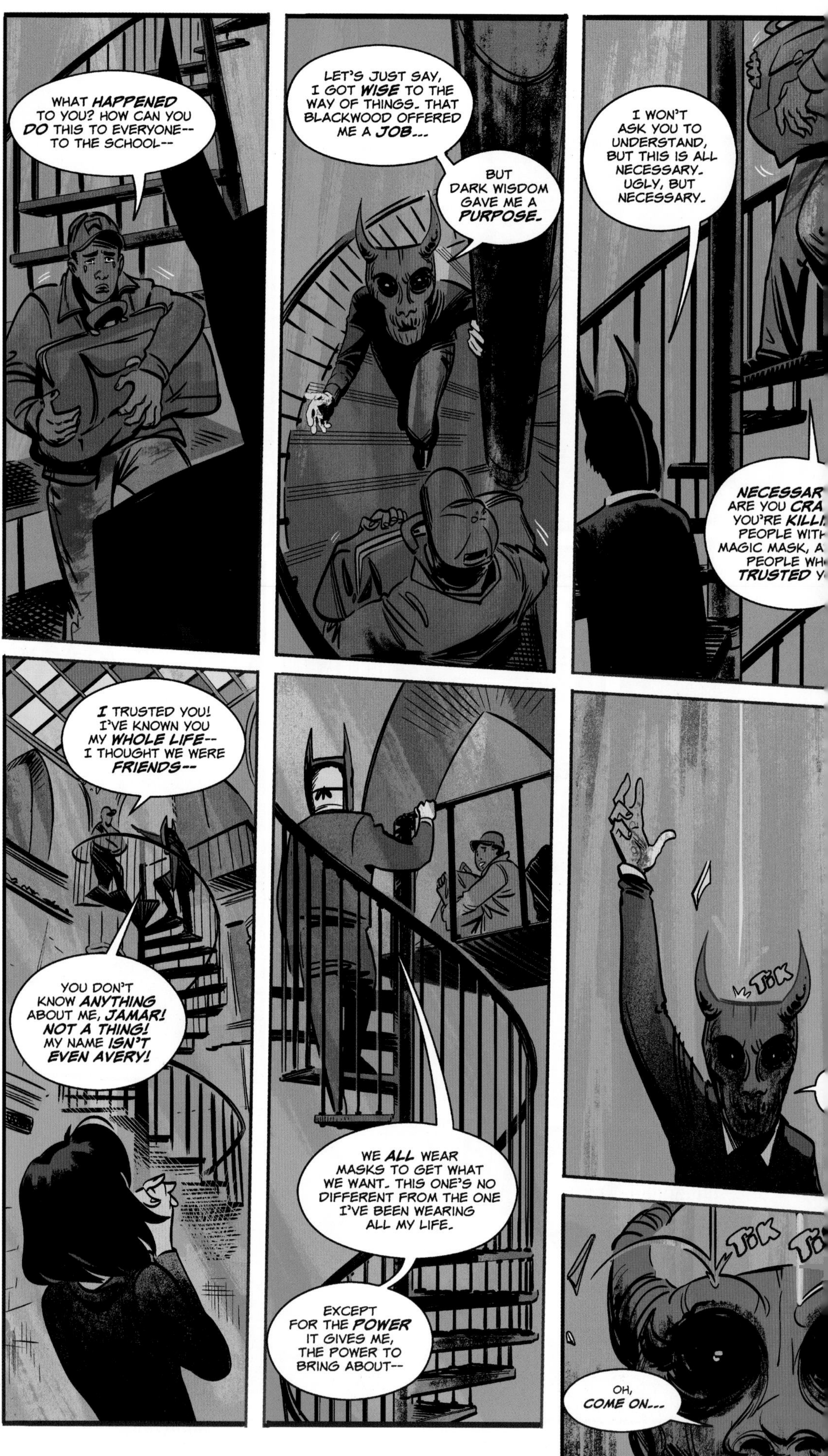
WHAT HAPPENED TO YOU? HOW CAN YOU DO THIS TO EVERYONE-- TO THE SCHOOL--
LET'S JUST SAY, I GOT WISE TO THE WAY OF THINGS. THAT BLACKWOOD OFFERED ME A JOB...
BUT DARK WISDOM GAVE ME A PURPOSE.
I WON'T ASK YOU TO UNDERSTAND, BUT THIS IS ALL NECESSARY. UGLY, BUT NECESSARY.
NECESSAR ARE YOU CRA YOU'RE KILLI PEOPLE WITH MAGIC MASK, A PEOPLE WH TRUSTED Y
I TRUSTED YOU! I'VE KNOWN YOU MY WHOLE LIFE-- I THOUGHT WE WERE FRIENDS--
YOU DON'T KNOW ANYTHING ABOUT ME, JAMAR! NOT A THING! MY NAME ISN'T EVEN AVERY!
WE ALL WEAR MASKS TO GET WHAT WE WANT. THIS ONE'S NO DIFFERENT FROM THE ONE I'VE BEEN WEARING ALL MY LIFE.
EXCEPT FOR THE POWER IT GIVES ME, THE POWER TO BRING ABOUT--
TOK
TOK
OH, COME ON...

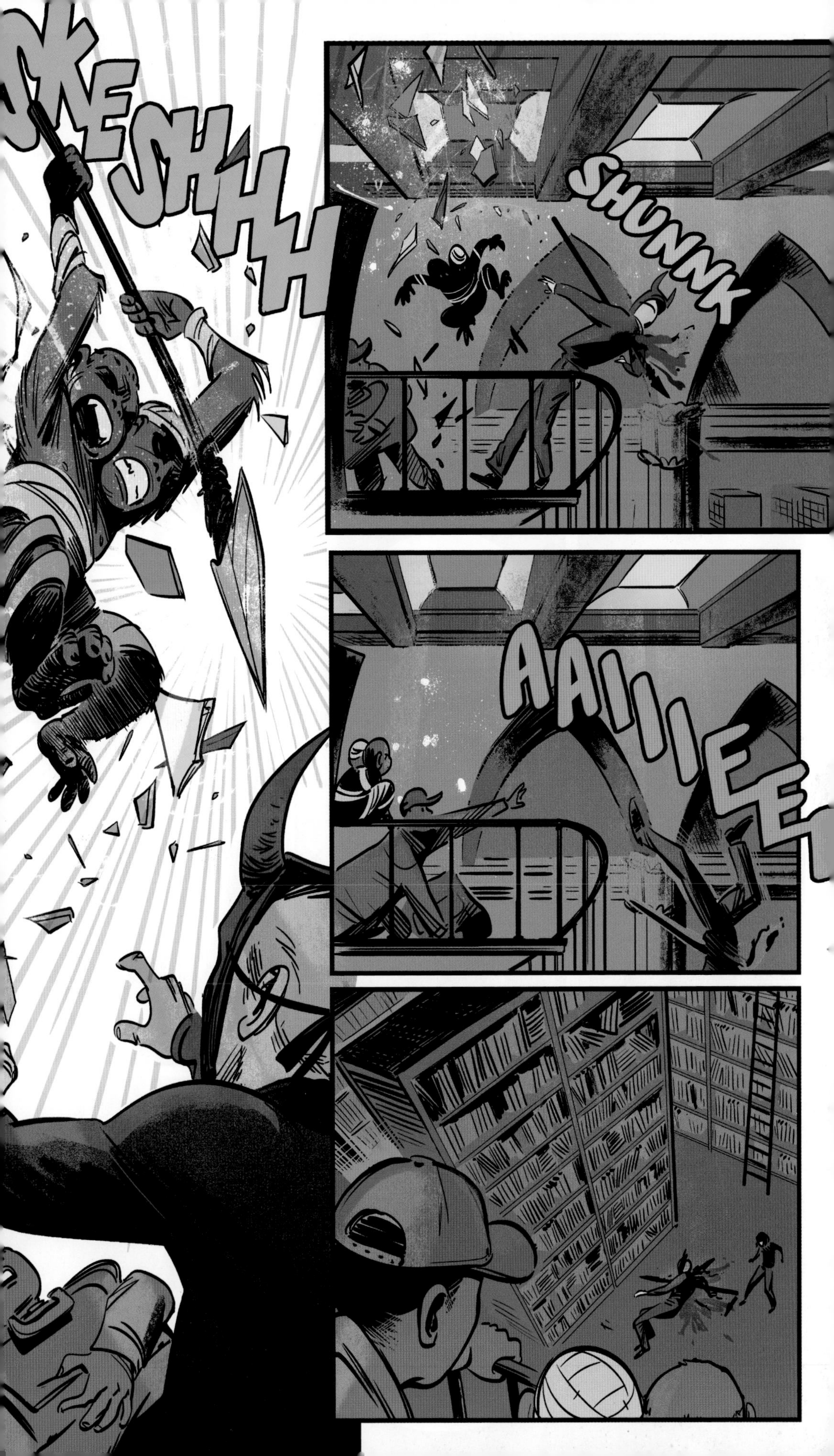

KESHHHH
SHUNNK
AAIIIIEE

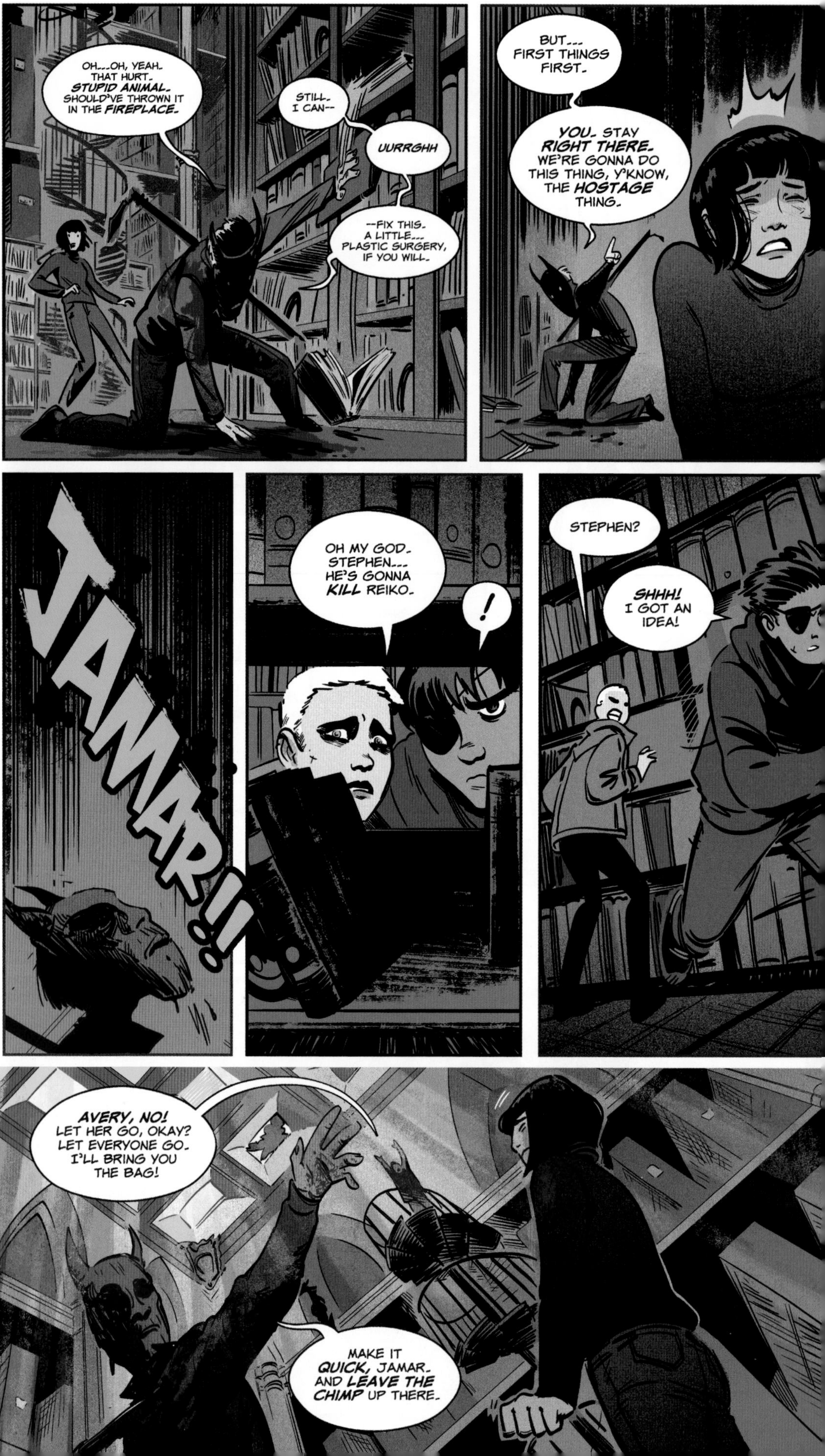
OH...OH, YEAH. THAT HURT. STUPID ANIMAL. SHOULD'VE THROWN IT IN THE FIREPLACE.
STILL. I CAN--
UURRGHH
--FIX THIS. A LITTLE... PLASTIC SURGERY, IF YOU WILL.
BUT... FIRST THINGS FIRST.
YOU. STAY RIGHT THERE. WE'RE GONNA DO THIS THING, Y'KNOW, THE HOSTAGE THING.
JAMAR!!!
OH MY GOD. STEPHEN... HE'S GONNA KILL REIKO.
!
STEPHEN?
SHHH! I GOT AN IDEA!
AVERY, NO! LET HER GO, OKAY? LET EVERYONE GO. I'LL BRING YOU THE BAG!
MAKE IT QUICK, JAMAR. AND LEAVE THE CHIMP UP THERE.

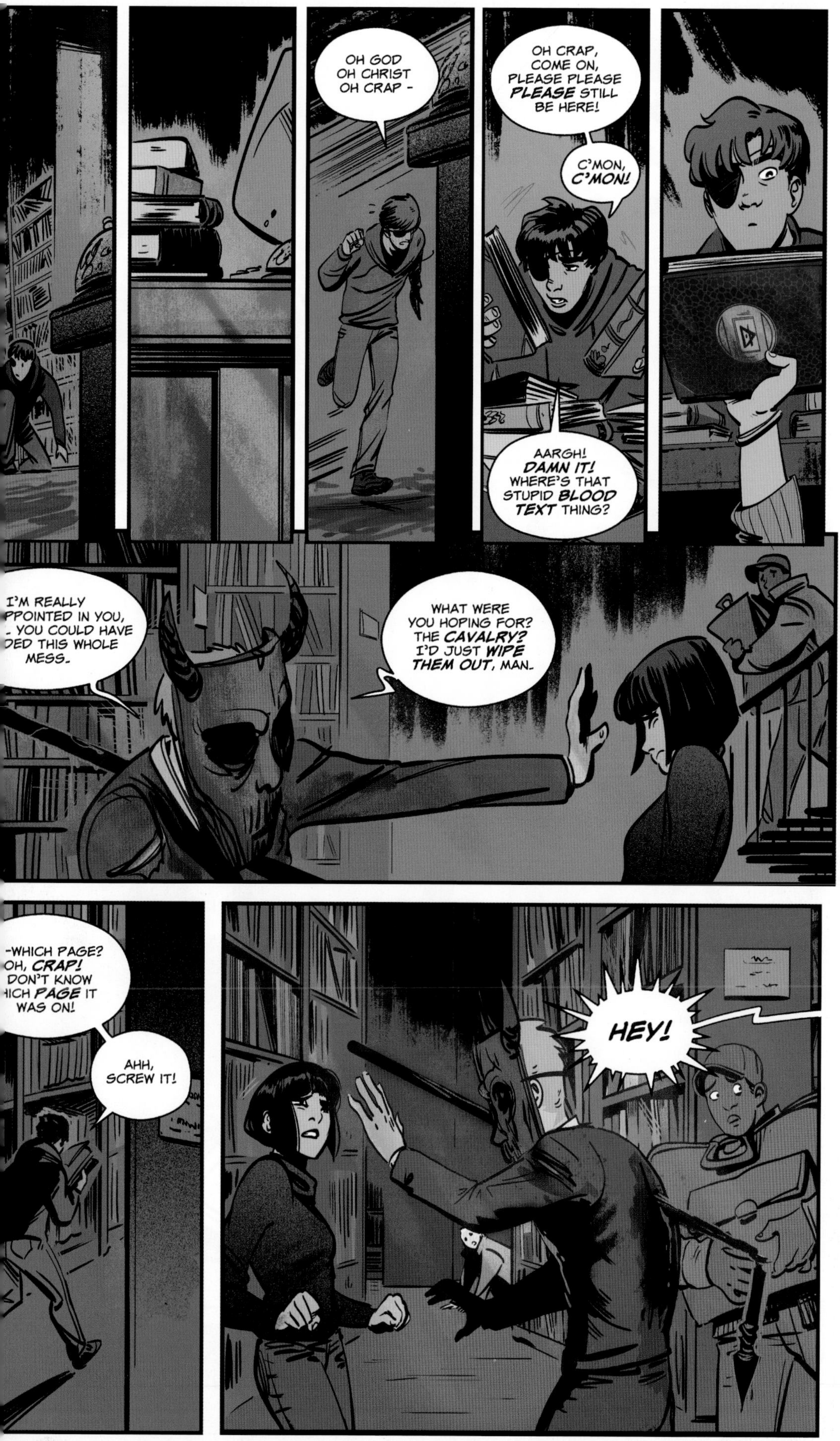
OH GOD
OH CHRIST
OH CRAP -
OH CRAP, COME ON, PLEASE PLEASE PLEASE STILL BE HERE!
C'MON, C'MON!
AARGH! DAMN IT! WHERE'S THAT STUPID BLOOD TEXT THING?
I'M REALLY PPOINTED IN YOU, . YOU COULD HAVE DED THIS WHOLE MESS.
WHAT WERE YOU HOPING FOR? THE CAVALRY? I'D JUST WIPE THEM OUT, MAN.
-WHICH PAGE? OH, CRAP! DON'T KNOW HICH PAGE IT WAS ON!
AHH, SCREW IT!
HEY!

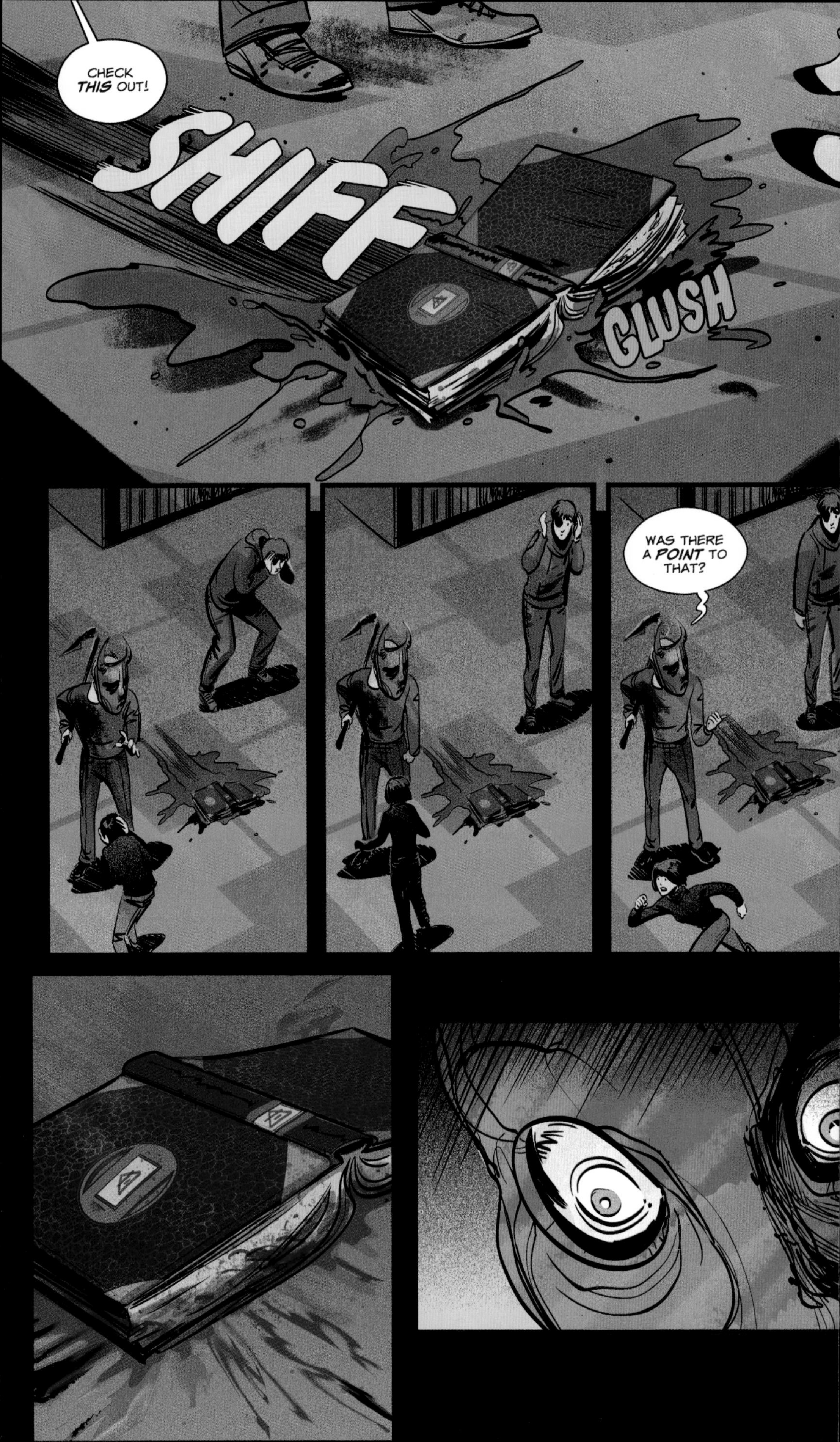
CHECK THIS OUT!
SHIFF
GLUSH
WAS THERE A POINT TO THAT?

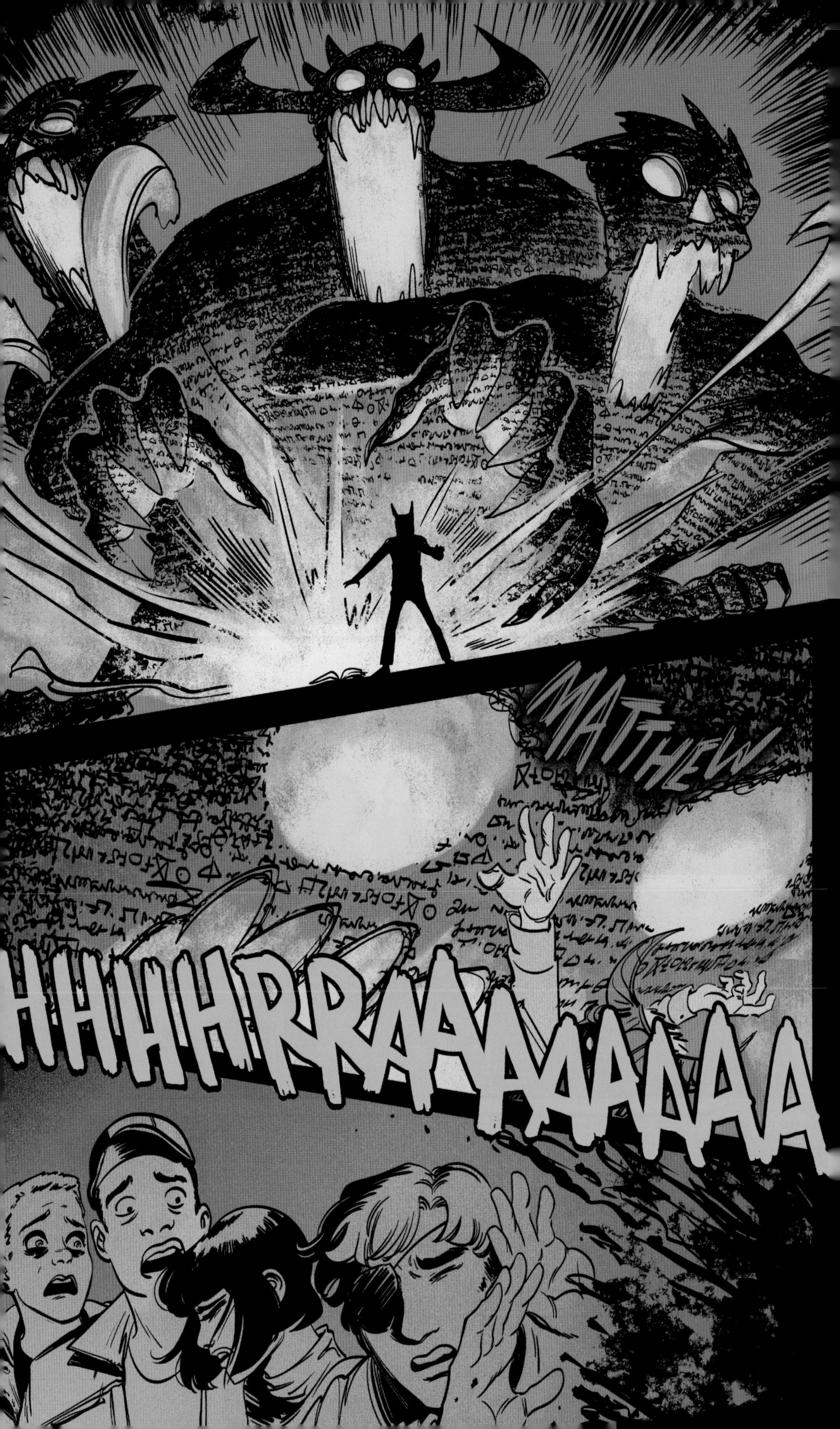
MATTHEW
HHHHRRAAAAAAA

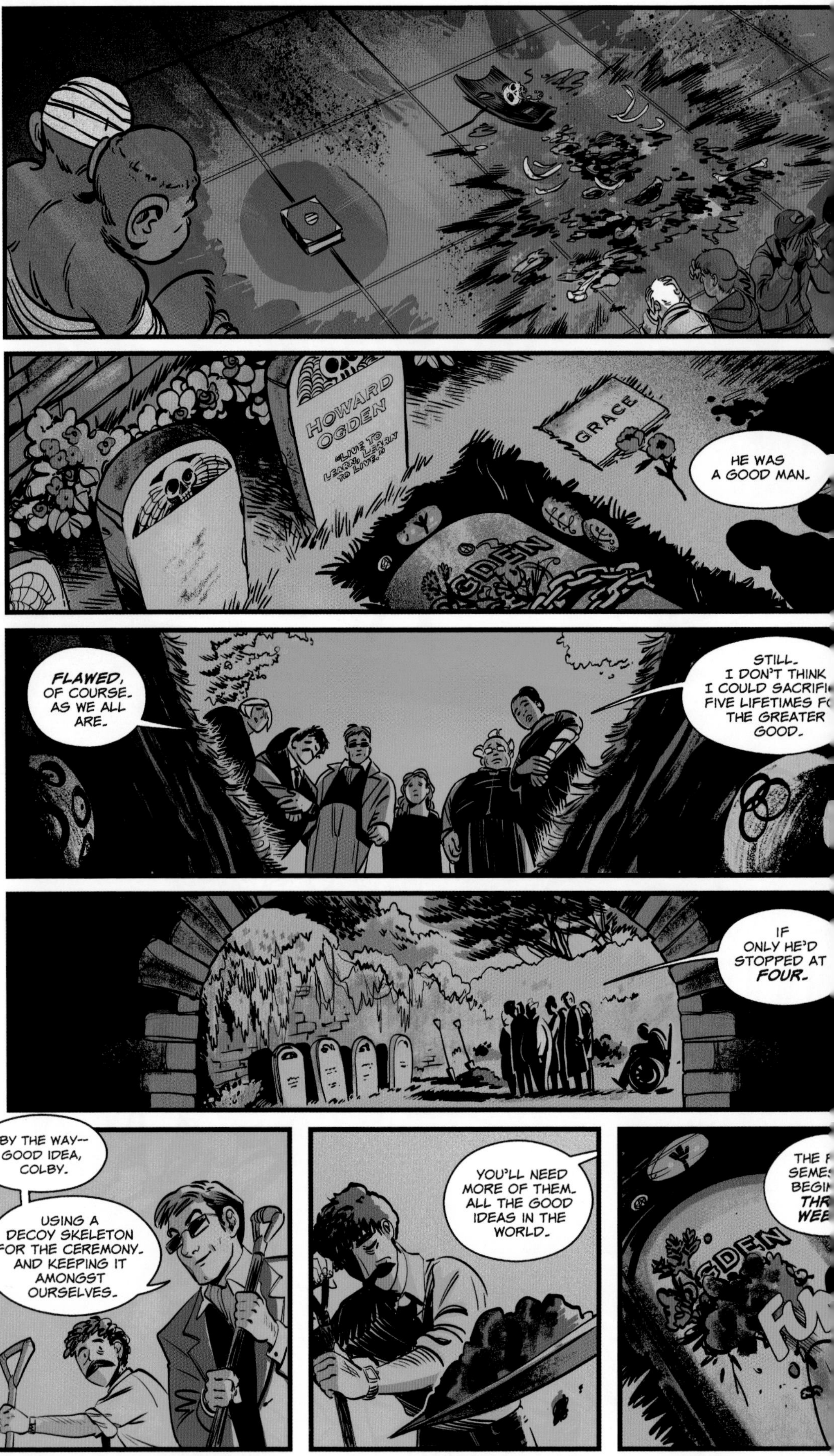
HOWARD OGDEN
"LIVE TO LEARN, LEARN TO LIVE."
GRACE
OGDEN
HE WAS A GOOD MAN.
FLAWED, OF COURSE. AS WE ALL ARE.
STILL. I DON'T THINK I COULD SACRIFI FIVE LIFETIMES FO THE GREATER GOOD.
IF ONLY HE'D STOPPED AT FOUR.
BY THE WAY-- GOOD IDEA, COLBY.
USING A DECOY SKELETON FOR THE CEREMONY. AND KEEPING IT AMONGST OURSELVES.
YOU'LL NEED MORE OF THEM. ALL THE GOOD IDEAS IN THE WORLD.
THE SEMES BEGI THR WEE
OGDEN

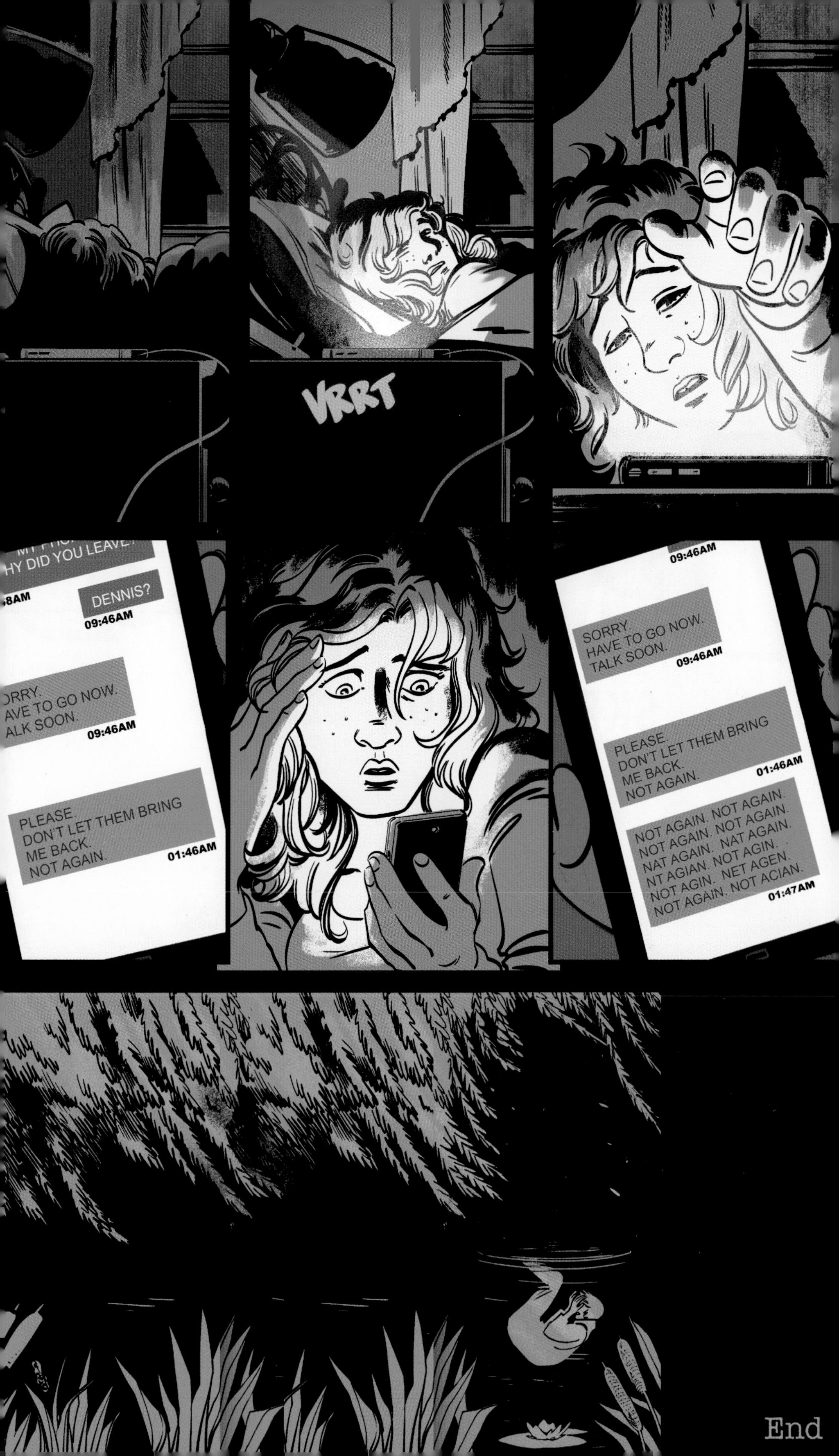

VRRT
HY DID YOU LEAVE?
DENNIS?
09:46AM
PLEASE. DON'T LET THEM BRING ME BACK. NOT AGAIN.
01:46AM
09:46AM
SORRY. HAVE TO GO NOW. TALK SOON.
09:46AM
PLEASE. DON'T LET THEM BRING ME BACK. NOT AGAIN.
01:46AM
NOT AGAIN. NOT AGAIN. NOT AGAIN. NOT AGAIN. NAT AGAIN. NAT AGAIN. NT AGIAN. NOT AGIN. NOT AGIN. NET AGEN. NOT AGAIN. NOT ACIAN.
01:47AM
End

BLACKWOOD

SKETCHBOOK

Notes by Veronica
and Andy Fish

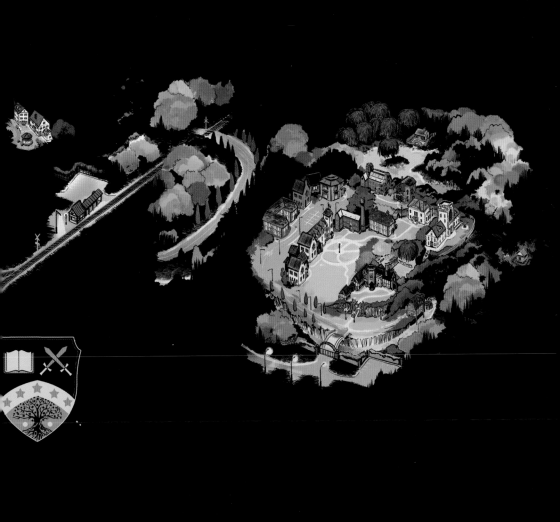

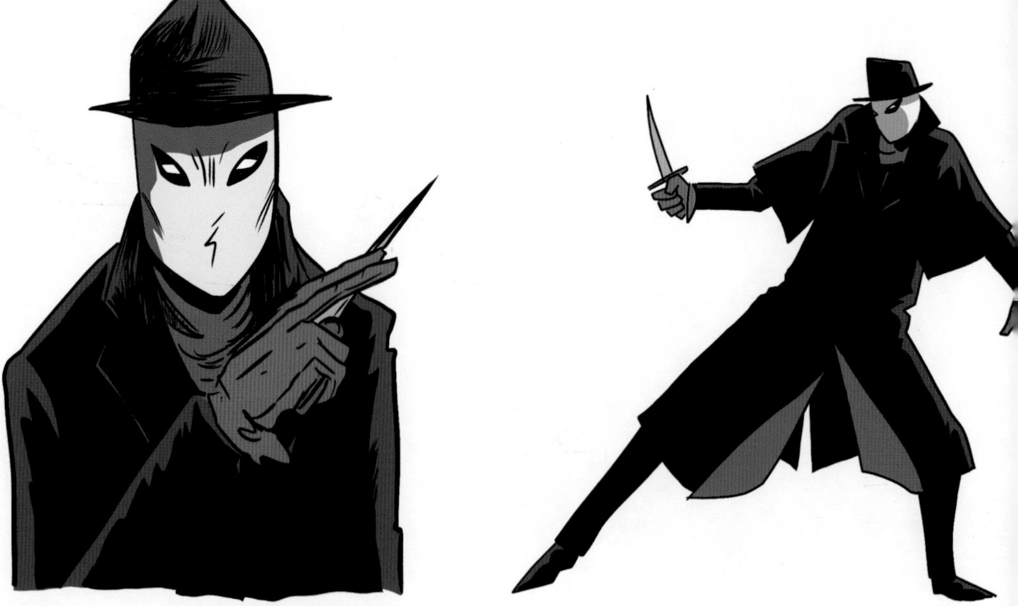

Giallo mask concept by Andy Fish.

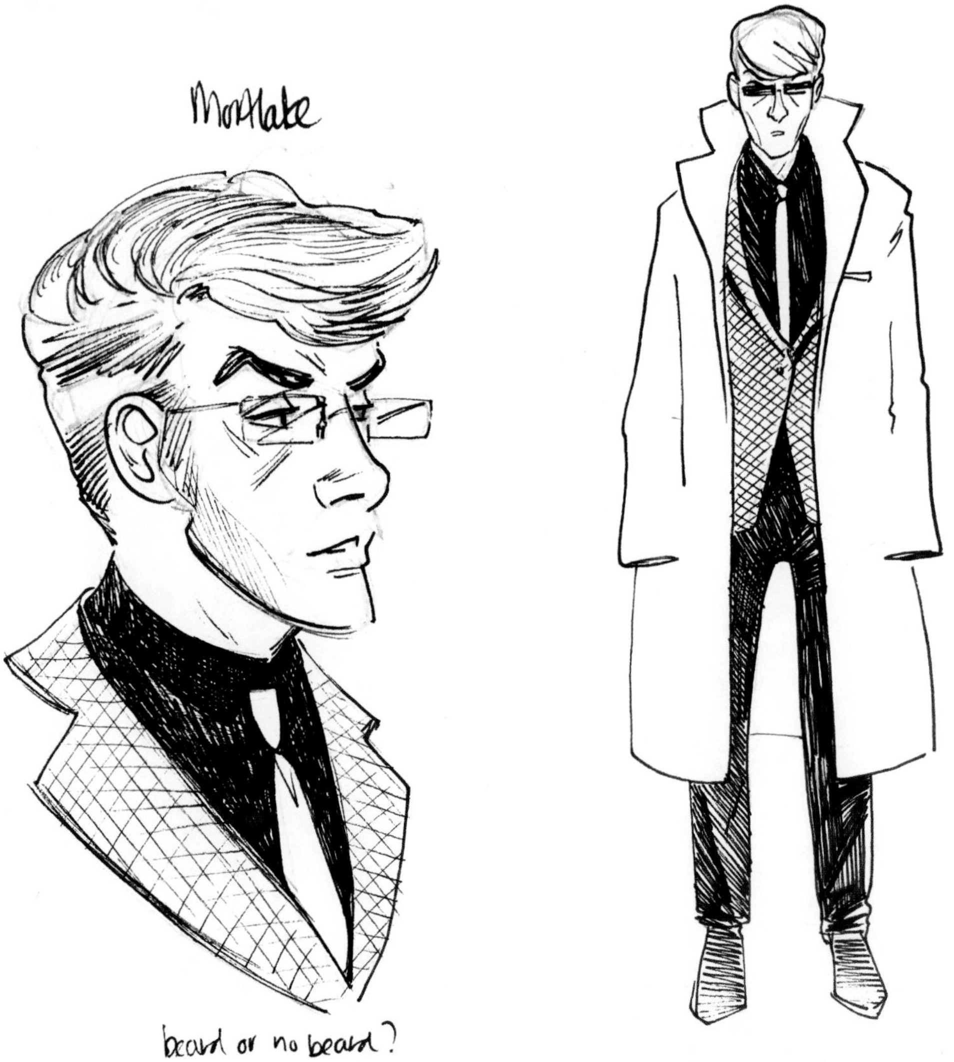
Mortlake
beard or no beard?

Mortlake concepts by Veronica Fish.

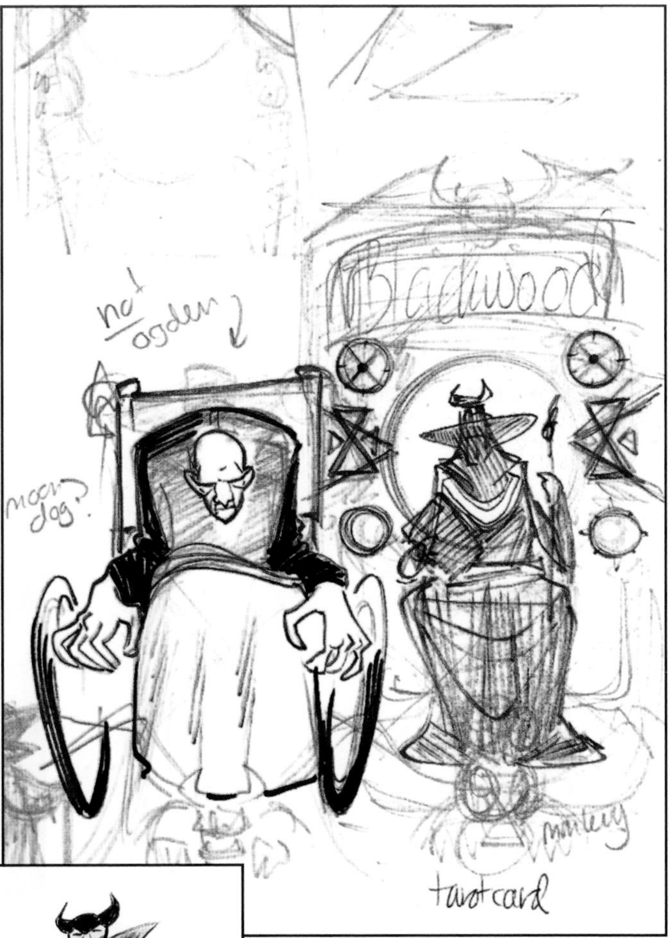

no† ogden
moon dog?
Blackwood
monkey
tarot card

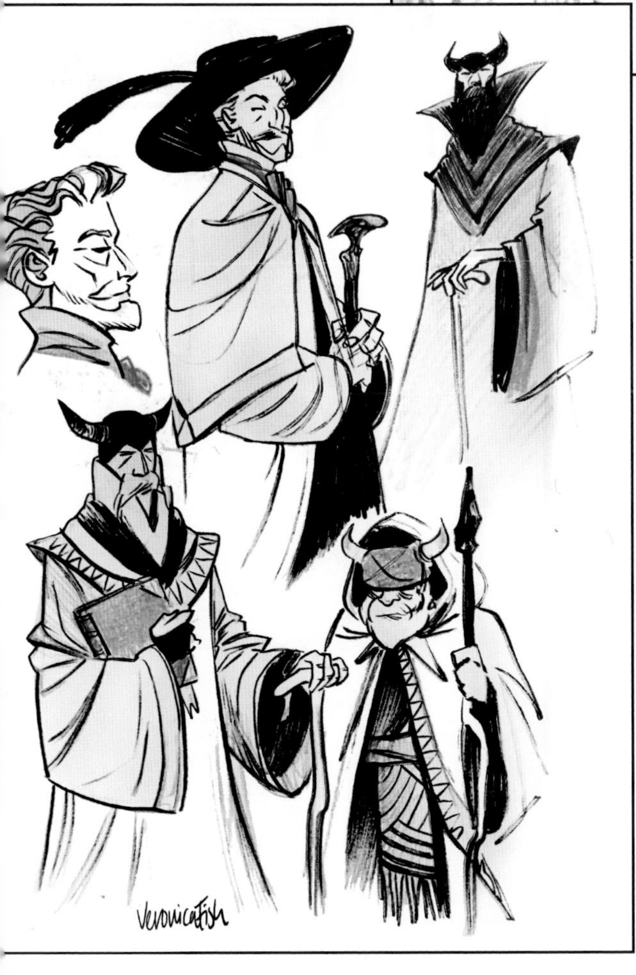

VeronicaFish

Prof. Kratchley sketches
by Veronica Fish.

I really liked Andy's design for the mirror shop owner, so he went ahead and penciled him into the layouts. Adjacent are my finishes over those layouts. Andy also designed Chimp Ho Tep's cute clown toy, which we thought could be reminiscent of a 1930s cartoon.

—Veronica

Veronica's finishes

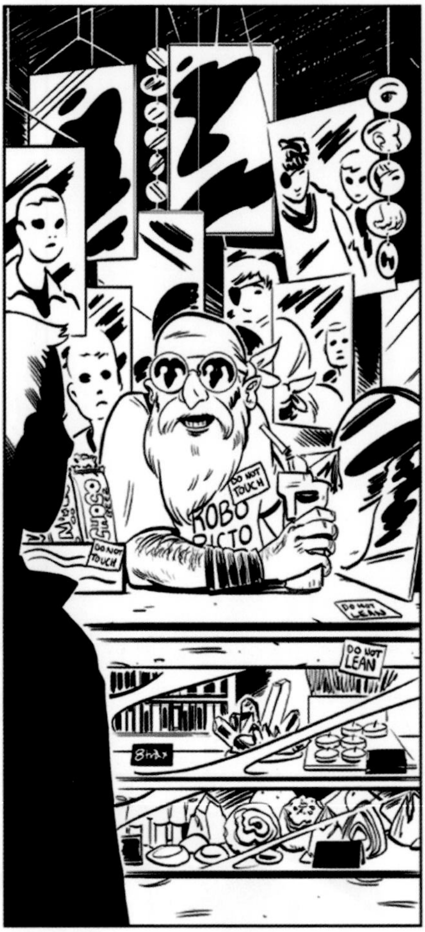
DO NOT TOUCH
ROBO PICTO
DO NOT TOUCH
DO NOT LEAN
DO NOT LEAN

Andy's pencils

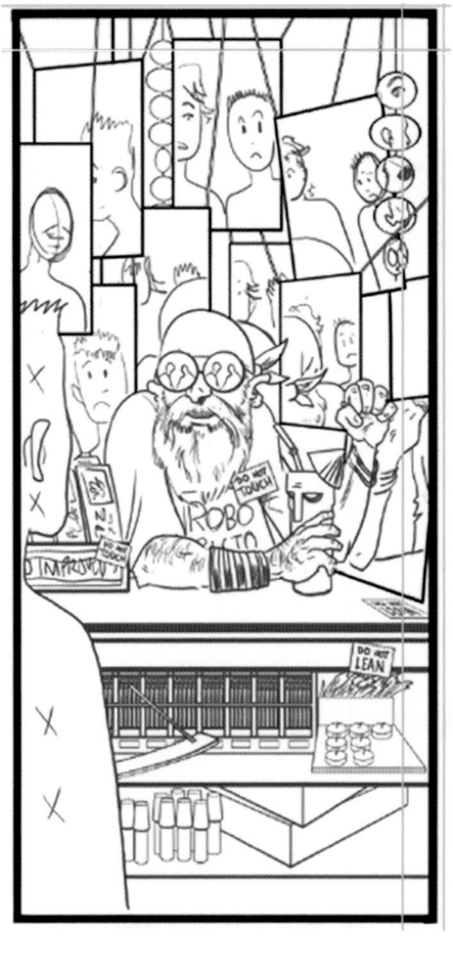
DO NOT TOUCH
ROBO
DO NOT LEAN

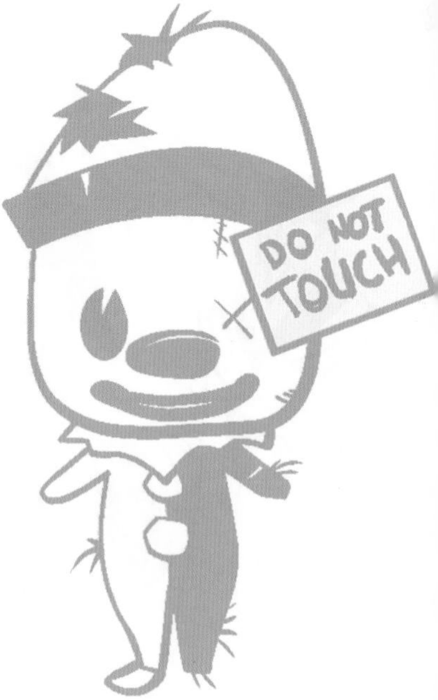
DO NOT TOUCH

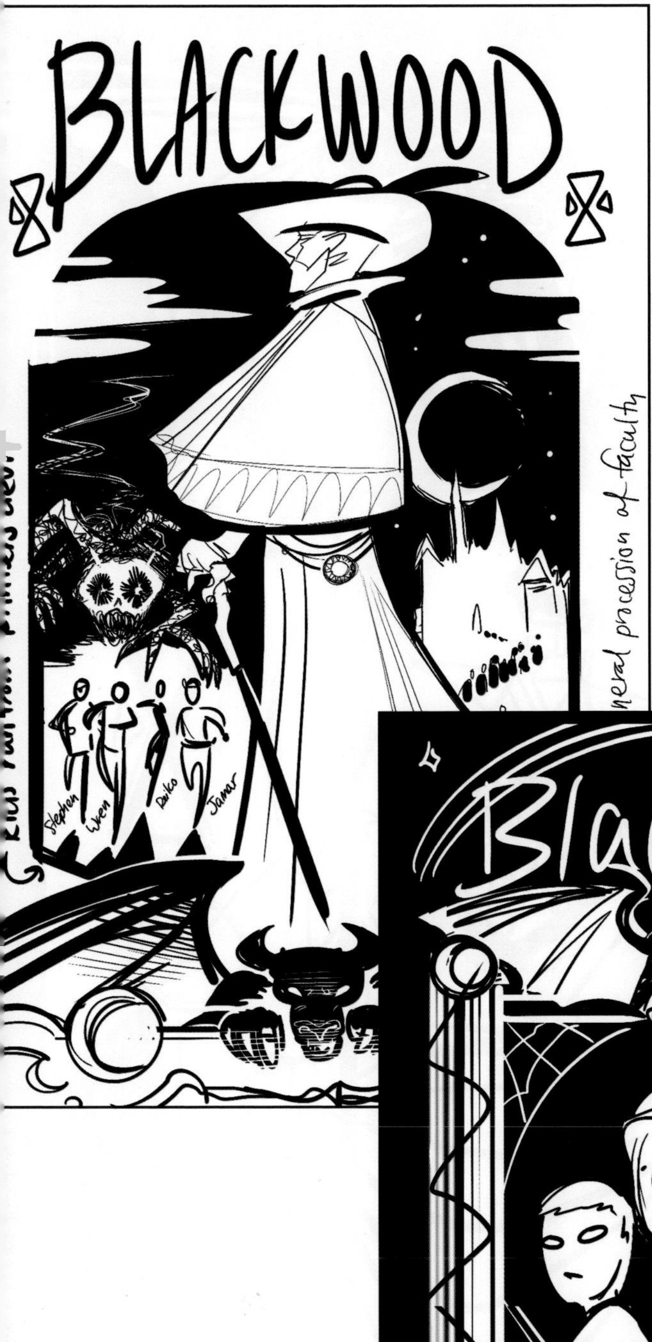
BLACKWOOD
Stephen
Wren
Reiko
Jamar
neral procession of faculty

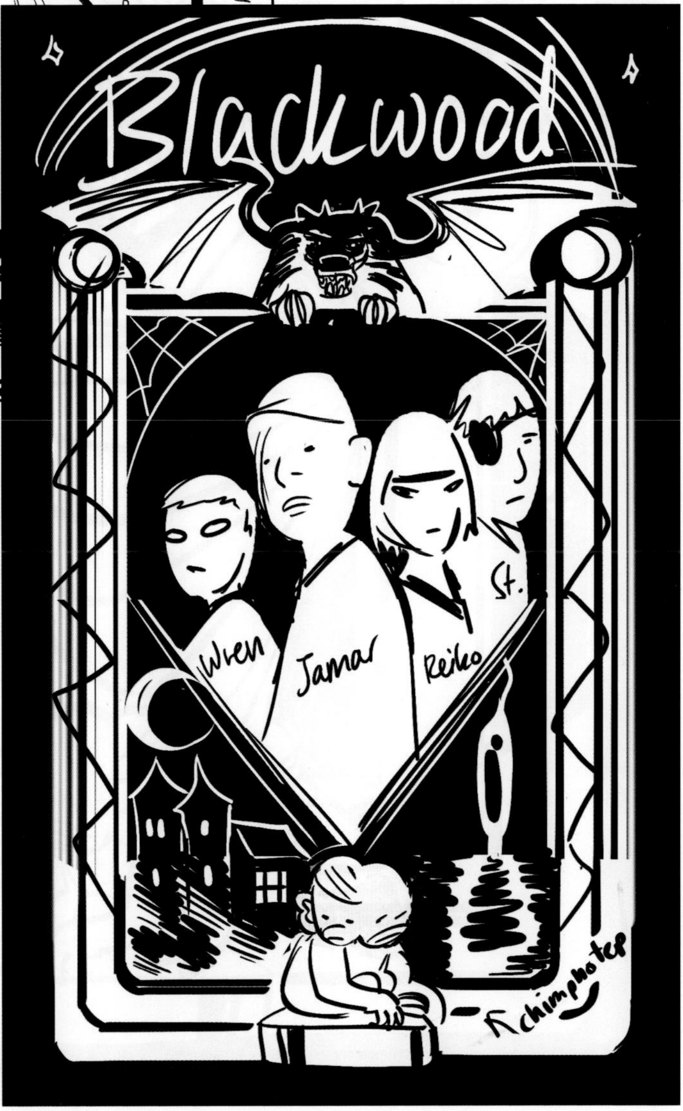
Blackwood
Wren
Jamar
Reiko
St.
chimphotep

Cover sketches for issues #1 and #2 by Veronica Fish.

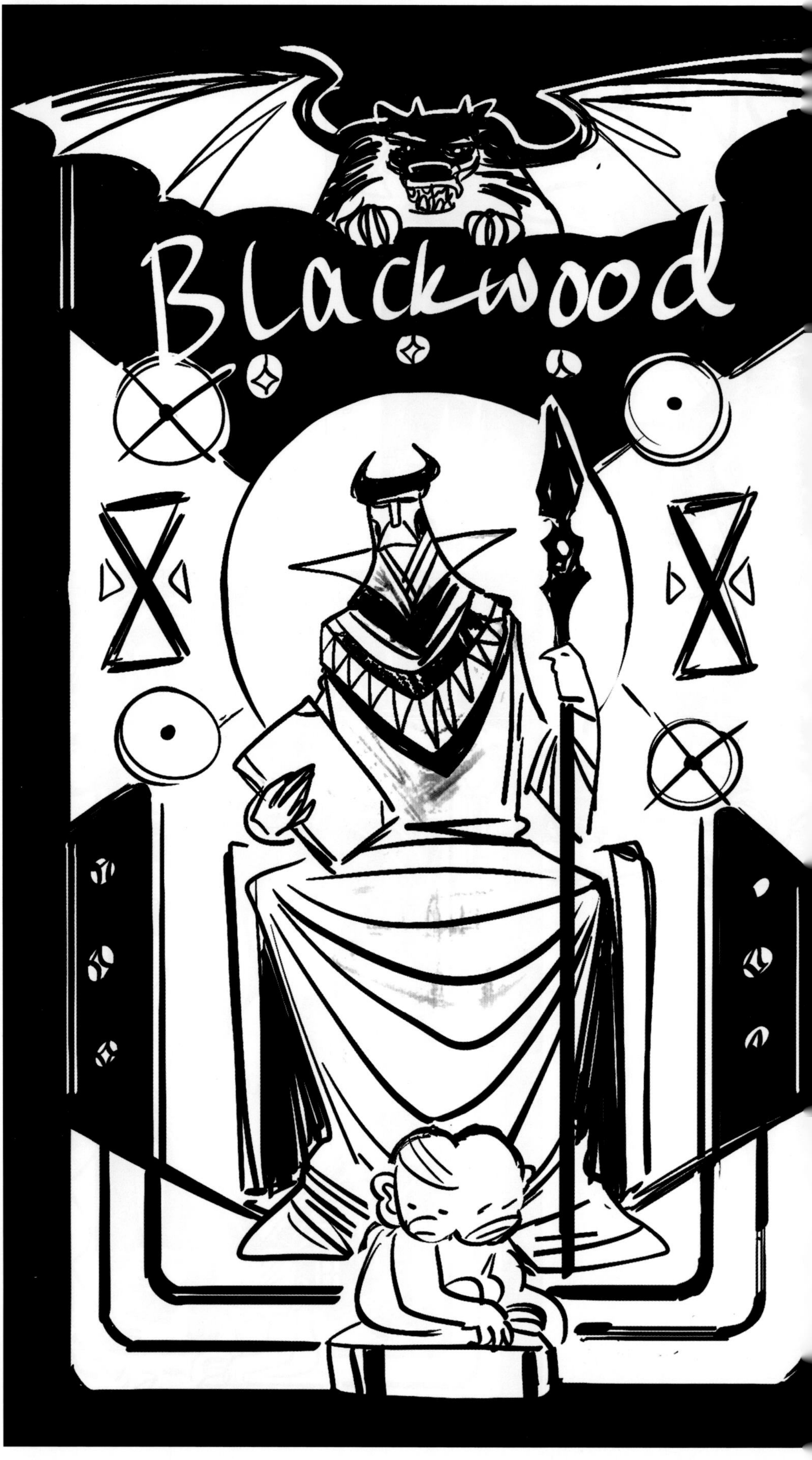
Blackwood

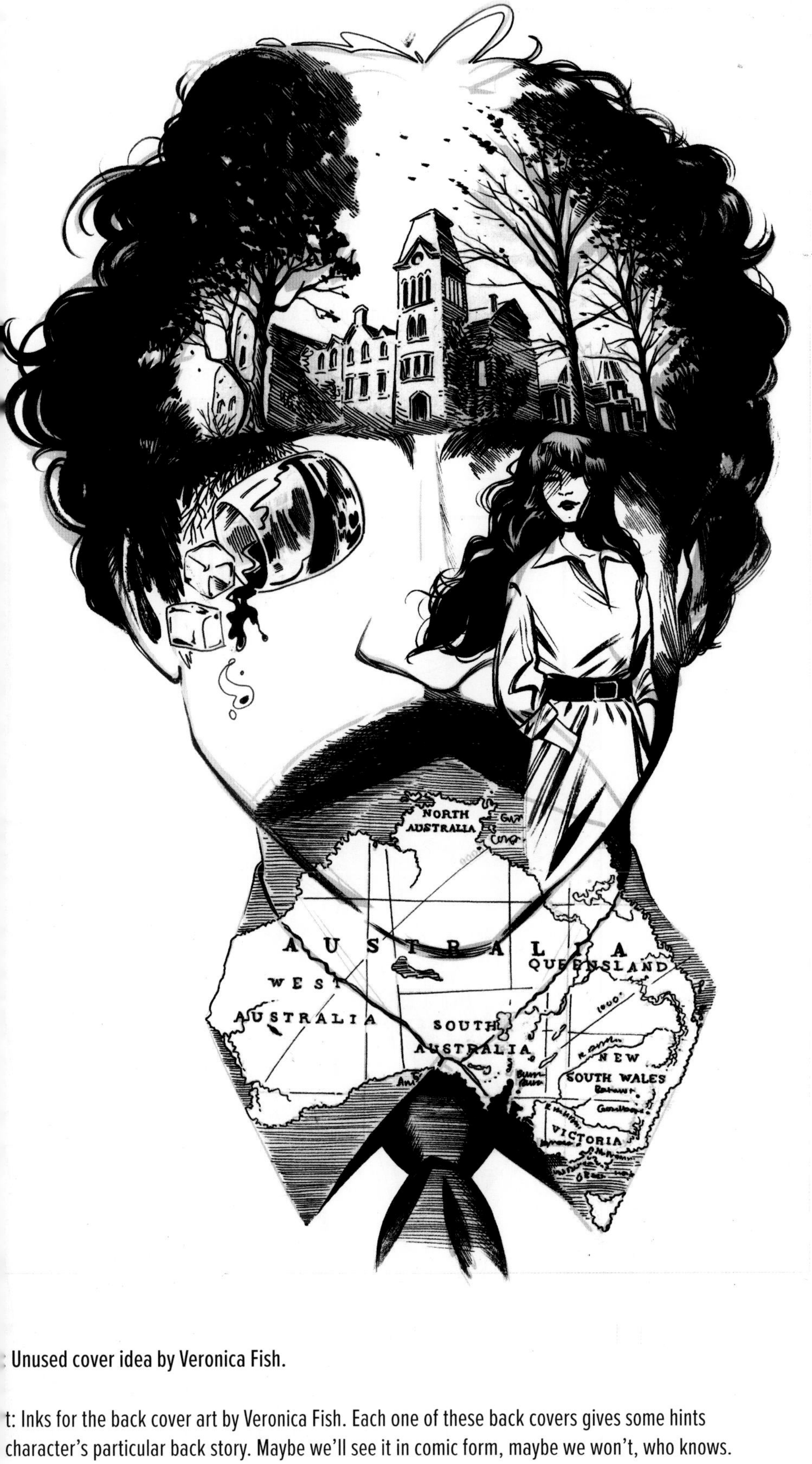
NORTH AUSTRALIA
AUSTRALIA
WEST AUSTRALIA
SOUTH AUSTRALIA
NEW SOUTH WALES
VICTORIA

: Unused cover idea by Veronica Fish.

t: Inks for the back cover art by Veronica Fish. Each one of these back covers gives some hints character's particular back story. Maybe we'll see it in comic form, maybe we won't, who knows.

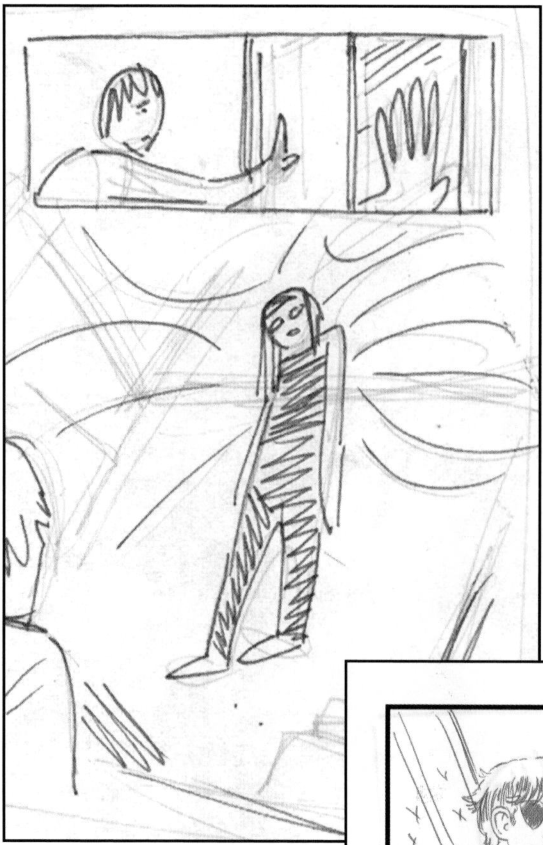

Here is an example of Andy and I jumping back and forth on a page together.

—Veronica Fish

Top left: This is Veronica's original thumbnail sketch.

Bottom left: Andy pencilled the art student's intricate "final project" web, complete with metal and new wave posters in back. Then it's back to Veronica for finished line art and colors.

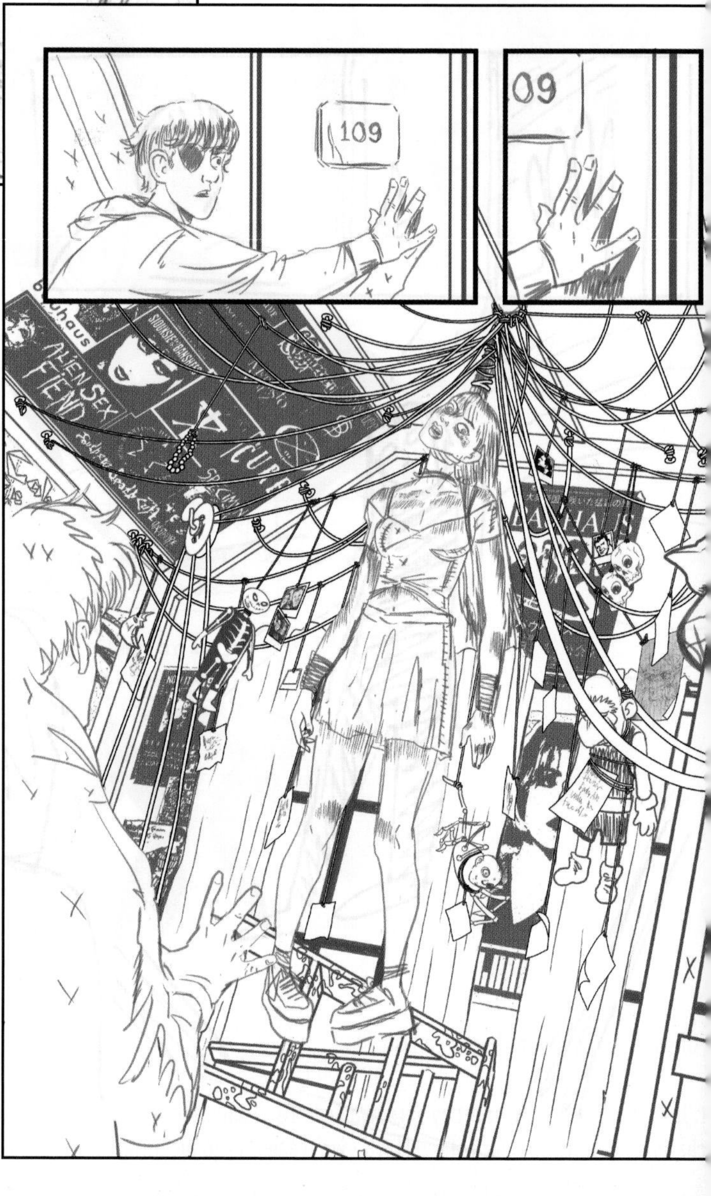
109
09
ALIEN SEX FIEND

Tiny Easter egg in the art school girl's room—those Polaroid photos are Evan and Sarah and the Fishes.

—Andy Fish

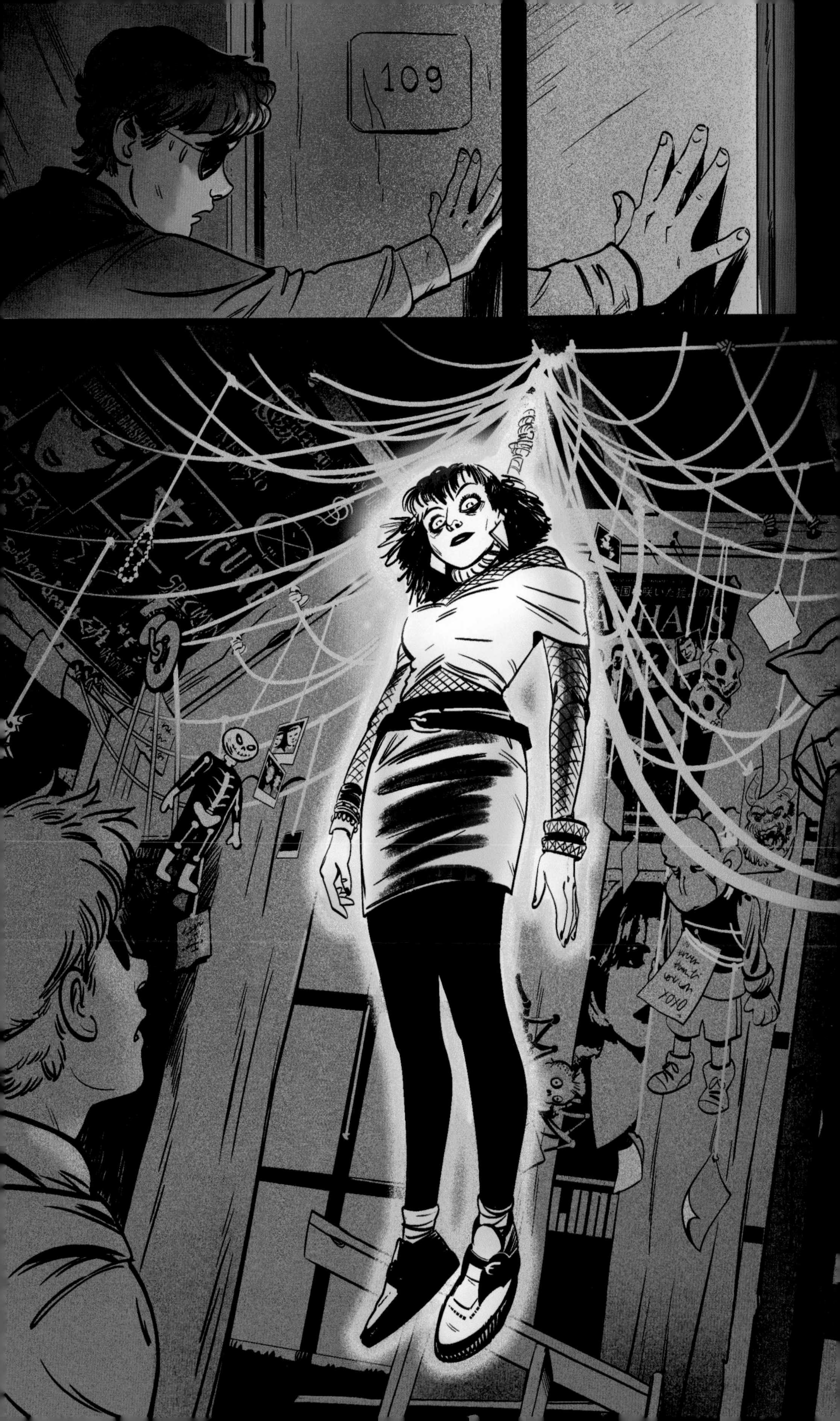
109
XOXO

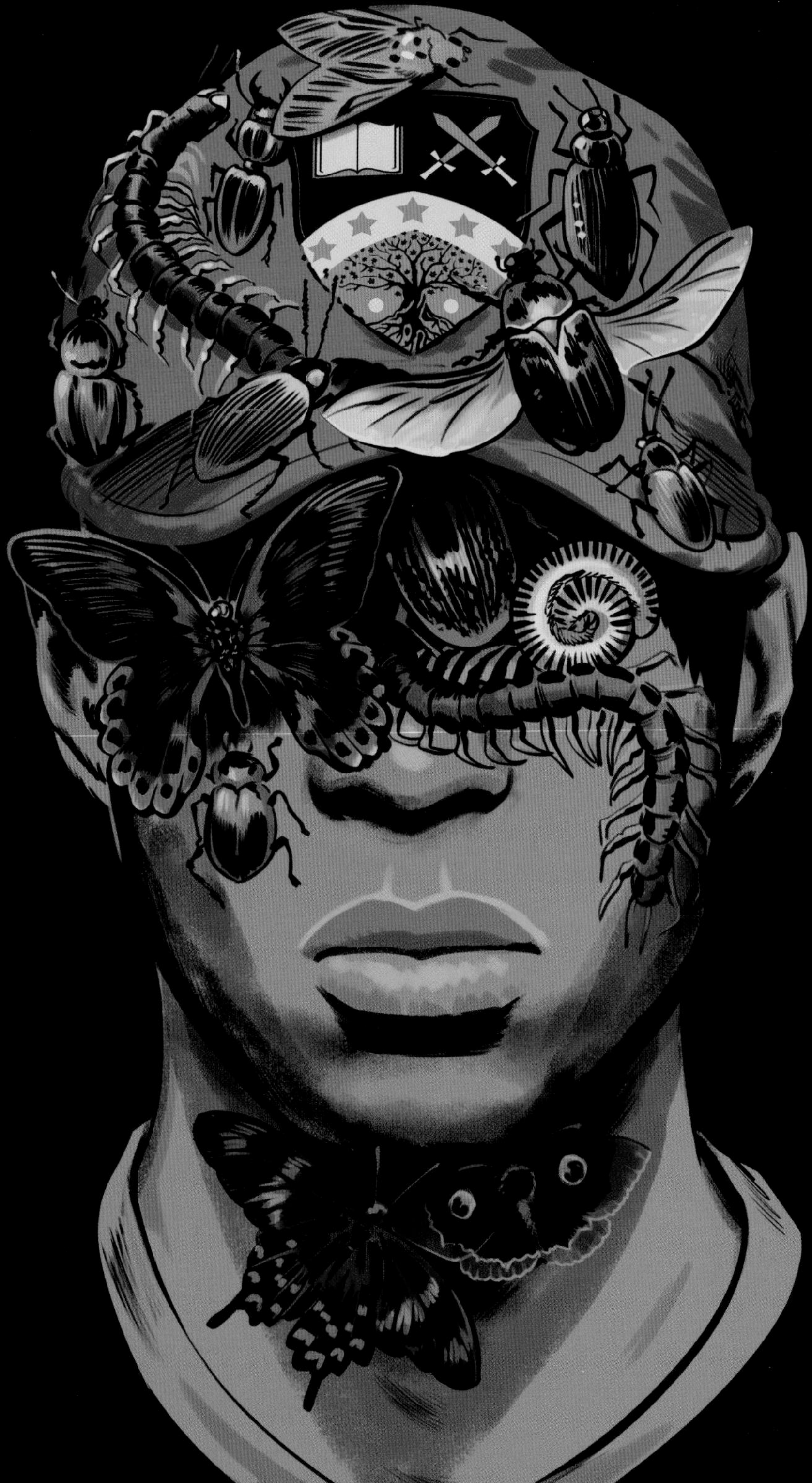
VFISH

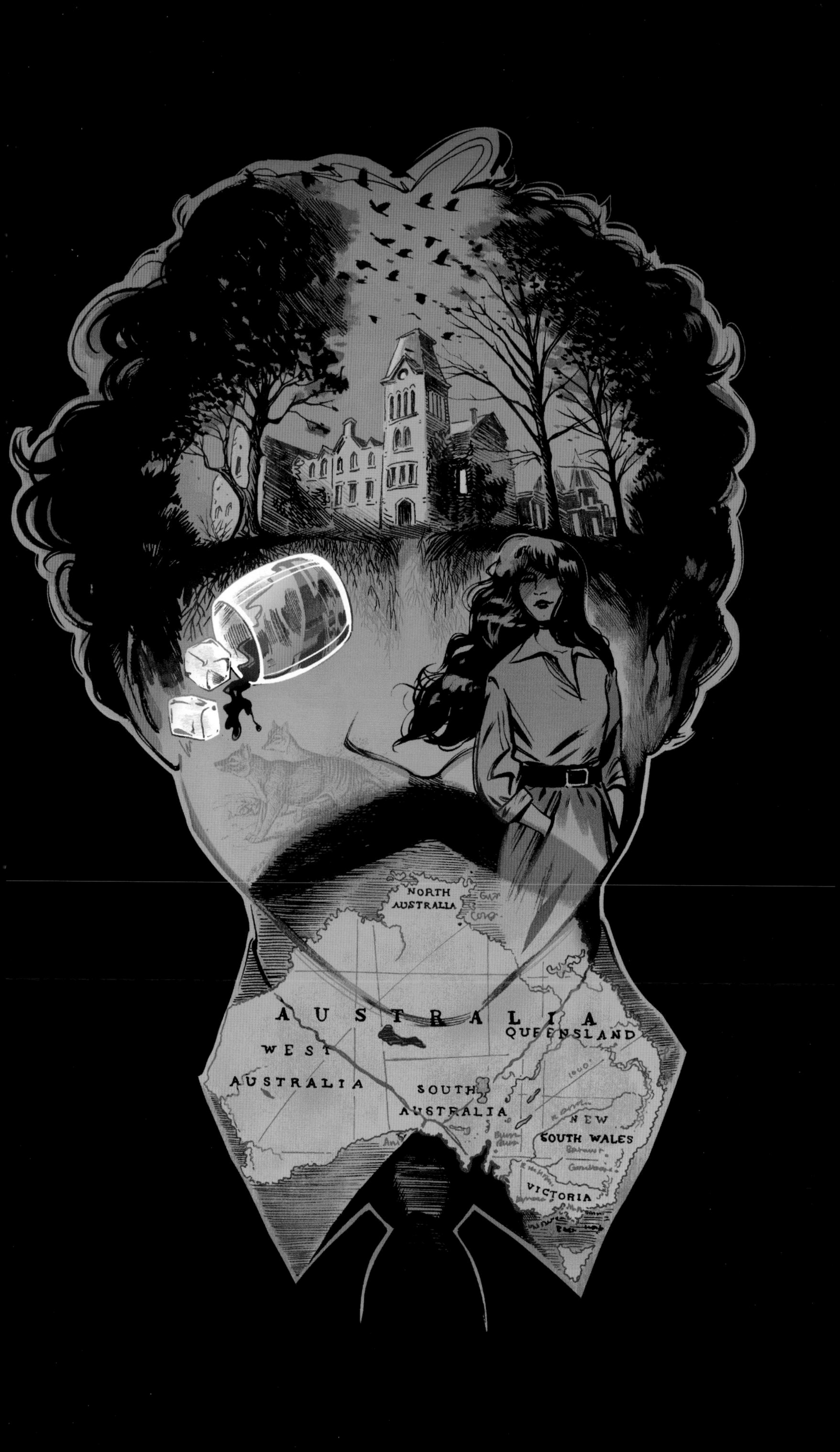
NORTH AUSTRALIA
AUSTRALIA
QUEENSLAND
WEST AUSTRALIA
SOUTH AUSTRALIA
NEW SOUTH WALES
VICTORIA

BLACKWOOD GARGOYLES

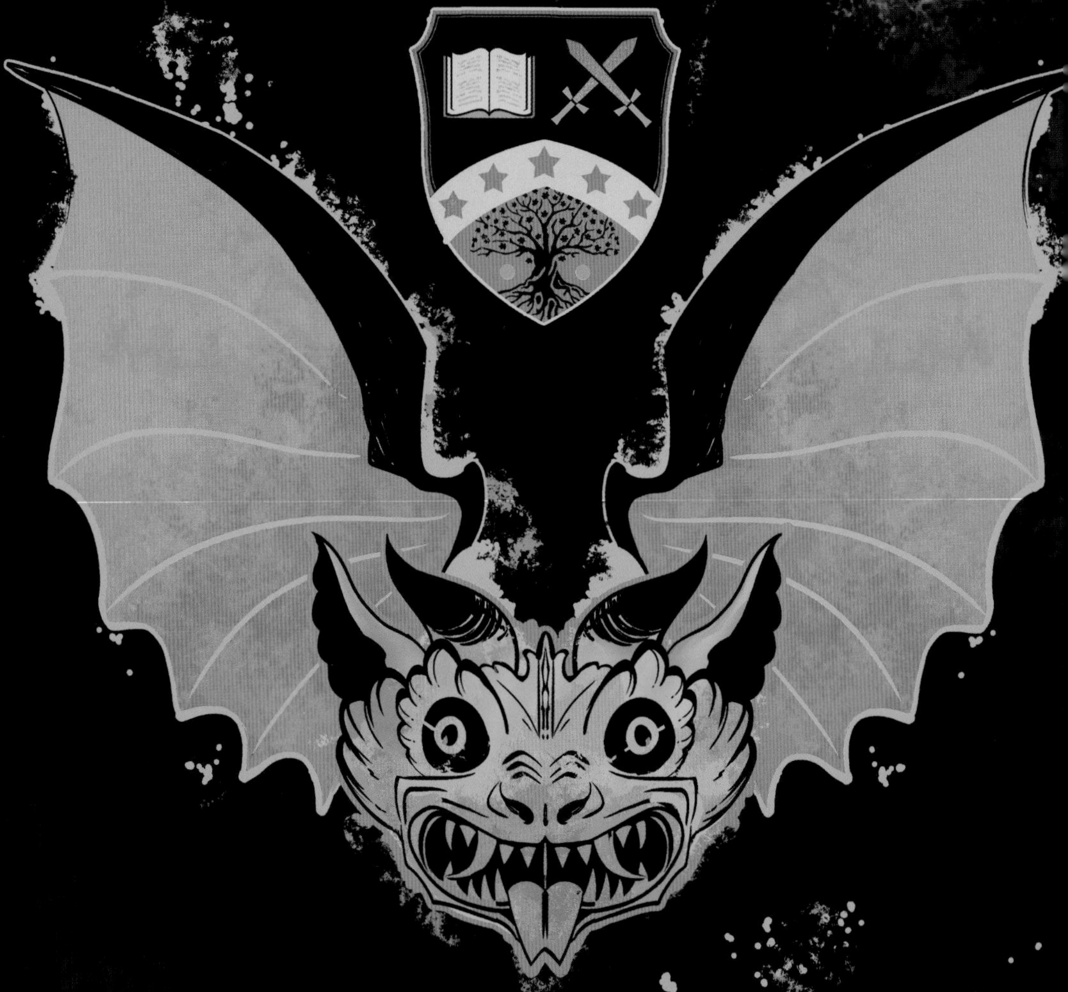

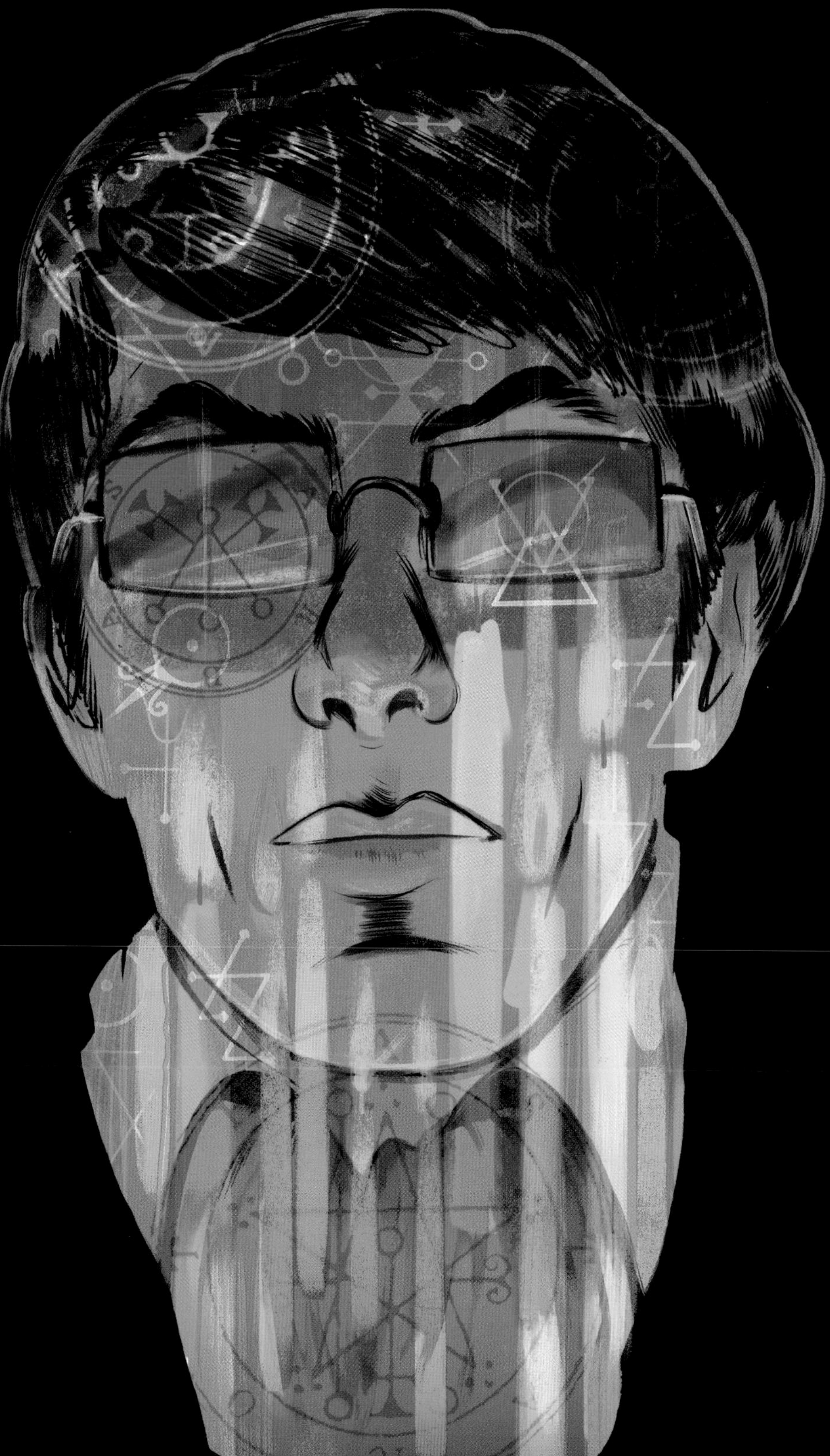

EVAN DORKIN with SARAH DYER

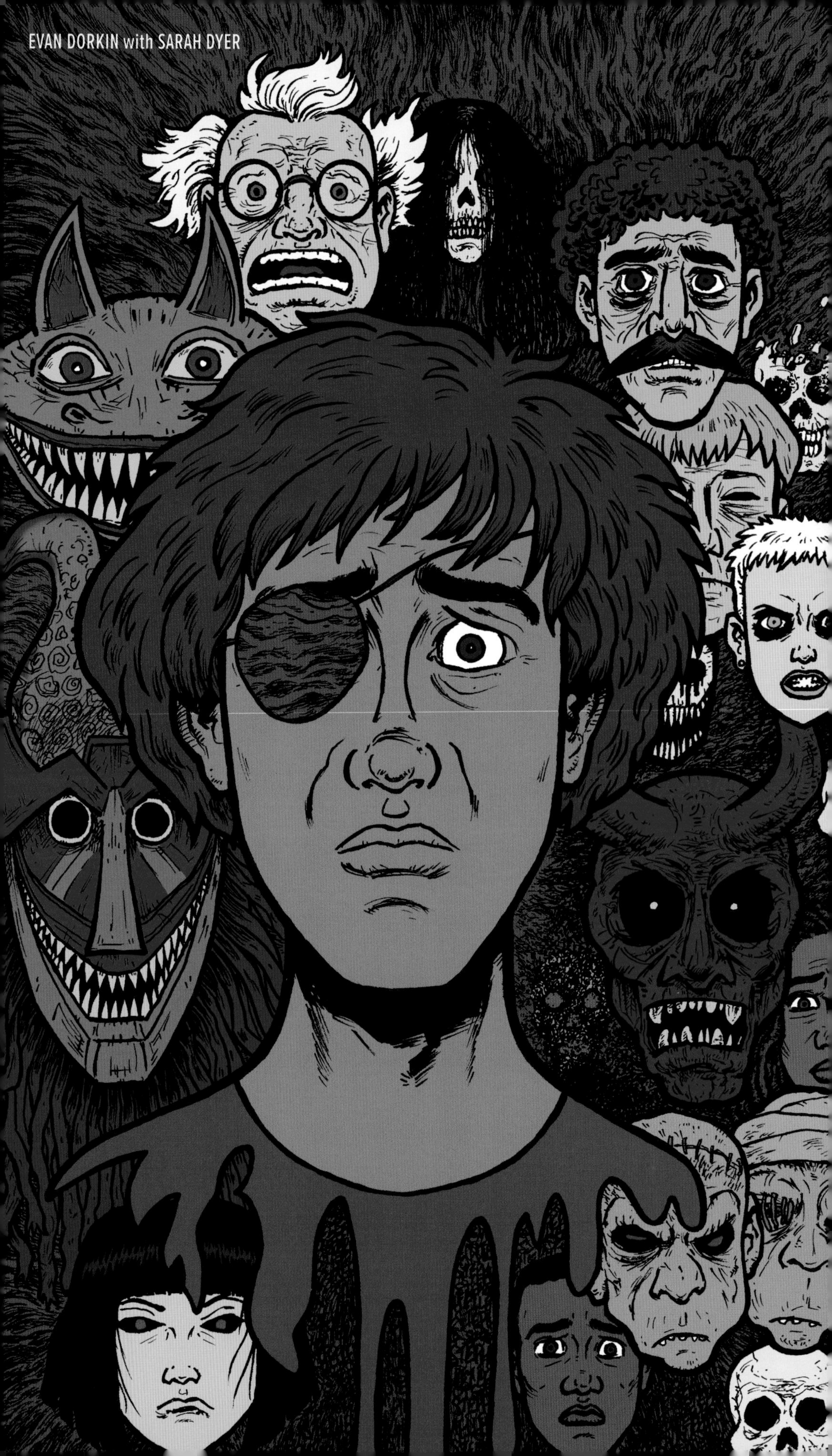

ANDREW MACLEAN

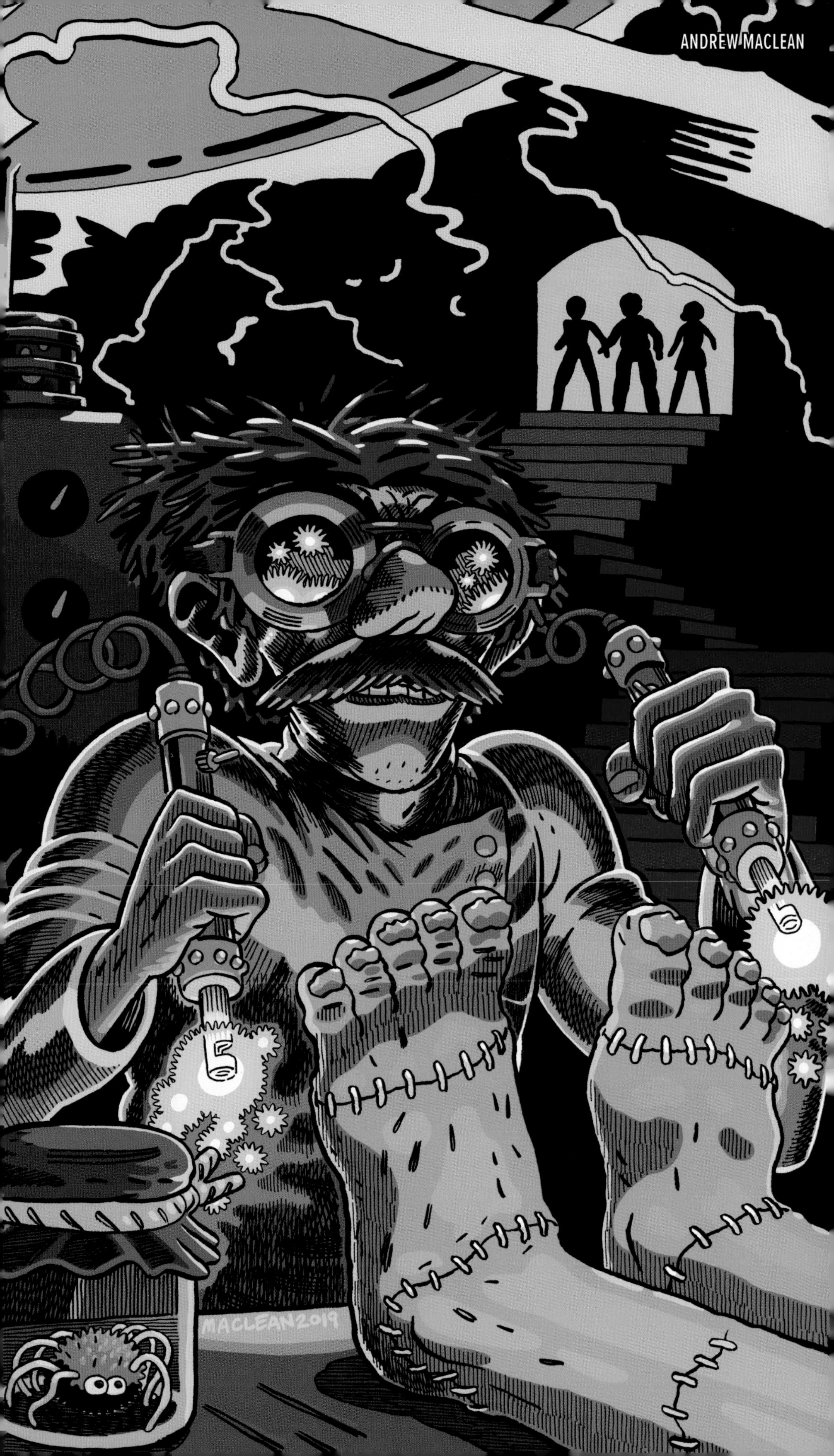
MACLEAN2019

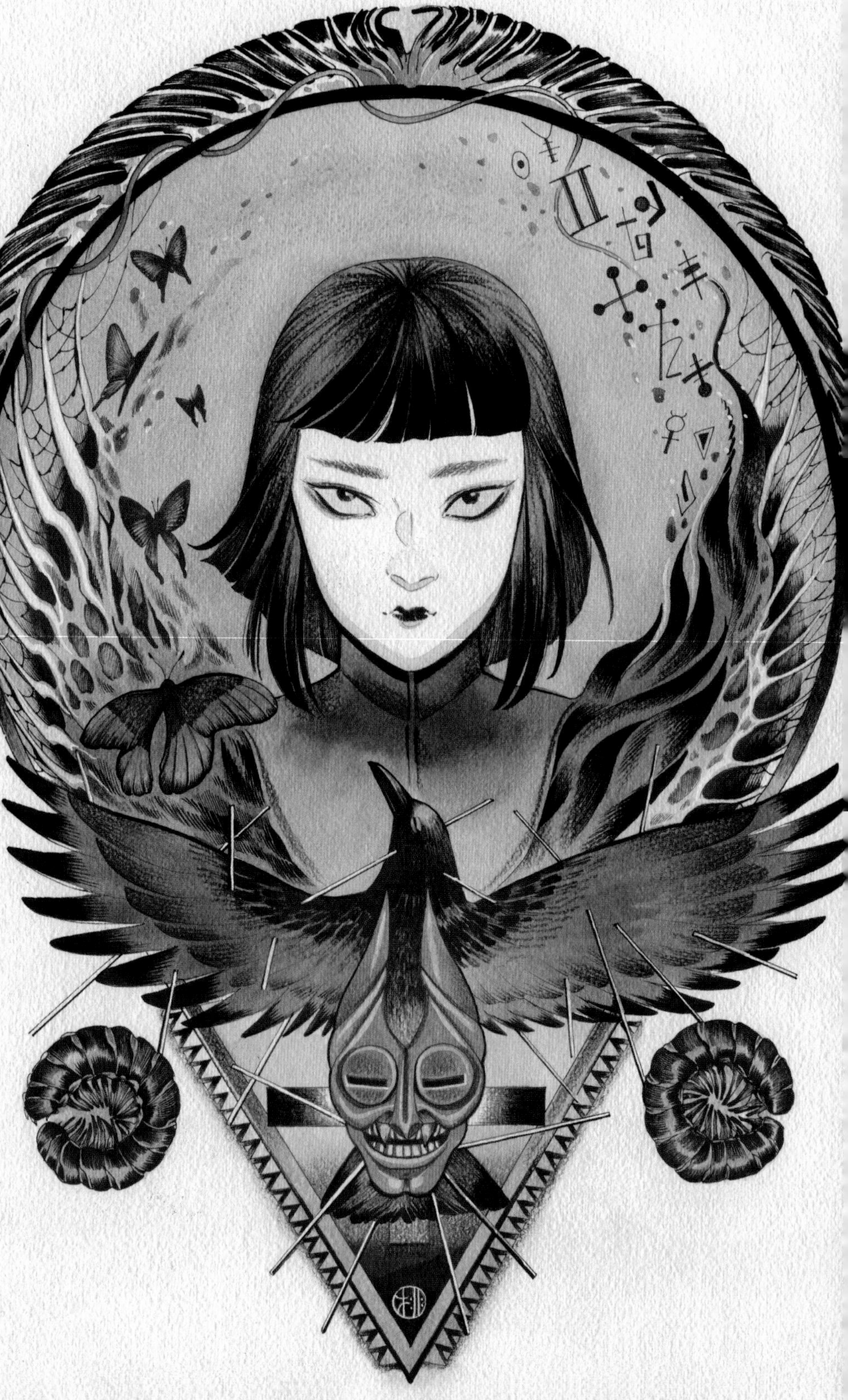

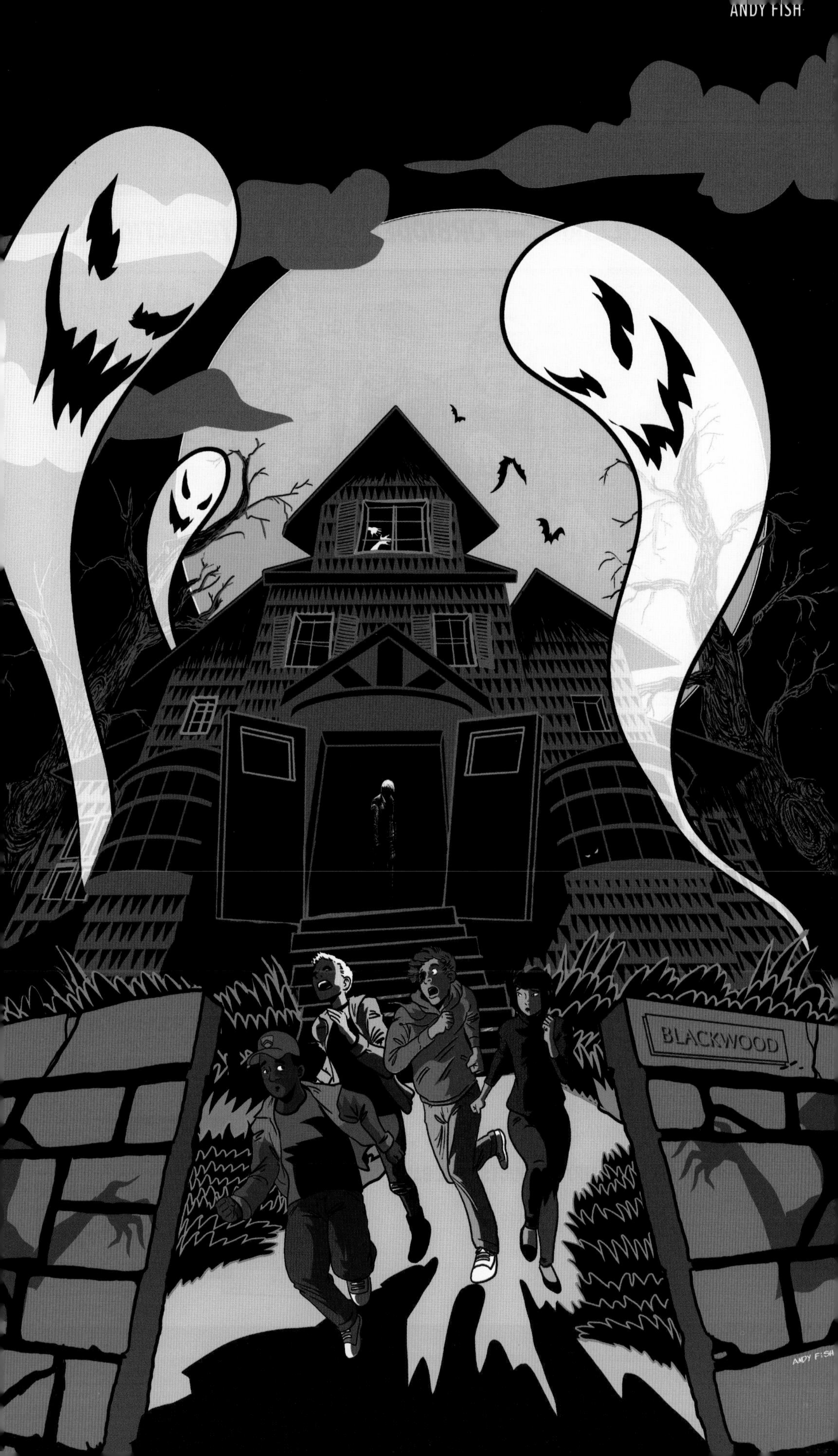
ANDY FISH
BLACKWOOD
ANDY FISH